IMAGES
of America

COMFORT

I0806483

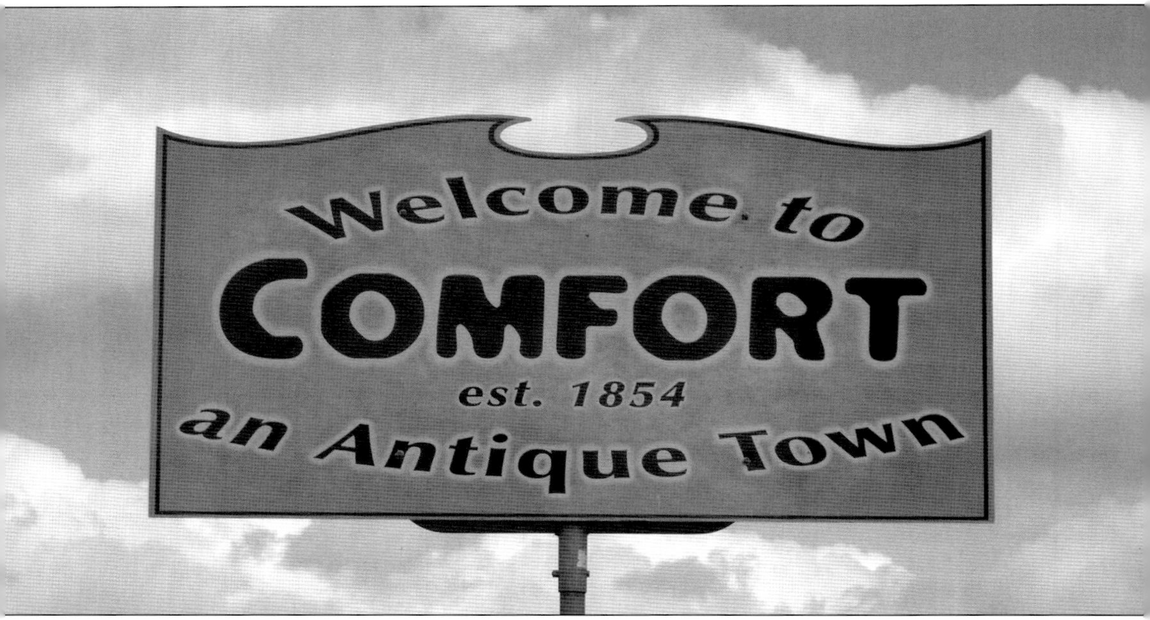

Welcome to Comfort. When drivers leave Interstate 10 and turn on Texas Highway 27, they will find this sign posted by the Comfort Chamber of Commerce. If they continue to the chamber office, they will find a friendly welcome, maps, and information about the area. They will begin to understand why the name given by the early settlers is still appropriate. (Photograph by Ruth Kiel.)

On the Cover: **Memorial Services at Treue der Union Monument, 1939.** The Treue der Union monument in Comfort was the location of the memorial services on Sunday, May 28, 1939. The Beethoven Maennerchor and Damenchor (men's and ladies' choruses) from San Antonio participated, as did the Hermann Sons Military Band of San Antonio. The groups marched from town to the monument on the hillside near the old community church. Three standard bearers led the way carrying the United States flag, the Texas flag, and the Beethoven Verein flag. During the parade, the band played Chopin's "Funeral March." The Maennerchor presented a large wreath for placement at the monument. Guido Ransleben gave an address, in German, about the men and events commemorated. The men and women's choirs sang "Wie Sie So Sanft Ruh'n," "Nearer My God to Thee," and "Altniederlaendisches Dankgebet." The assembly then paraded back to town for lunch at the spacious and shady yard of Alex Brinkmann. The photograph was taken by Ernst Wilhelm Raba (1874–1951), a German photographer who worked in San Antonio. (Comfort Heritage Foundation archives.)

IMAGES
of America

COMFORT

Ruth Kiel and Frank Kiel

ARCADIA
PUBLISHING

ISBN 978-0-7385-7948-1

Published by Arcadia Publishing
Charleston, South Carolina

Printed in the United States of America

Library of Congress Control Number: 2010929730

For all general information, please contact Arcadia Publishing:
Telephone 843-853-2070
Fax 843-853-0044
E-mail sales@arcadiapublishing.com
For customer service and orders:
Toll-Free 1-888-313-2665

Visit us on the Internet at www.arcadiapublishing.com

Contents

Acknowledgments

The archives of the Comfort Heritage Foundation preserve the history of Comfort through photographs, oral histories, copies of the research for designation of Comfort as a Texas State Historic District, and bound volumes of the *Comfort News* from 1903 to the present. We are grateful to Margaret Kutzer Morries, archivist and descendant of original settlers to the Comfort area, for her help. Anne Seidensticker Stewart, another descendant of original settlers, has written books about them and has helped many people researching the history of the area, including the authors. Research, articles, and pictures from Esther Wiedenfeld are treasured; her presence is missed by all. Roy Perkins, whose ancestors donated the building for the Comfort Museum, shared his pictures and his memories, as did Joyce Behr, Steven Bohnert, Lois Haufler, Jonathan Letz, Tina Martin Neumann, A. C. Schwethelm, Lillian Soell, and Ruth Lindner Zoeller (all descendants of early settlers), and William "Bill" Terry of the *Comfort News*. Sgt. Kieth Rose of the U.S. Army MedCom Band confirmed the identification of instruments of the Comfort Band. The Texana Section of the Comfort Public Library includes volumes of local history and biographies of early settlers; we are grateful to Patti Miles, library director, and her staff for their help in finding rare books in the library collection and through interlibrary loan.

We also thank Hannah Carney and Kristie Kelly, our editors at Arcadia Publishing, for their suggestions and encouragement.

INTRODUCTION

In 1851, after the German uprisings of 1848, Ernst Hermann Altgelt (1832–1878) left his home in Düsseldorf in North Rhineland to sail from Bremen to New Orleans. In 1854, his new American employer, John Vles, sent him to the Texas frontier to survey and determine the value of a league and a labor (4,605 acres) of land that Vles had bought in 1846. It was a valley in the Hill Country where Cypress Creek flows into the Guadalupe River, a lovely and peaceful area that the settlers named Comfort. Guido Ransleben reports in *A Hundred Years of Comfort in Texas* that Altgelt persuaded his father to give him money to buy 1,000 acres next to Vles's land. Completing the survey in August 1854, Altgelt divided his portion and 1,500 acres of Vles's land into residential lots. The official founding took place on September 3, 1854. More settlers soon came. By the time of the 1860 U.S. Federal Census of Kerr County, which then included Comfort, 328 persons had a Comfort post office address. Of those, 120 were adult white men of whom 97 were foreign born, including 93 Germans.

Soon after the arrival of the early pioneers, Texas became embroiled in the question of secession. These German settlers who had just pledged their loyalty to the United States faced a difficult decision. Some men enlisted in the Confederate Army, while others accepted conscription. Some chose to join a group of Union loyalists, who started to Mexico where they hoped to get passage to New Orleans in order to join the Union army. At the Nueces River on August 10, 1862, a Confederate detachment from Col. James Duff's 33rd Cavalry Regiment, under the command of Lt. C. D. McRae, found them. In the ensuing battle, many were killed, while others who were wounded were later shot by their captors; all were left unburied. Some men escaped and, with the help of the U.S. consul in Matamoros, went on as planned; others stayed in Mexico, including commander Fritz Tegener.

In 1865, a group of their friends and families brought the remains of those killed back to Comfort for burial, not in the established Comfort Cemetery but in a plot of land on a hill near the end of High Street where they were interred in a mass grave. A detachment of federal troops from Camp Verde accompanied the cortege to the grave site and fired a rifle volley salute over the grave.

On August 10, 1866, the community dedicated an obelisk at the grave site with the inscription "*Treue der Union*" (True to the Union) and the names of the fallen. It is one of several such monuments in the South, such as Greeneville, Tennessee, and Vanceburg, Kentucky, where the local population remained loyal to the Union and sent men to fight in the Union army.

The war years were a difficult time, with some families divided—one son fighting for the South and another for the North. Conditions became desperate. Ernst Altgelt himself favored the Confederacy, and he wrote a letter (now in the author's possession) on May 21, 1863, to John Thurmond, secretary of a San Antonio aid association, seeking help for needy wives:

> I had the pleasure to address you a few weeks ago, giving you a statement about team affairs, etc., and asking at the same time for certificates to trade in your Aid Store for Mrs. A. Rosenthal,

> Mrs. C. Beseler, Mrs. W. Schultze—all three of them wifes [sic] of private soldiers in Duff's Battalion. They are in a suffering condition up here and can get nothing for paper money and there is a report that the goods of the Association will arrive the latter end of this month. Dr. Kingsbury left word with me that in a case or cases as the above stated I could make application for such women and the Directors would consider the same favorably. Please let me know what to answer the said women.
>
> —Most respectfully yours, Ernest Altgelt

In 1866, after the war with its hardships and tragedies, the Comfort School Association built a new school near the present Comfort Park with a well for drinking water. The community had built its first public school in 1856, two years after its founding. It was a one-room cabin with a gravel floor on Michael Lindner's Lot 258. Several teachers, including Emma Altgelt, conducted school in their homes. In 1866, the Comfort School Association built a new school near the present Comfort Park, with a well for drinking water. By 1870, enrollment had increased so that an addition was needed. In 1893, a three-room rock schoolhouse with a bell tower was built that was accompanied by a playground on two adjacent lots. Nearby ranching communities of Cypress Creek, Holiday, Brownsboro, Waring, and Welfare built one-room schools that have since closed and been incorporated into the Comfort Independent School District. Comfort recently built a new high school on the outskirts of town. The excellence of Comfort's schools reflects the philosophy of the freethinkers with its emphasis on education.

In 1892, after the coming of the railroad and new arrivals, Comfort built its first church for the Deutsche Evangelische Geminde (the German Evangelical Congregation). Prior to that time, services were held in private homes and sometimes in the railroad depot.

Following the Civil War, economic development took place. Ranching and farming continued, as did the making of shingles from the cypress trees bordering the river and creeks. In 1887, the San Antonio and Aransas Pass Railroad came from San Antonio to Comfort, providing freight and passenger service. Hotels were built for businessmen and for summer visitors. Summer camps were developed for children, church members, and working women from San Antonio. One unique business was an armadillo farm, which made lamps, purses, and baskets from armadillo shells. The Gousha Map Company began operation in 1966 and built a new plant that employed over 100 people. It moved away in 1987, and the James Avery Jewelry Company took over the building. The lumberyard, established in 1879 by Edward Steves and Sons, is still active, although in a new location that is now owned by Steven and Randolph Bohnert. Three generations of the Lindner family have managed a feed mill. Artists and antique dealers lure visitors to the area.

Descendants of original settlers live on family ranches and in town in houses built by their ancestors. The Comfort Historic District, listed on the National Register of Historic Places, encompasses the original town site and includes over 100 buildings. The cut limestone structure, built in 1917 at the corner of Seventh and High Streets (now the Comfort Public Library), was originally the Schwethelm mercantile establishment. Across the street is the Comfort State Bank building, constructed in 1907, which is now home of the Comfort Heritage Foundation.

Comfort remains independent and freethinking. It is unincorporated and has no elected local officials. Law enforcement and road maintenance are by the county, and fire protection is by a volunteer fire department. When a catastrophe strikes, such as a fire, flood, or illness, the community—whether it be a church or family friends or a restaurant or local pub—will hold a fund-raiser. New subdivisions are home to people seeking the beauty and tranquility of the Hill Country. They have contributed to the prosperity of the community and have joined the volunteers who make possible the unique ambiance of this small town.

One

Founding and Early Development

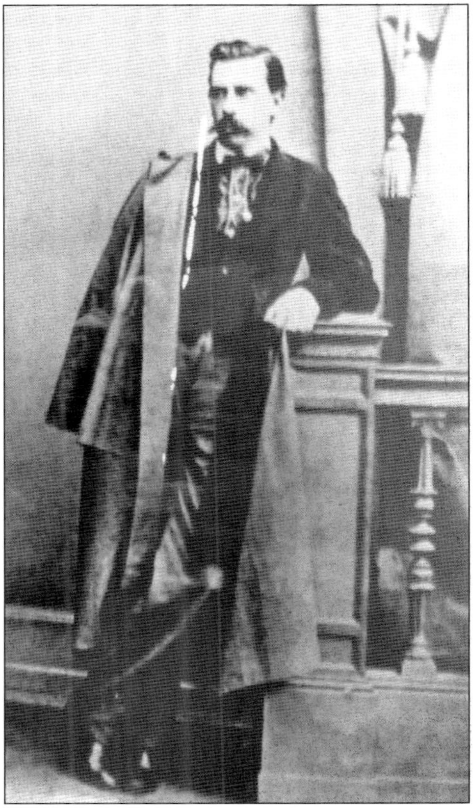

Ernst Hermann Altgelt (1832–1878). In Bexar County District Court on February 25, 1852, Altgelt filed a declaration of intention to become a U.S. citizen, proclaiming he was a subject of the king of Prussia, born in Düsseldorf, 18 years of age, and that he arrived in New Orleans about October 15, 1851. He came with a surveying party in 1854 to lay out the town of Comfort. (Roy Perkins collection.)

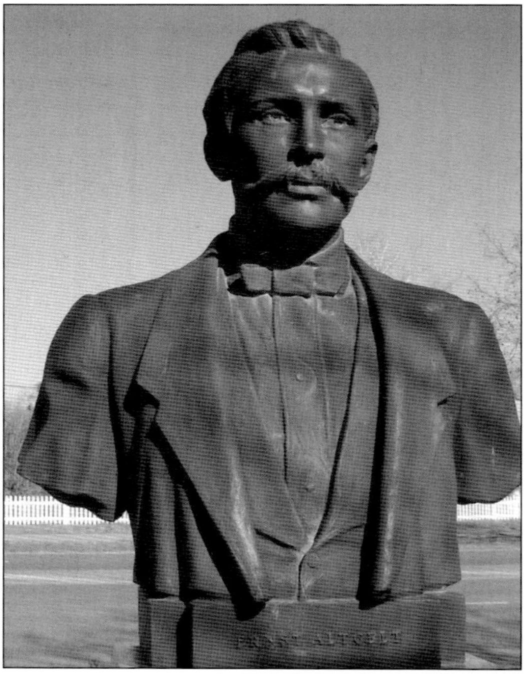

ALTGELT BUST IN COMFORT PARK. At the time of the 1860 U.S. Federal Census, Altgelt was in Comfort as a lawyer; he was the richest man in town with real estate valued at $18,000. During the Civil War, he aligned himself with the Confederate cause. After the war, he practiced law in San Antonio. On July 3, 1971, during the Homecoming Celebration, the Comfort Historical Society honored him as the town founder with a sculptured bust by Waldine Tauch of the Copini Institute of Fine Arts in San Antonio. Harry Jersig, who was born in Comfort and became president of the Lone Star Brewing Company, gave the dedication address. Congressman O. C. Fisher from Junction followed with a speech, and descendants of Ernst and Emma Altgelt unveiled the statue. A. C. Schwethelm was the master of ceremonies. (At left, photograph by Ruth Kiel; below, the *Comfort News* July 8, 1971, from Comfort Heritage Foundation archives.)

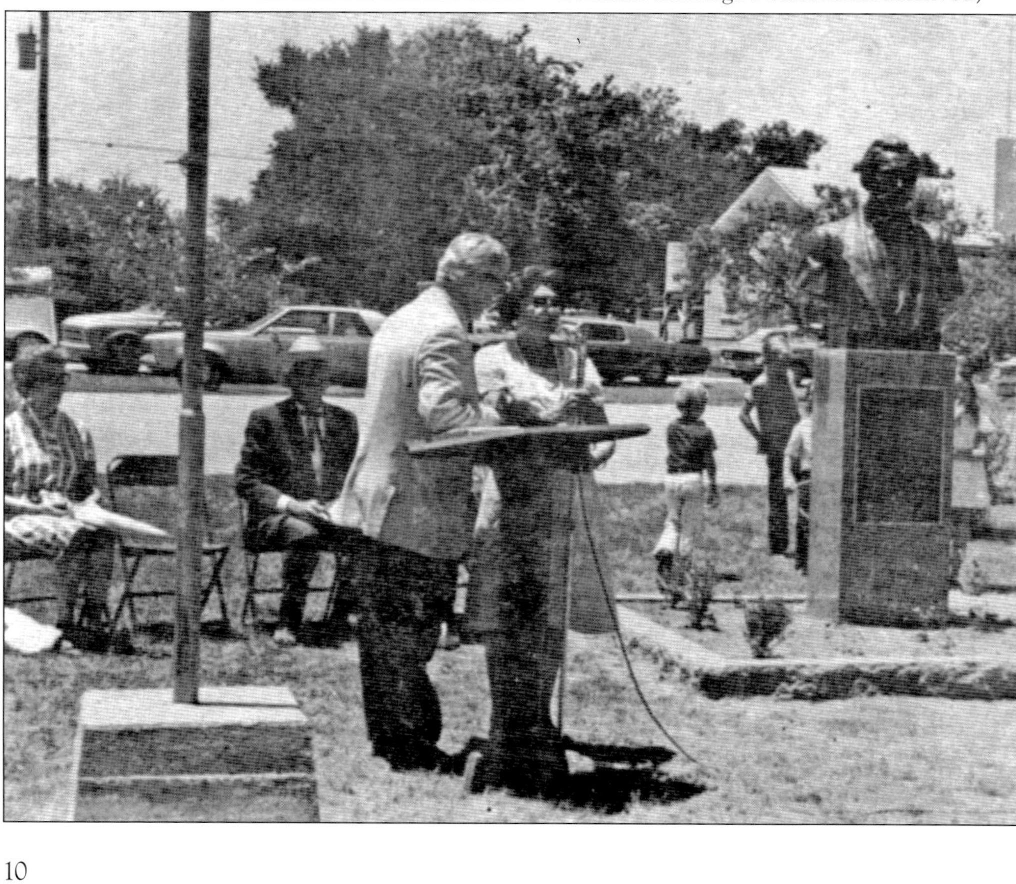

EMMA FRANZISKA MURCK ALTGELT (1833–1922). Born in Barmen, Prussia (now part of Wuppertal, Germany), on December 4, 1833, she sailed from Bremen on the *Franziska* in October 1854 and landed in Galveston. After marrying Ernst Altgelt in 1855, their residence for 12 years was Comfort. Emma conducted school in her home. Her published works include a collection entitled *Beobachtungen und Erinnerungen* ("Observations and Memories"), published in 1930 by the Neu-Braunfelser Zeitung, and *Schilderungen aus texanischen Leben* ("Descriptions of Texas Life"). Guido Ransleben translated them for serial publication in the *Comfort News* from May 22, 1969, through July 9, 1970. (At right, Texana collection, San Antonio Central Library; below, Roy Perkins collection.)

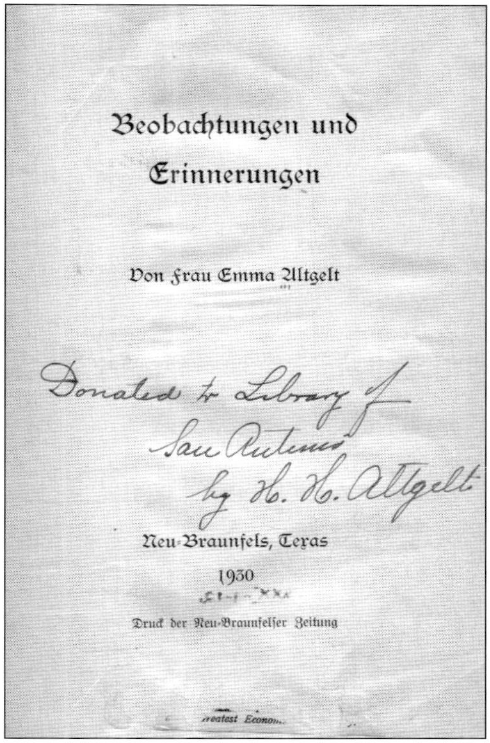

Beobachtungen und Erinnerungen

Von Frau Emma Altgelt

Donated to Library of San Antonio by H. H. Altgelt

Neu-Braunfels, Texas

1930

Druck der Neu-Braunfelser Zeitung

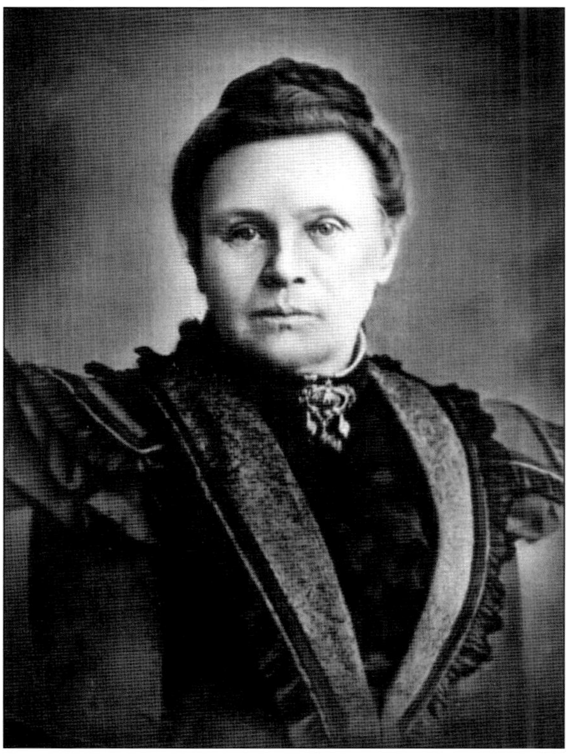

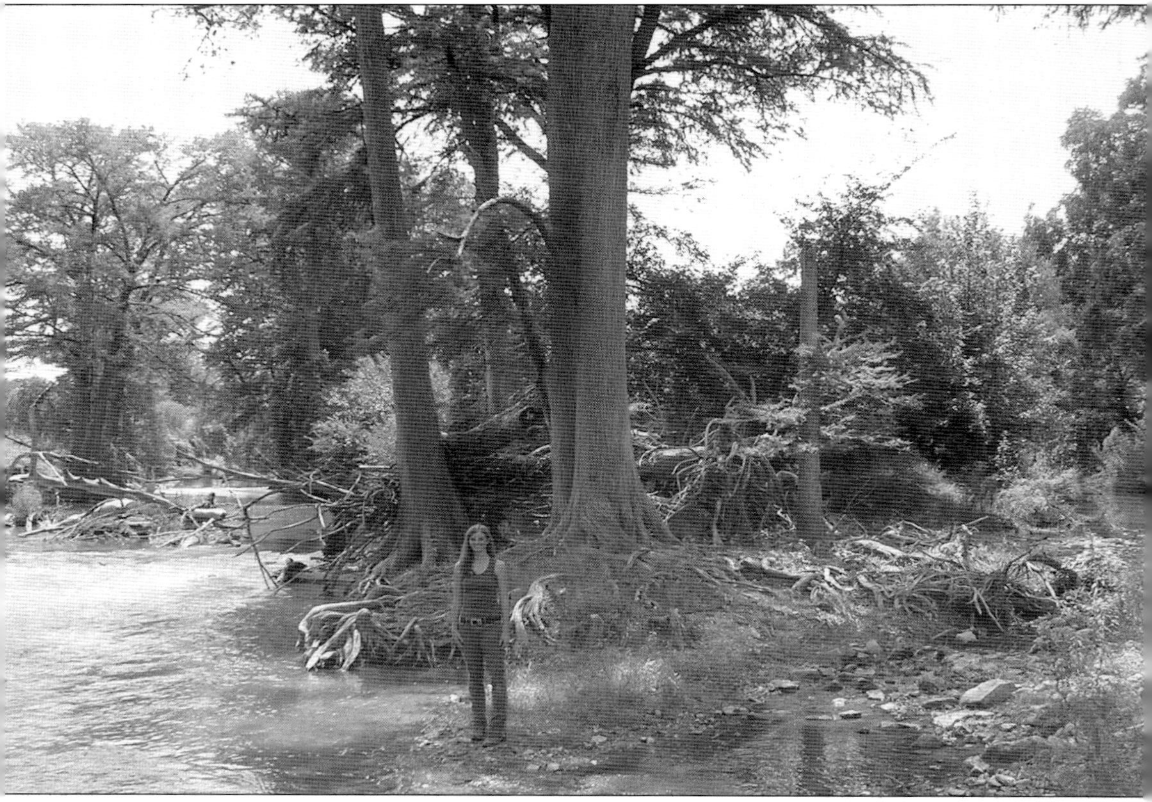

CYPRESS TREES ALONG GUADALUPE RIVER. Daryn Petermann is standing at the point where Flat Rock Creek on the right flows into the Guadalupe River. Alonzo de Leon, governor of Coahuilla in 1689, followed the course of this river and named it after Our Lady of Guadalupe, whose statue traveled with his exploration party and whose image was on the party's banner. The stretch above the junction with the Comal River went by the designation of San Ybón River until 1727 when use of the present name began. The length of the river is 250 miles. It originates in western Kerr County, flows through Comfort, continues through New Braunfels and Victoria, and enters San Antonio Bay near Seadrift. The tall cypress trees were a source of shingles for early builders. The valley's northern boundary is the Guadalupe-Pedernales Divide, and the southern boundary is the Guadalupe-Medina Divide; hills on both exceed 2,000 feet. (Photograph by Ruth Kiel.)

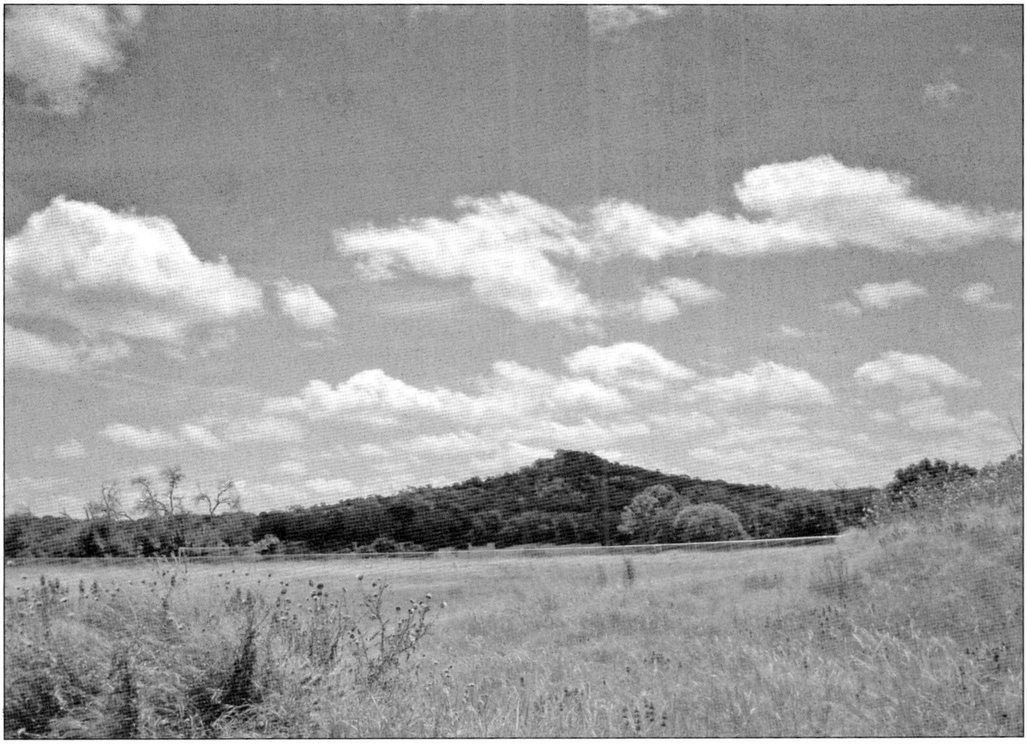

Mount Rigi at Comfort and Lake Lucerne. At 1,801 feet, this conical hill behind the current high school was a prominent landmark for travelers. Its name probably derives from 5,896-foot Mount Rigi, south of Lake Lucerne in Switzerland, which was a favorite destination for 19th-century climbers, including William Wordsworth and Mark Twain. A cable car goes from the village of Weggis to the top of the mountain. In Comfort, ascent of the hill was a popular day trip for local residents. Farther north, the Stieler Hill (formerly called Der Hohe Berg) was too steep for commercial traffic until the state constructed U.S. Route 87 in 1931. (Both photographs by Ruth Kiel.)

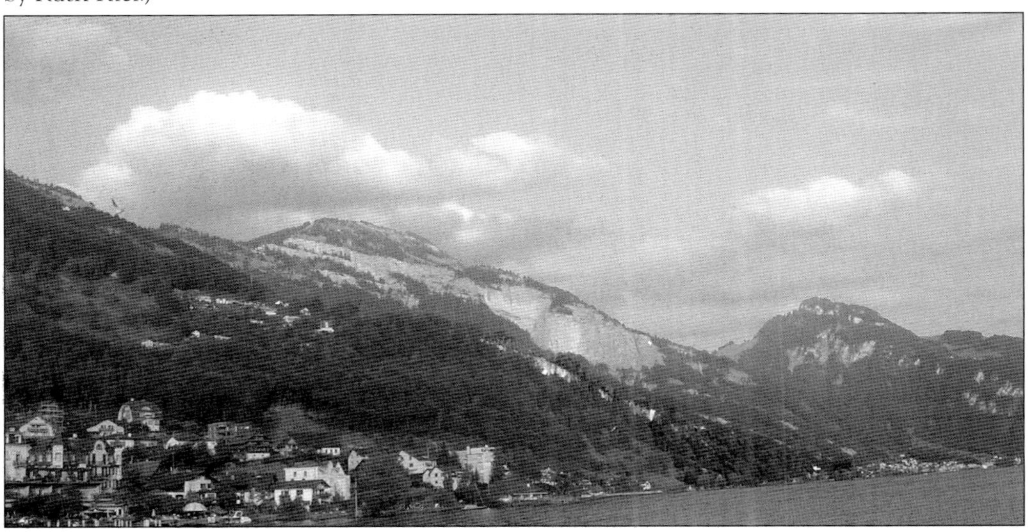

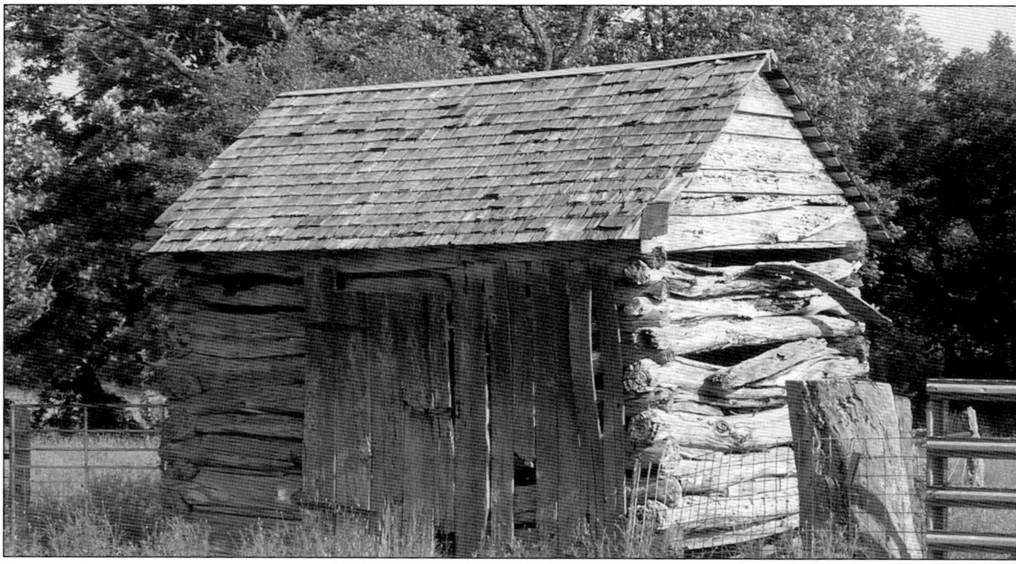

Early Log Cabin. The Michael Lindner place is a Texas Family Land Heritage 100–Year Ranch, which is a Texas Department of Agriculture program that honors continuous family ownership of farms and ranches. Purchased by Bavarian Michael Lindner in 1875, son Leo Lindner enlarged the place to 640 acres. Still standing is this old log cabin built by the founder. (Photograph by Ruth Kiel.)

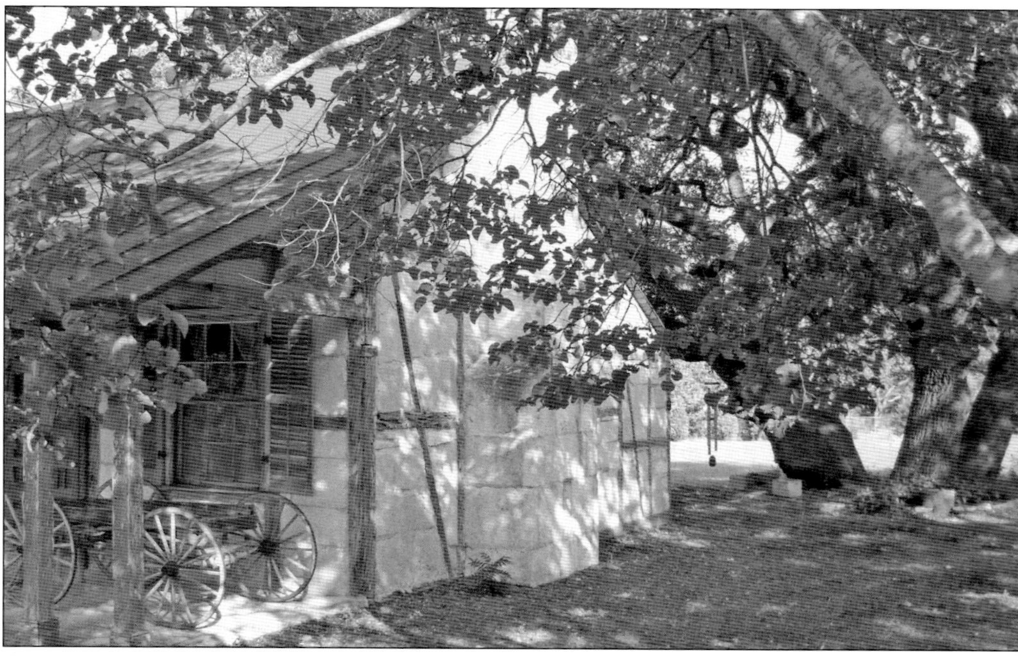

German *Fachwerk* Construction. The Goldbeck-Faltin cabin, adjacent to Comfort Crockery (formerly the Faltin and Company store) at Main and Seventh Streets, is the oldest building on an original site in town, built in 1854 by Theodore Goldbeck and purchased in 1856 by August Faltin. Fachwerk (compartmented construction) features diagonal, heavy timbers to brace the walls of limestone rock. (Photograph by Ruth Kiel.)

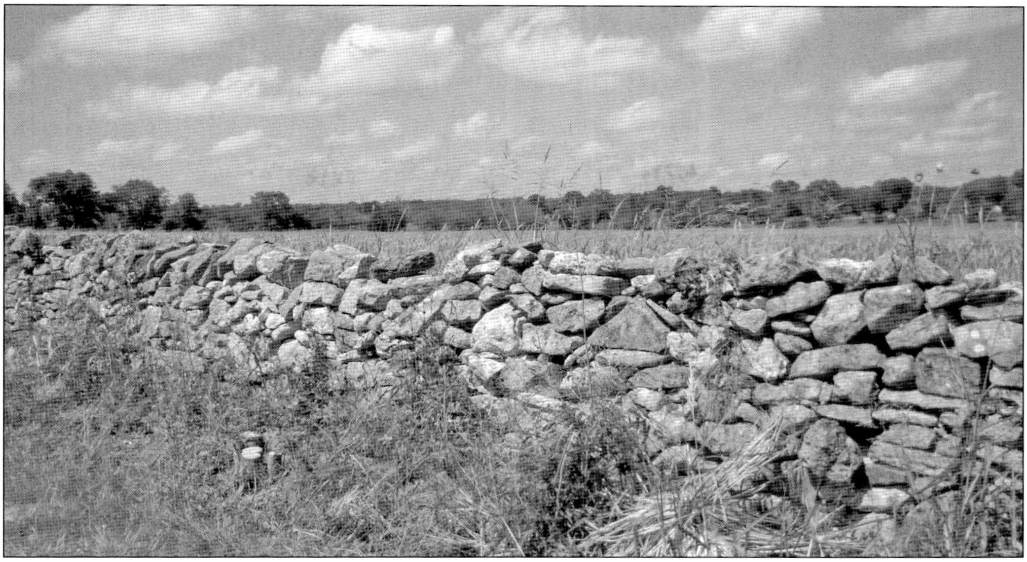

Old German Stone Wall. This dry-stacked rock wall on Old Number 9 Highway is typical of boundary fences employed by German settlers to demarcate their land and restrict their livestock. This example is on the Marquardt Ranch on Block Creek east of Comfort. Johann Christian Marquardt founded the ranch in 1871, and it is in the Texas Family Heritage Program as a 100-Year Family Ranch. Another example was on the Nelson Minor ranch on Gaddis Bluff Road north of Comfort, where the old stone wall now acts as a retaining wall for the soil that shifted over the years. (Both photographs by Ruth Kiel.)

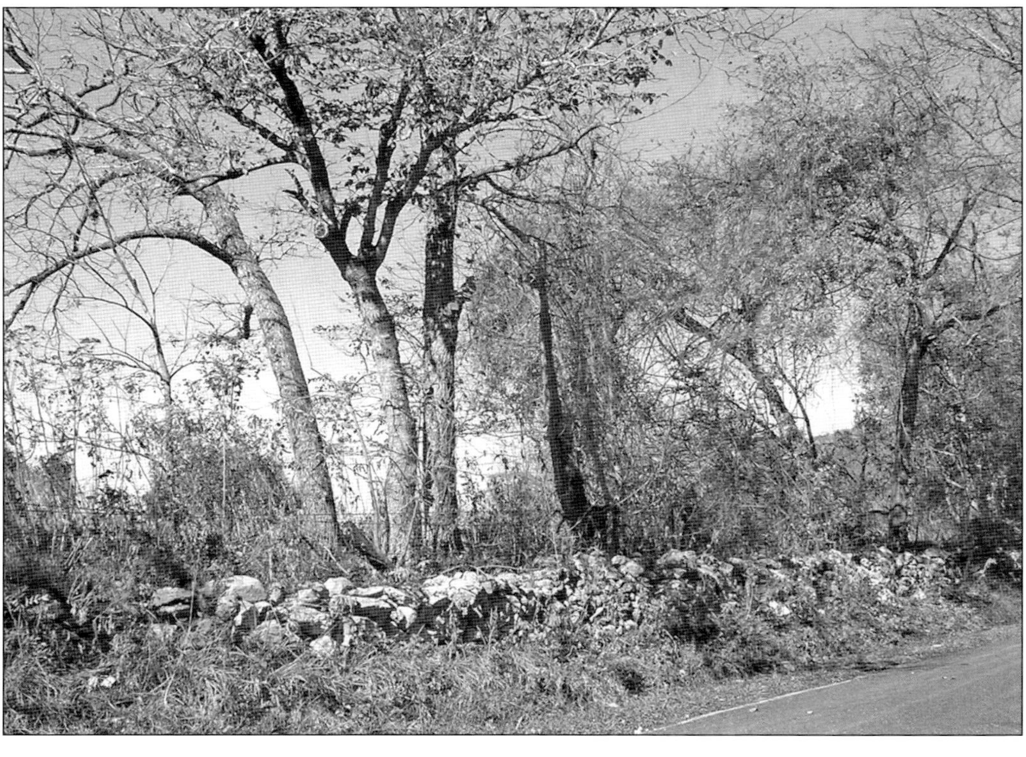

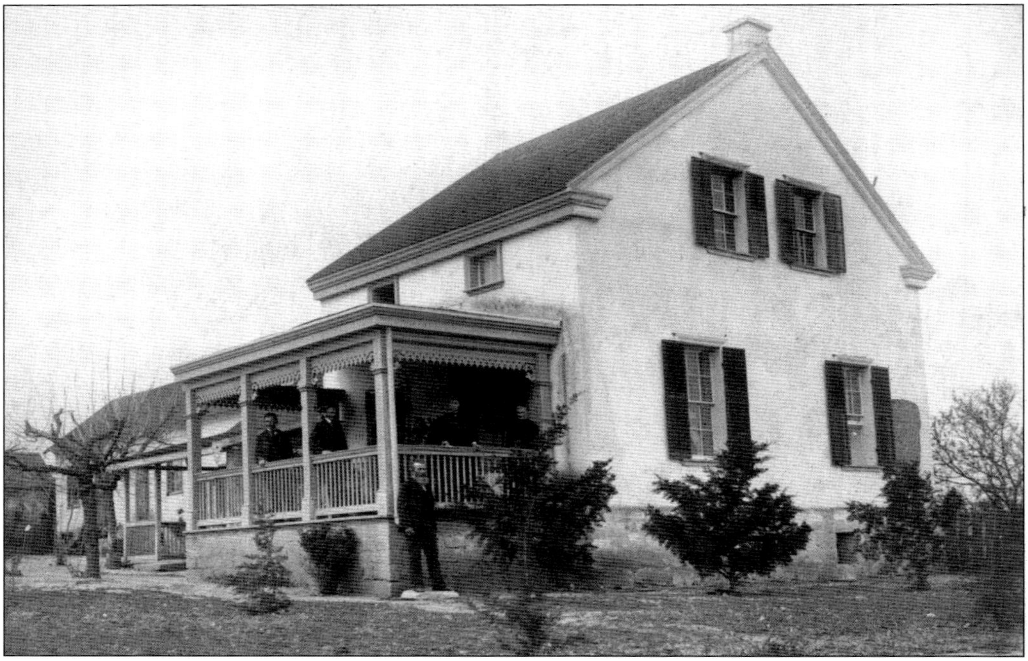

Lantana Farms. Using trees growing on nearby Cypress Creek, Emil Serger built the 10-foot-by-10-foot log portion of the house in 1857. He added the west wing in 1870 and rented part of it to Paul Hanisch. Hanisch was the first pharmacist in Comfort. The second story also dates from 1870; restoration began in 1951. In 1954, Comfort had a live historical pageant presented here on the grounds for the 100th anniversary when guests gathered on the lawn to watch the tableau on the other side of the stream. The pageant recurred in 1979 and 2004. (Above, Roy Perkins collection; below, photograph by Ruth Kiel.)

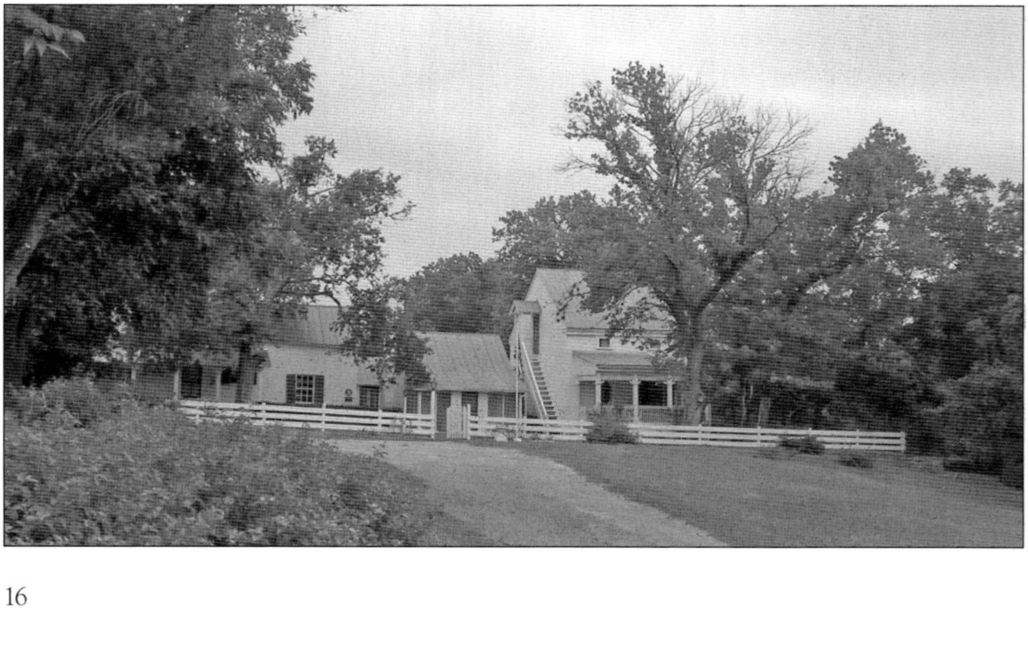

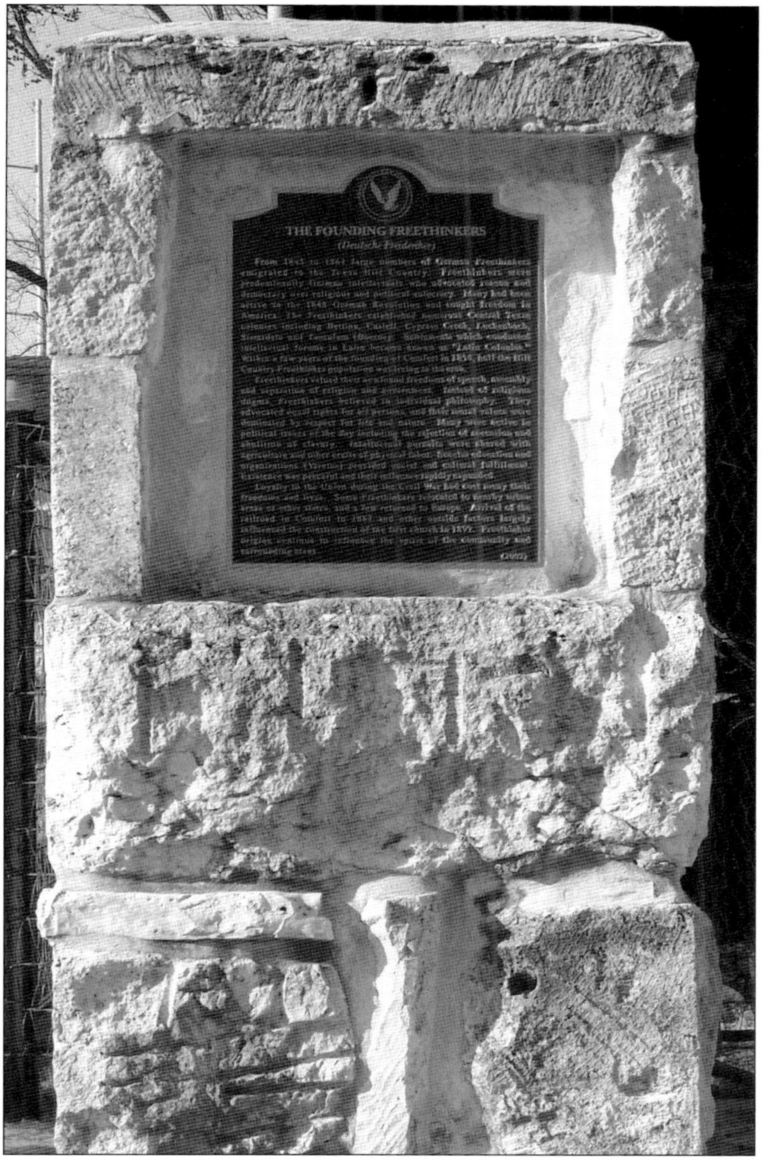

The Founding Freethinkers. Gregory Krauter erected this stone monument next to the Ingenhuett Store on High Street in 2002. It reads, in part, "From 1845 to 1861, large numbers of German Freethinkers emigrated to the Texas Hill Country. Freethinkers were predominantly German intellectuals who advocated reason and democracy over religious and political autocracy. . . . The Freethinkers established numerous Central Texas colonies, including Bettina, Castell, Cypress Creek, Luckenbach, Sisterdale, and Tusculum. Within a few years of the founding of Comfort in 1854, half the Hill Country Freethinker population was living in the area. Freethinkers valued their newfound freedoms of speech, assembly, and separation of religion and government. Instead of religious dogma, Freethinkers believed in individual philosophy. They advocated equal rights for all persons, and their moral values were dominated by respect for life and nature. . . . Freethinker origins continue to influence the spirit of the community and surrounding areas." (Photograph by Ruth Kiel.)

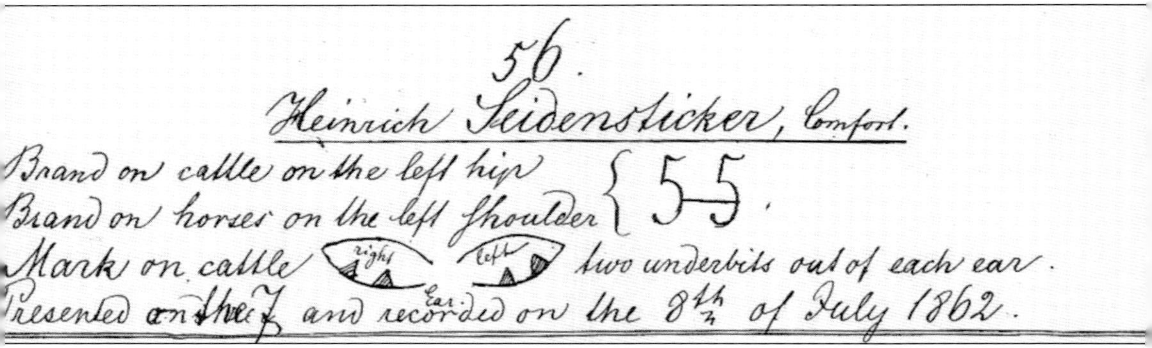
56.
Heinrich Seidensticker, Comfort.
Brand on cattle on the left hip
Brand on horses on the left shoulder { 5-5.
Mark on cattle right left two underbits out of each ear.
Presented on the 7 and recorded on the 8th of July 1862.

Seidensticker Cattle Brand. Heinrich Seidensticker came to Comfort in 1855. He was a tailor and lived in town, but he also operated a dairy. Descendants live on the land where he grazed his cattle near the old town of Brownsboro at Big Bend of the Guadalupe River. The Seidensticker ranch still uses the "5–5" cattle brand, which was first registered at the Kendall County Courthouse in 1862. It commemorates the year of the immigrant's arrival. (Record of Marks and Brands, Book E–1, Kendall County Clerk Office, Boerne, Texas.)

Two

Treue der Union Monument

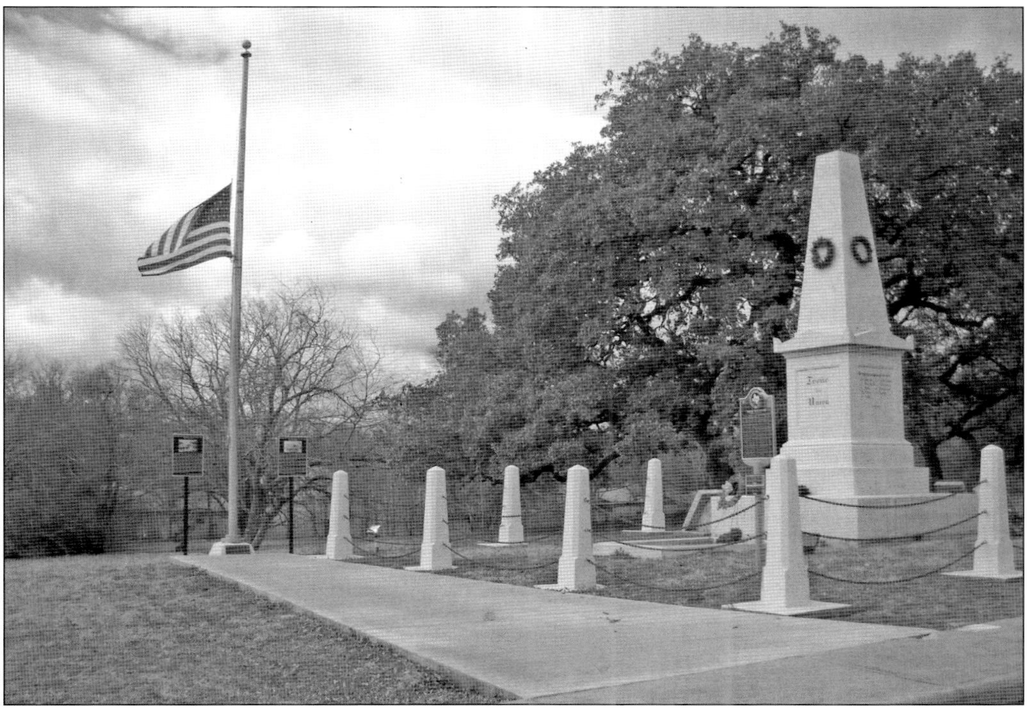

Comfort's Iconic Monument. The Treue der Union monument in Comfort has been the community's pride ever since civic leaders dedicated it in 1866. It was reconstructed and rededicated in 1996. The Comfort Heritage Foundation has a long-term lease on the monument and is responsible for its care. (Photograph by Ruth Kiel.)

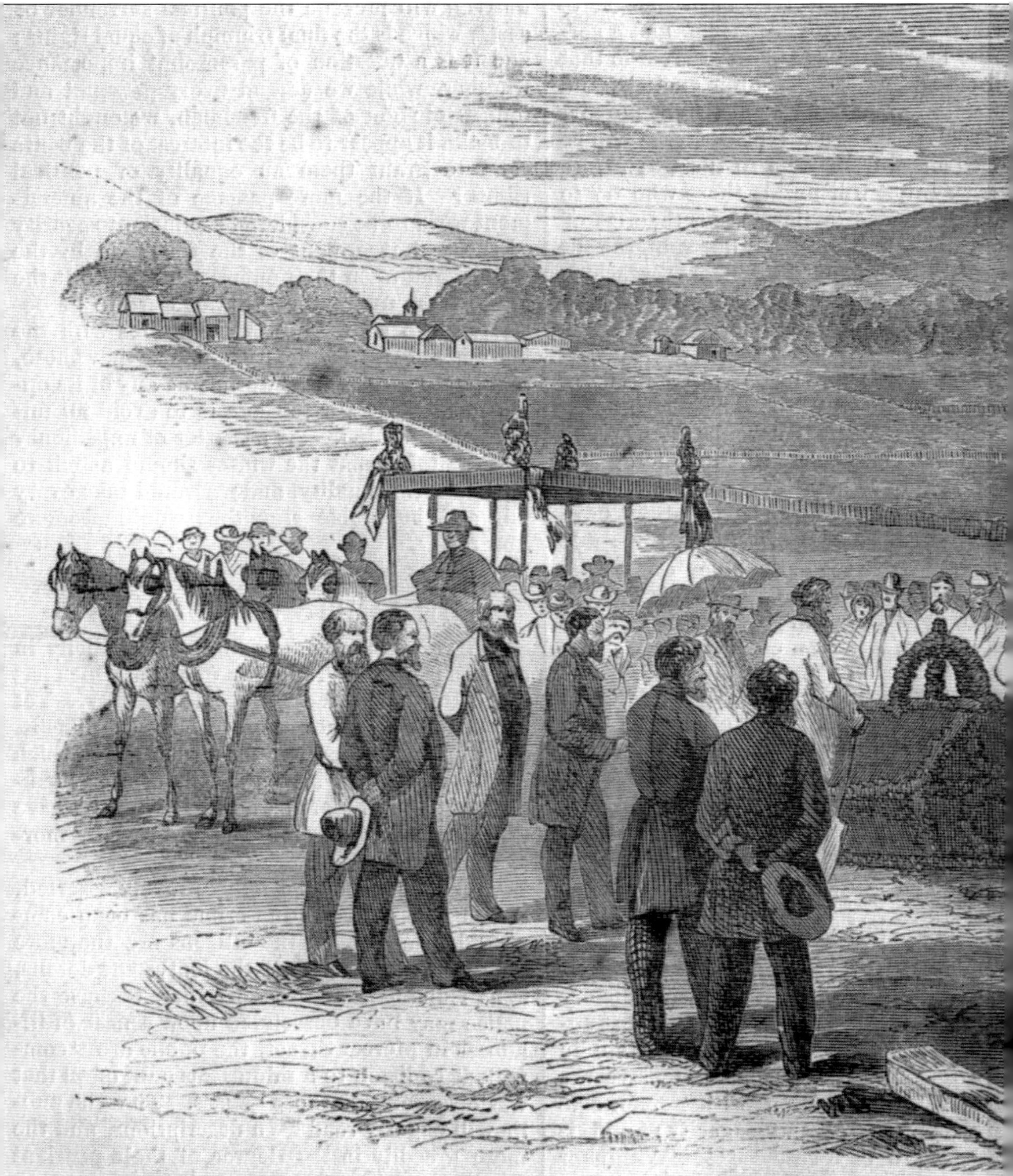

Funeral of German Patriots, 1865. In August 1865, after travel restrictions were eased, a party of men went from Comfort to the Nueces battlefield to recover the remains of the slain. The group had eight Confederate veterans whose units had disbanded by that time. The only Union representatives were two soldiers with deserter status, as all of the units were still on active duty en route from Mississippi to Texas and would not be discharged until

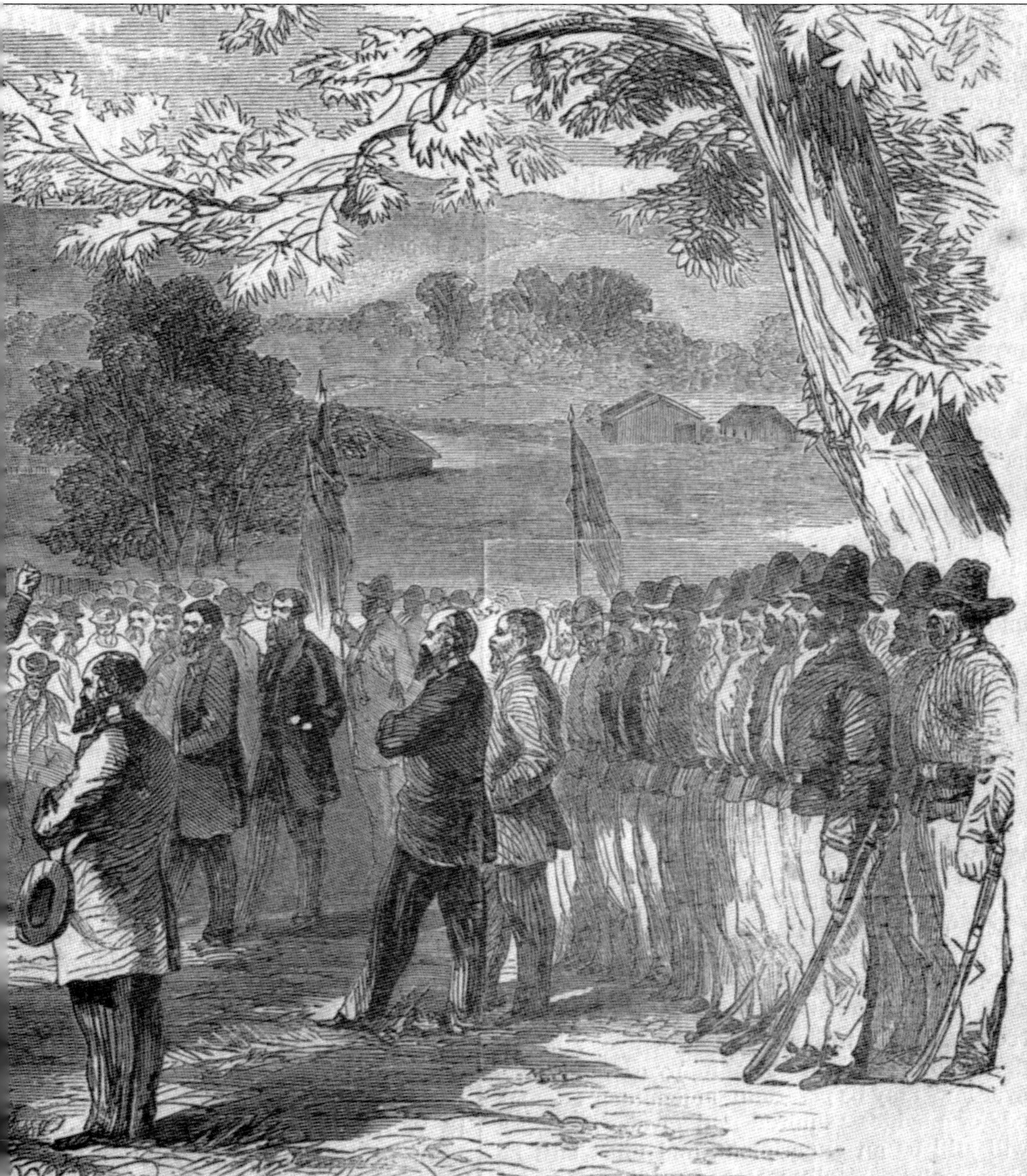

October 1865. Burial was not in the Comfort Cemetery, but rather in a site at the end of High Street overlooking the town. Edward Degener, father of two of the victims, gave the funeral oration. A detachment of Union soldiers, in the area to reoccupy Camp Verde and negotiate with Native Americans, attended the ceremony and fired a salute over the grave. (Comfort Heritage Foundation archives, originally published in *Harper's Weekly*, January 20, 1866.)

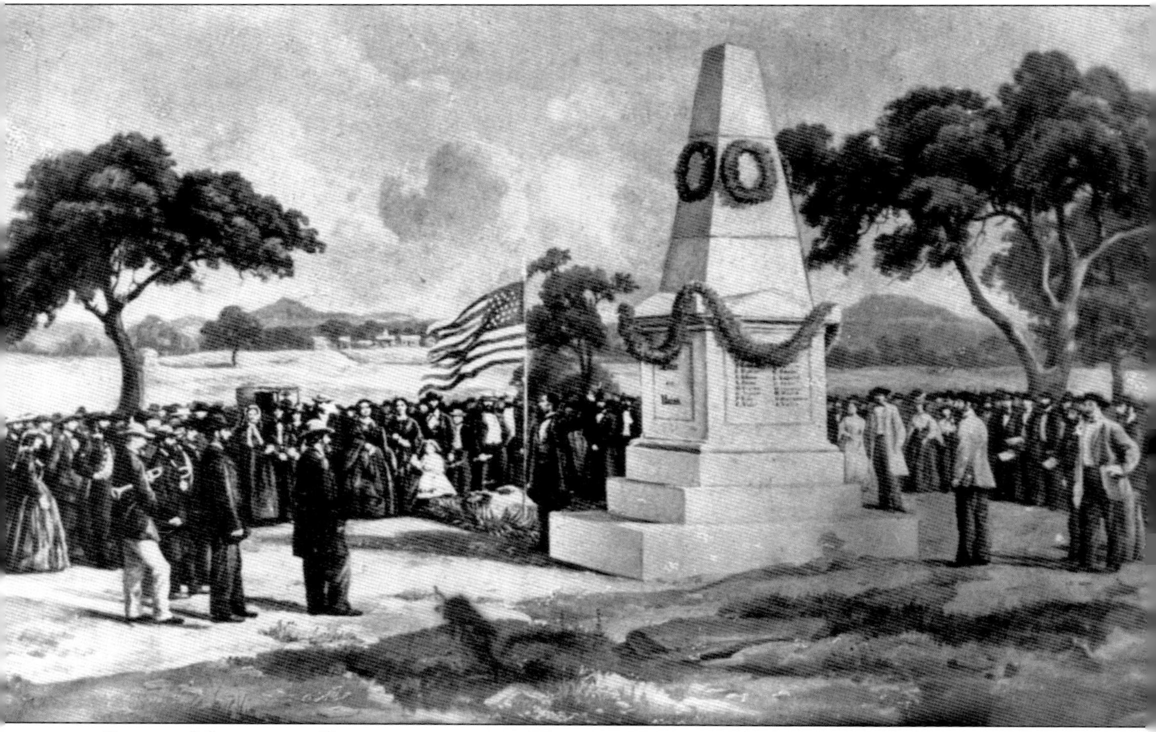

INITIAL MONUMENT DEDICATION, 1866. The Texas Historical Survey Committee historical marker states, "*Treue der Union* (Loyalty to the Union). This German language monument, erected 1866, honors the memory of 68 men (mostly Germans) from this region who were loyal to the Union during the Civil War. Trying desperately to reach U.S. Federal troops by way of Mexico, about 40 of the men were killed by vengeful Confederates bent on annihilating them, in the Battle of the Nueces (August 10, 1862) and a later fight (October 18). The bodies of the slain and those who drowned swimming the Rio Grande were left unburied. A group of Germans gathered the bones of their friends and buried them at this site in 1865." (Comfort Heritage Foundation archives.)

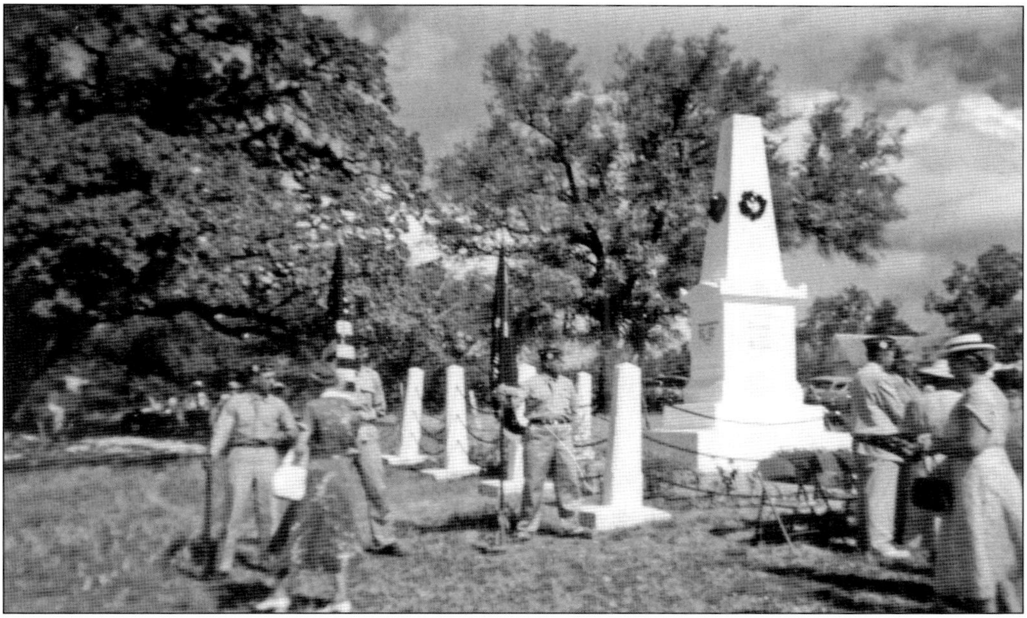

EARLY CELEBRATIONS AT MONUMENT. Annual ceremonies at the monument became customary. The picture on the cover of this book is a 1939 Memorial Day event. The 1954 picture taken at the centennial of the founding of Comfort shows it to be less formal. It includes several uniformed men standing at ease, possibly serving as the color guard. The dark flag may be that of the local American Legion. For many years in early August on the anniversary of the battle, the San Antonio Tent of the Daughters of Union Veterans honored those interred. On September 10, 1988, Roberta Stieler Smith, Irene and Bernard Stieler, and Esther Wiedenfeld participated in the dedication of bronze name markers that duplicated the names chiseled on the monument, which were deteriorating. After historical reflections and a roll call of the victims, descendants of victims unveiled the markers. (Both Comfort Heritage Foundation archives.)

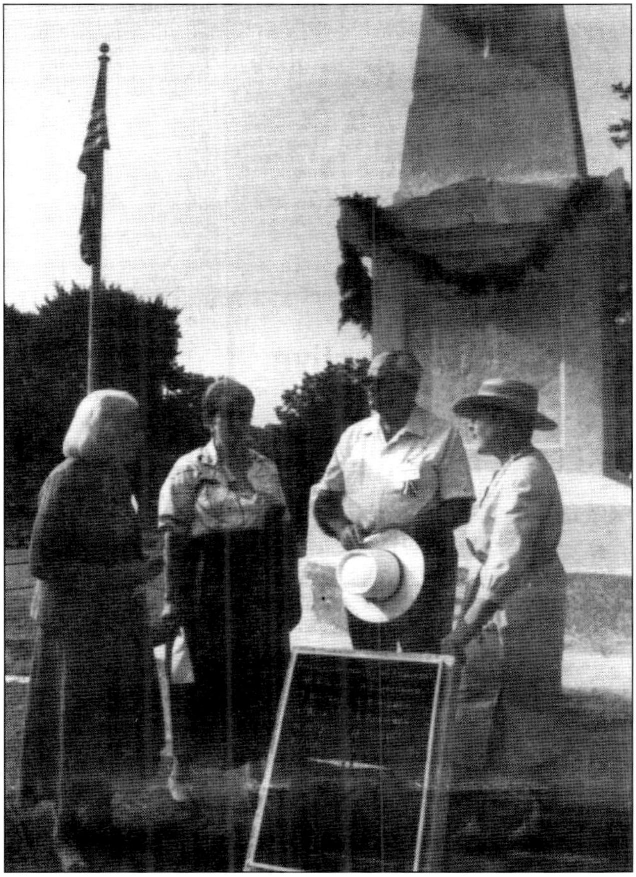

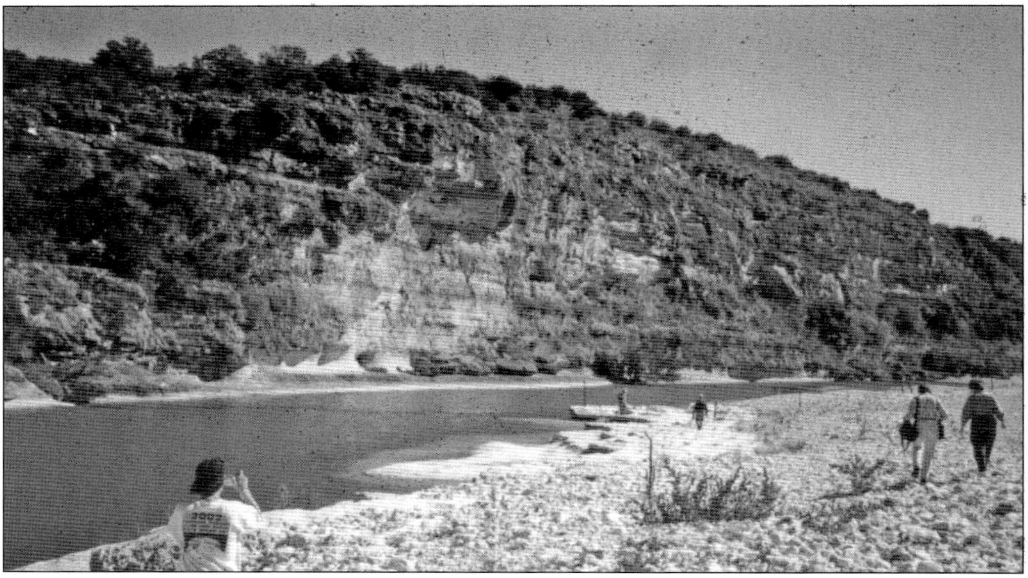

Nueces Battlefield. The site on the North Prong of the Nueces River had abundant water and grass for horses, and a pleasant cedar brake in which the men could sleep, but it had no cover for defense. Observation of the Unionists by the Confederates on the bluff was possible. Although the battle site is often placed in Kinney County at the time of the encounter in 1862, the location was actually Dawson County, which existed from 1857 to 1866. In 1866, the Texas Legislature eliminated Dawson County by drawing new boundaries for Uvalde and Kinney Counties, with Kinney County taking the west part of Dawson County. (Both photographs by Ruth Kiel.)

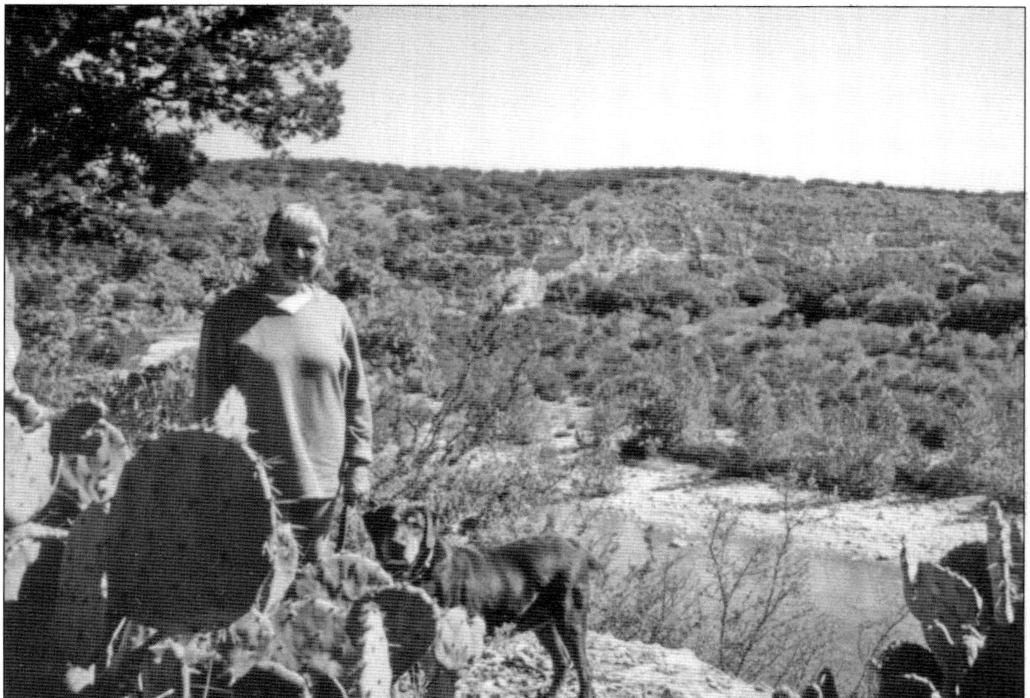

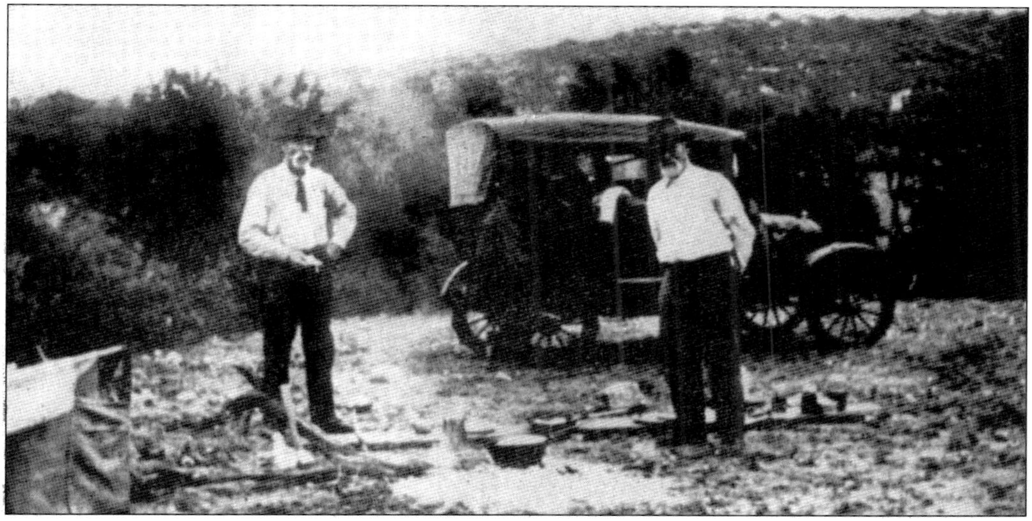

Visits to the Battlefield. Visits to the battlefield are uncommon because it is beyond Rock Springs on a private ranch; the distance from Comfort is 141 miles to the ranch gate and then another 7 miles over an unpaved road to the battle site. In 1923, Alex Brinkmann, Henry Schwethelm, and Richard Doebbler made the trip in Doebbler's Ford Model T, leaving before sunrise and arriving in late afternoon; they visited the battlefield the next day. The Comfort Heritage Foundation occasionally sponsors visits such as that on May 5, 2008, when Col. (Ret.) Paul Burrier explained the tactics of the battle. (Above, Comfort Heritage Foundation archives; below, photograph by Ruth Kiel.)

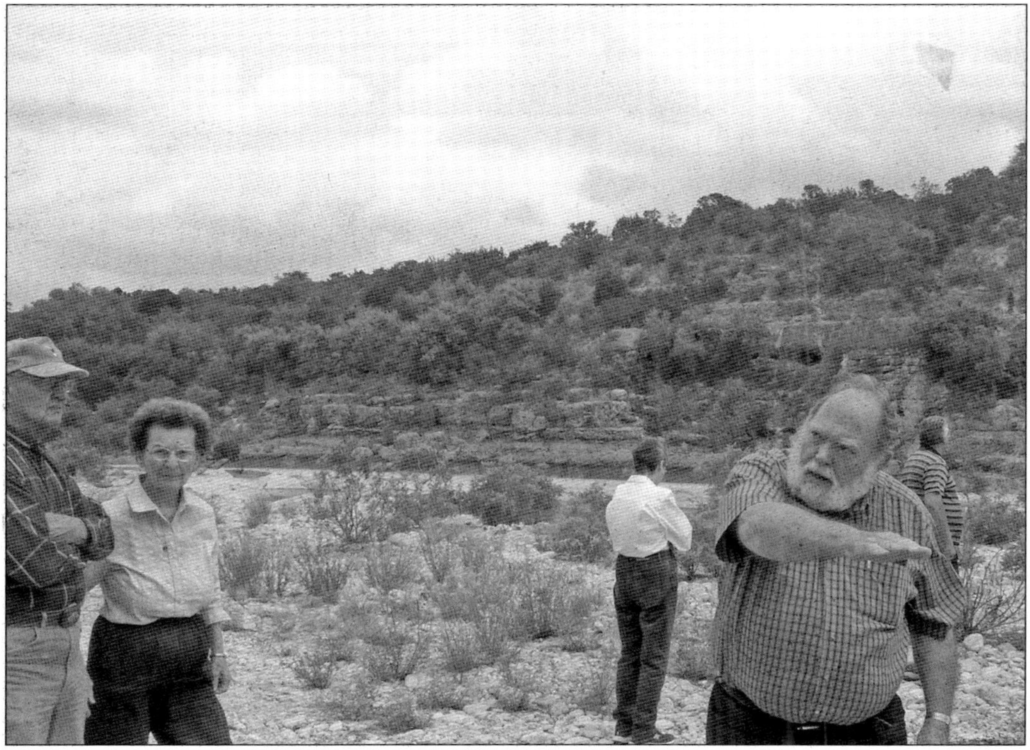

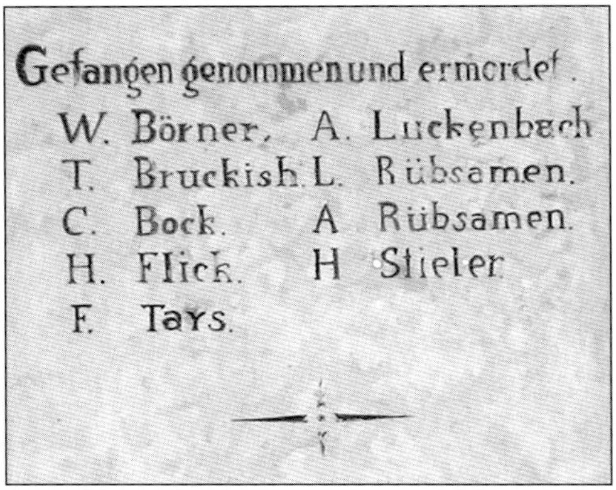

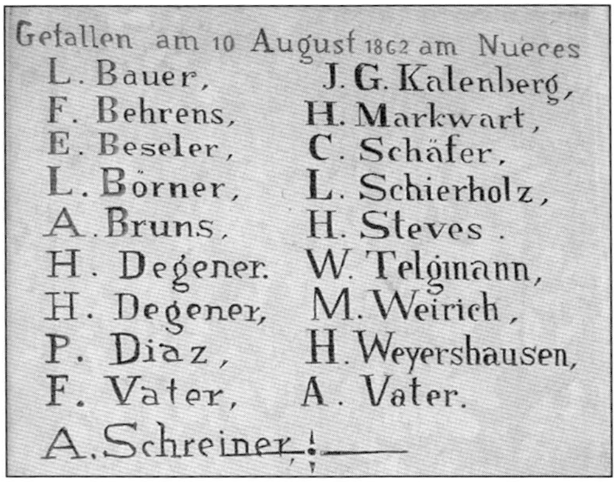

The Honored Dead. Although not the only monument of its kind south of the Mason-Dixon line in Confederate territory (Vanceburg, Kentucky, and Greenville, Tennessee, have similar monuments), it is special in being the only German-language monument to the Union in the South where remains of those killed in battle are buried and where an 1866 period flag is flown at half-staff. (All photographs by Ruth Kiel.)

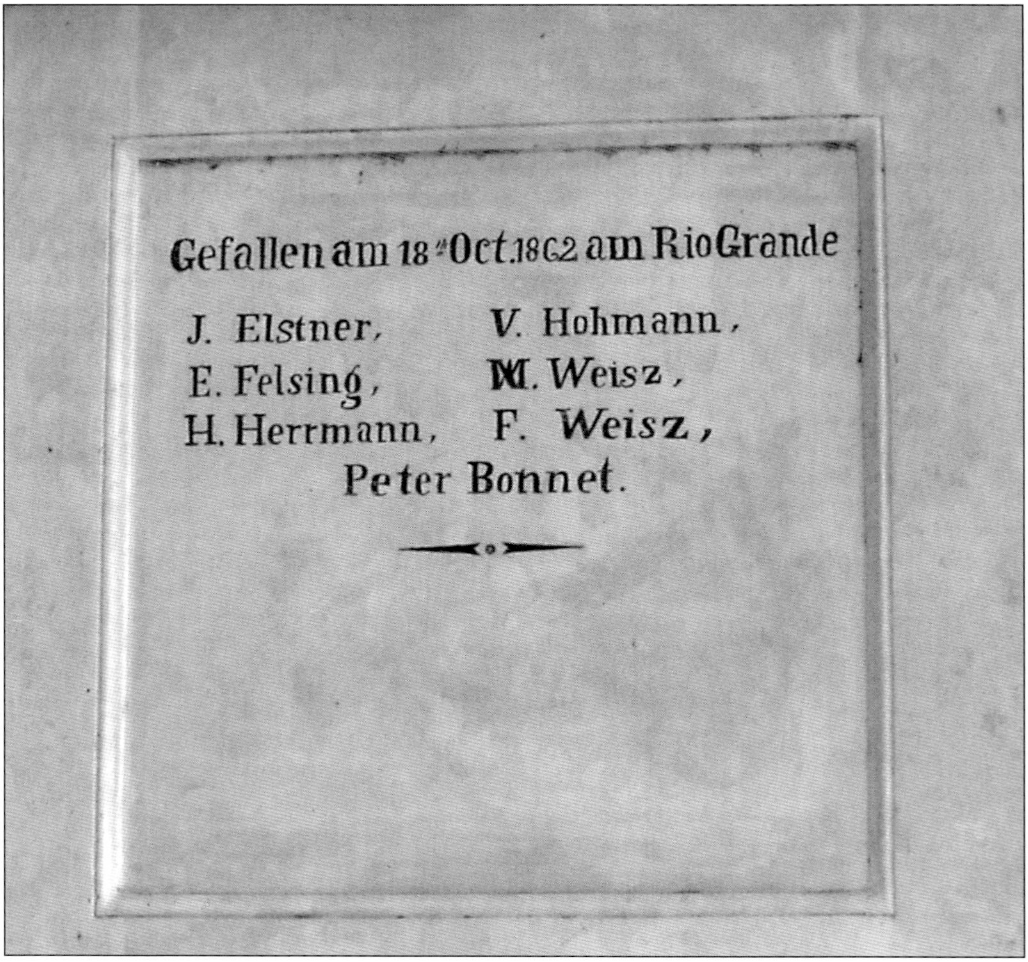

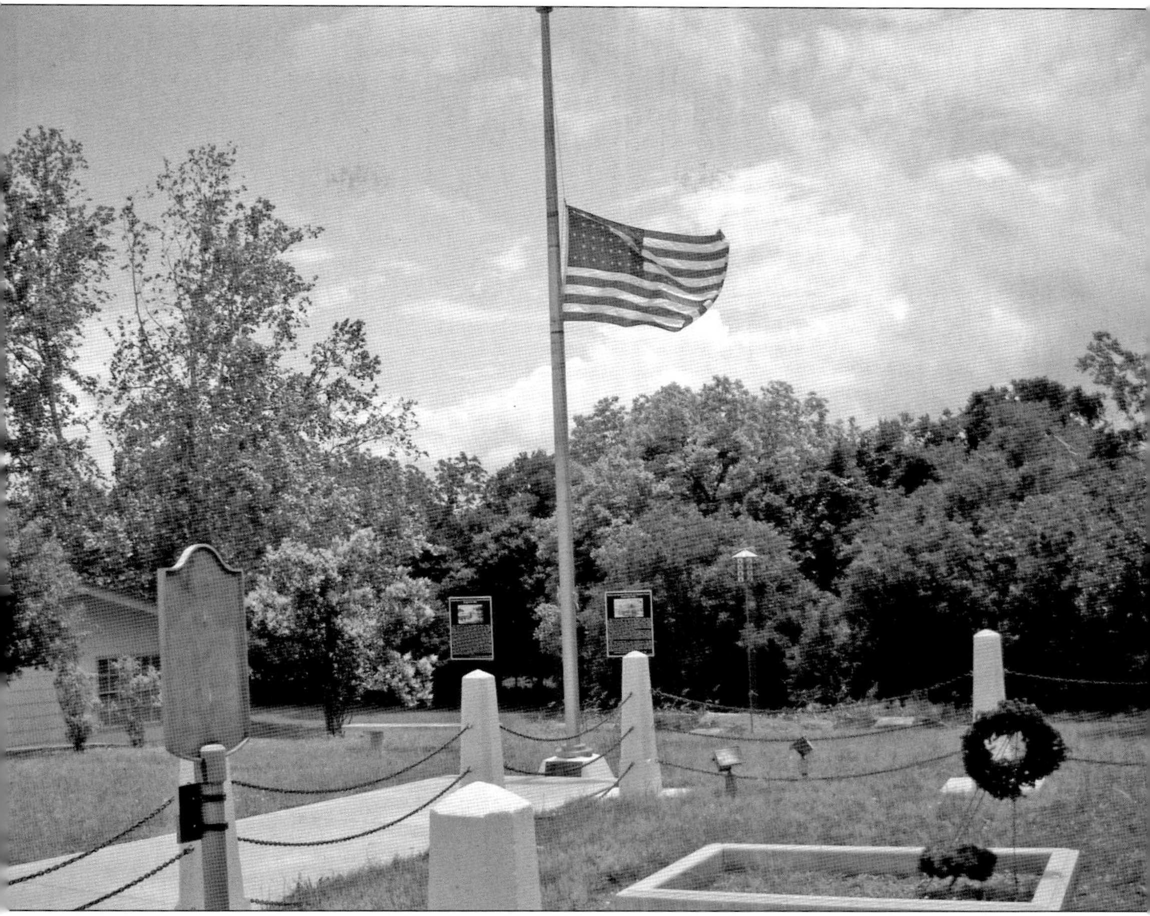

The 36-Star Flag. At the start of the Civil War there were 33 states, thus there were 33 stars on the flag. States subsequently admitted to the Union were Kansas in 1861, West Virginia in 1863, and Nevada in 1865. The Treue der Union monument has the 36-star flag of 1865, the date of the funeral for the victims. Other places that fly replica flags include Flag House in Baltimore, Maryland, which uses a 15-star, 15-stripe flag; Fort McHenry in Baltimore, which also uses a 15-star, 15-stripe flag; and Fort Sumter, in Charleston, South Carolina, which flies five flags from the 1861–1865 time, including the 33-star U.S. flag of 1861 and the 35-star flag of early 1865. In Texas, places that fly replica flags include Fort Davis, which on different occasions uses a 31-star flag, a 37-star flag, and a 38-star flag; Fort McKavett, which uses a 37-star flag; and Fort Concho, which uses a 39-star flag. (Photograph by Ruth Kiel.)

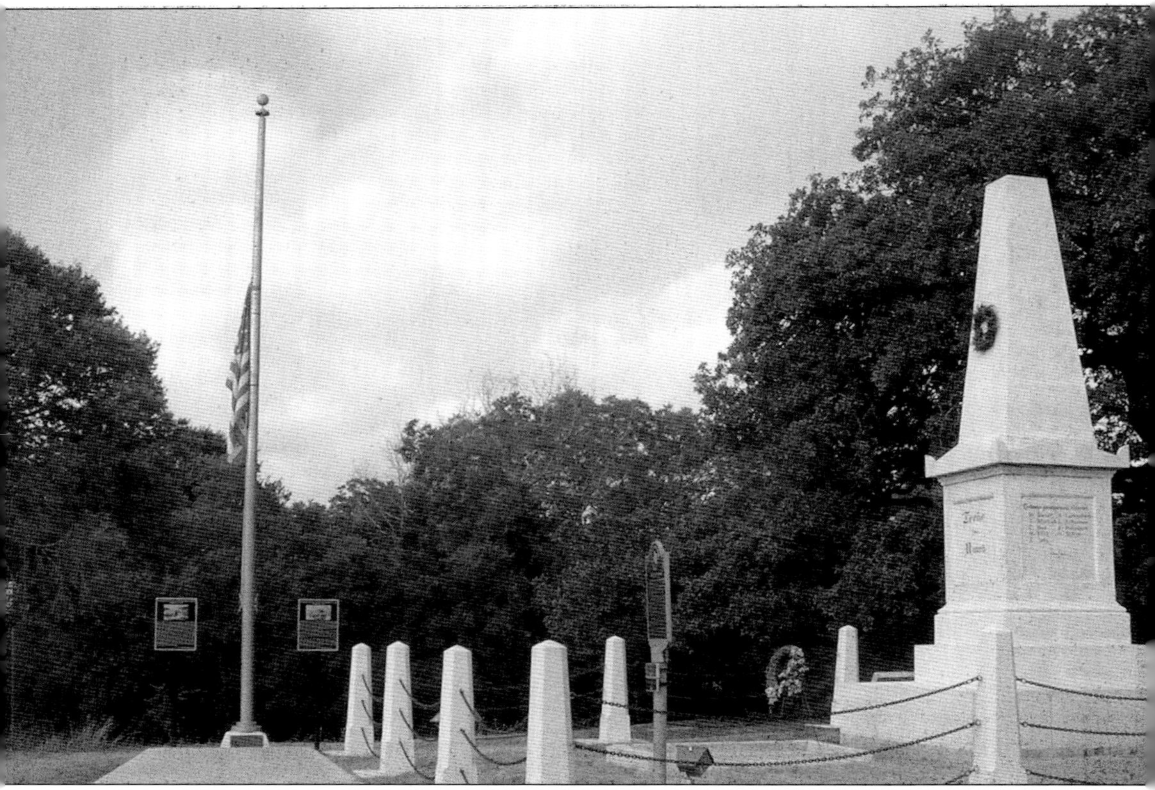

FLAG AT HALF-STAFF. Starting with the 125th anniversary in 1991, the flag at the monument has flown at half-staff, 24 hours a day. Although newspaper accounts relate that Congress authorized such a policy, and that only five other sites have been awarded this distinction, recent research indicates neither statement is true. Congressional authorization regarding flag protocol takes the form of a presidential proclamation or a public law, such as those that authorize the flag to be flown 24 hours per day, seven days per week (but not at half-staff): Fort McHenry, Flag House Square, the Iwo Jima Monument, Town Green, the White House, the Washington Monument, U.S. Customs ports of entry, and Valley Forge. Regarding the alleged claims of five other places to fly the flag at half-staff, recent research indicates none are true: the USS *Arizona* only lowers the flag when other ships fly their flags at half-mast; in Arlington, a half hour before the first funeral and a half hour after the last, five days per week; Gettysburg, where it is not a policy; Little Bighorn, which is only at half-staff on June 24, the date of the battle (but then only until noon); and Fort Mackinac State Historic Park, which has no congressional authorization but a long-standing tradition to fly the flag at half-staff over the post cemetery that is raised every morning. (Photograph by Ruth Kiel.)

Three

Historic Buildings

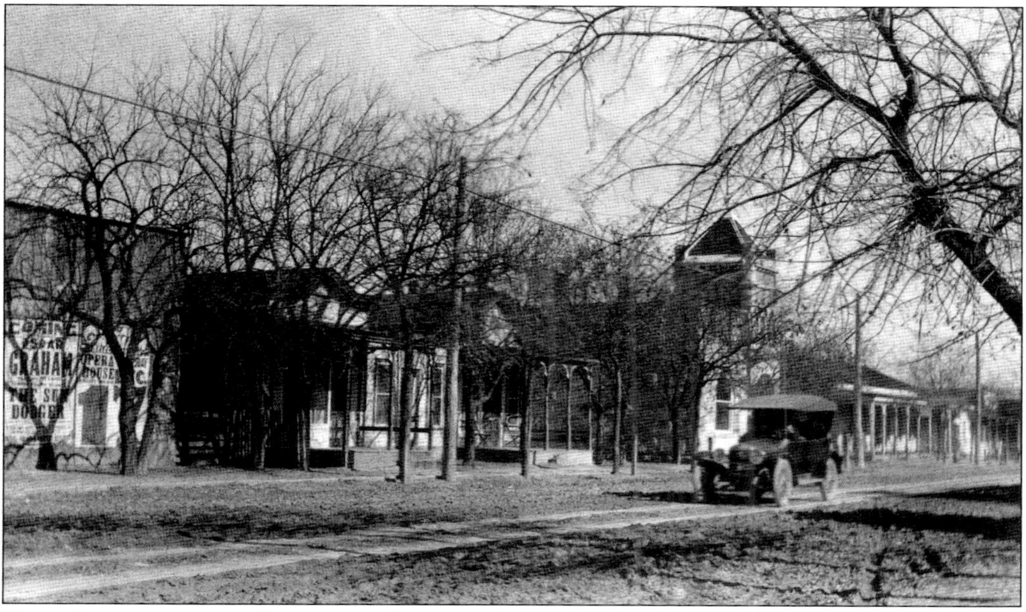

High Street between Sixth and Seventh Streets, 1920. On the left are the Ludwig Hein blacksmith shop, the Alex Brinkmann building, and the Comfort State Bank. The sign on the blacksmith shop advertised the Oscar Graham Company scheduled to perform *The Sun Dodger* on December 17, 1919, at the Steves and Stahmann's Opera House. (Comfort Heritage Foundation archives.)

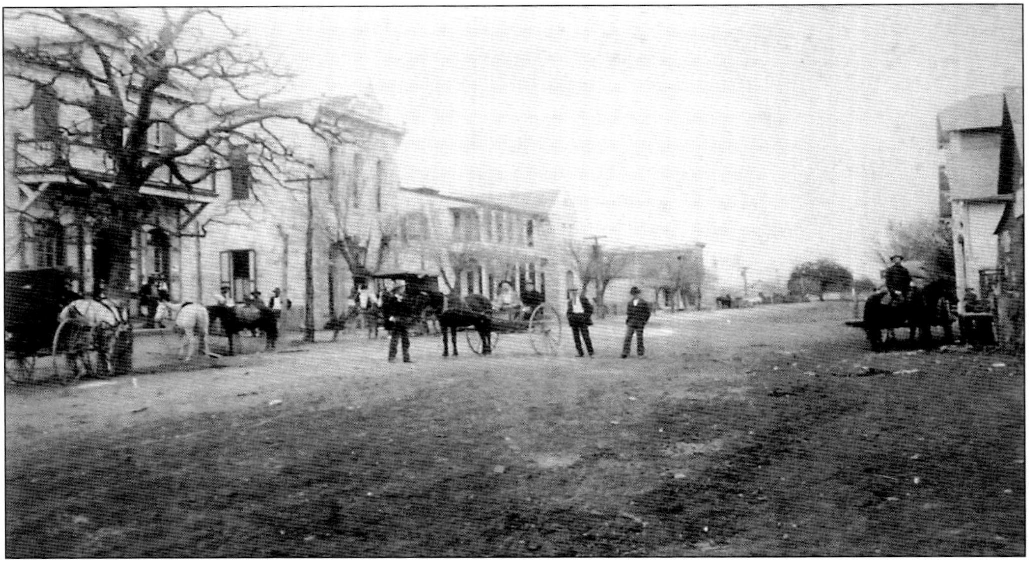

HIGH STREET FROM EIGHTH STREET, BEFORE 1913. Visible on the left are the Ingenhuett Store, Ingenhuett-Karger Saloon, and Faust Hotel. On the right are blacksmith shops owned by Henry Weber and Ernst Letz. The presence of a horse-drawn cart in the street, a rider on horseback on the right at the livery stable, and horses tied up in front of the saloon suggests this is an early-1900s scene. (Comfort Heritage Foundation archives.)

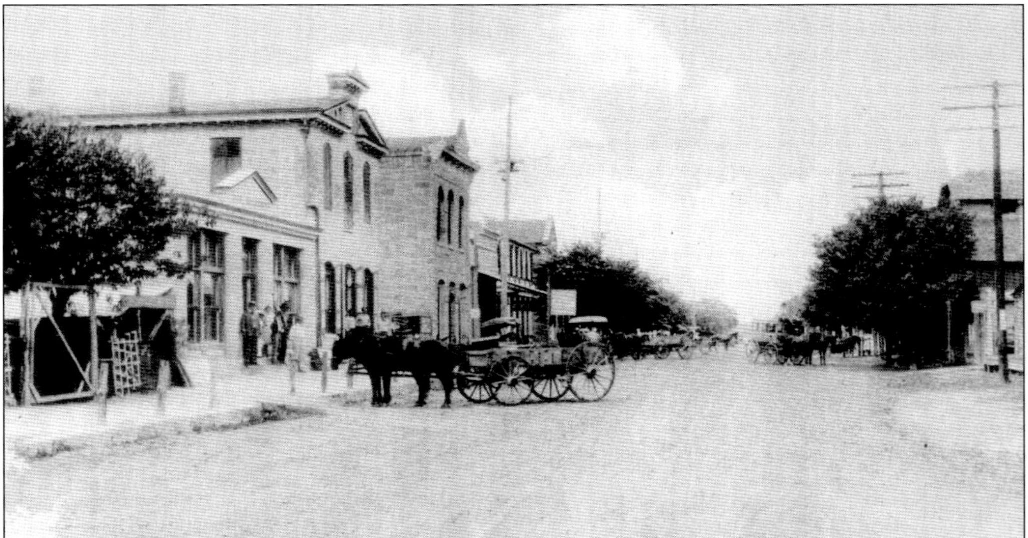

HIGH STREET, AFTER 1913. The "Pool Hall" sign at the Karger Building suggests a date after 1913. The *Comfort News* of November 28, 1913 wrote, "A contract has been made between Ernst Karger and Fritz Anderwald whereby the latter will move his pool hall into the new building which is being erected next to Ernst Karger's saloon." (Comfort Heritage Foundation archives.)

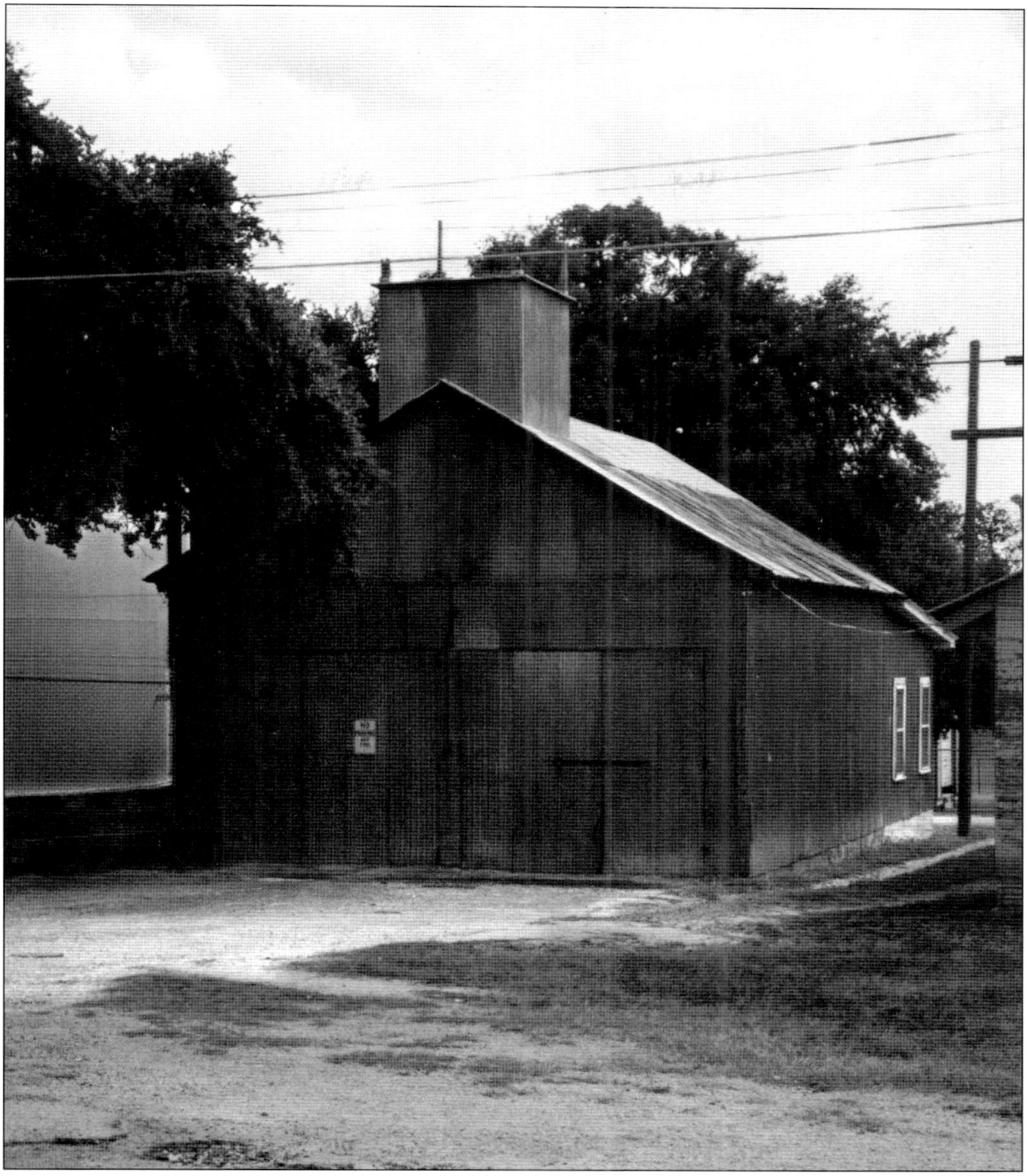

First Firehouse of Comfort Volunteer Fire Department. The first firehouse at the southwest corner of Seventh and Main Streets was used from 1912 to 1962, when a larger brick building was erected on High Street. The Comfort Volunteer Fire Department is a corporation governed by a board of directors. It is financed by voluntary donations from the citizens of Commissioners Precincts 1 and 4 of Kendall County, Commissioners Precincts 2 and 3 of Kerr County, and by contributions at the annual fish fry. (Comfort Volunteer Fire Department collection.)

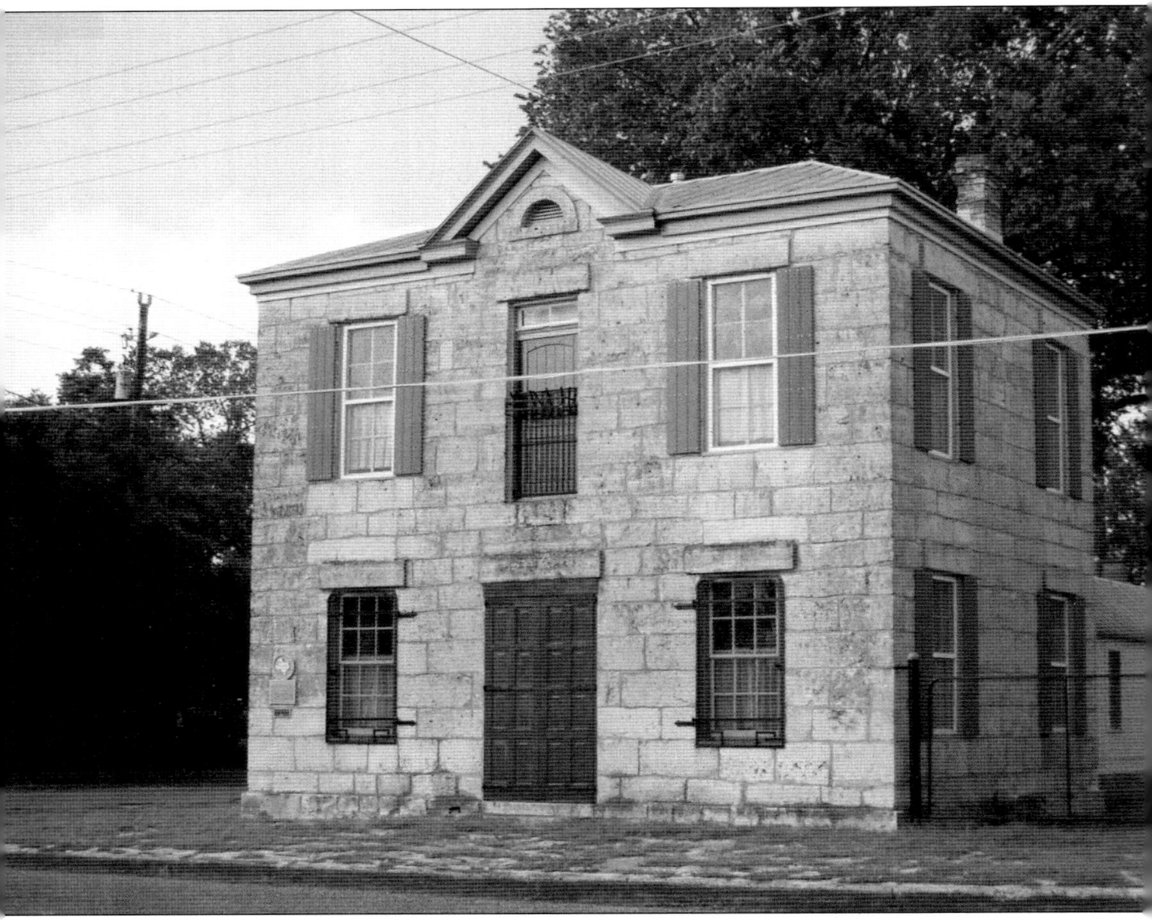

GASS *SCHMIEDE* (BLACKSMITH SHOP). According to the Texas Historic Landmark plaque of 1986, "This limestone-block building was built in 1890 as a blacksmith shop (Schmiede) for Jacob Gass (1845–1913). Rock mason J. Gottlieb Lorbeer worked on the lower level for almost a year, walking to the job each week from Sisterdale (15 miles east). The upper level was finished quickly with machinery and was used as a residence. Paul Ingenhuett bought the building in 1903. His family made it available for a museum and public library in 1932." (Photograph by Ruth Kiel.)

Ingenhuett Store. Peter Ingenhuett built the two-story original store in 1883 using the design of architect Alfred Giles. He added the one-story east wing in 1900. Products sold included hardware, farm equipment, groceries, and dry goods. "If you can't find it anywhere else, go to Ingenhuett's," said Comfort residents. The store also did banking and served as the post office. The older picture at right has a balcony for the upstairs apartment, while the lower part has a saloon sign. The one-story addition is in the later picture below. (At right, Roy Perkins collection; below, Comfort Heritage Foundation archives.)

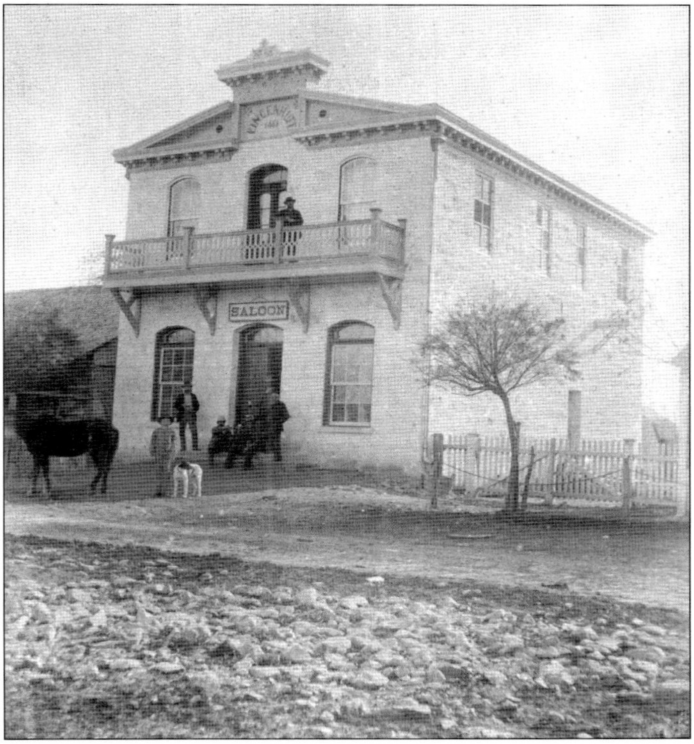

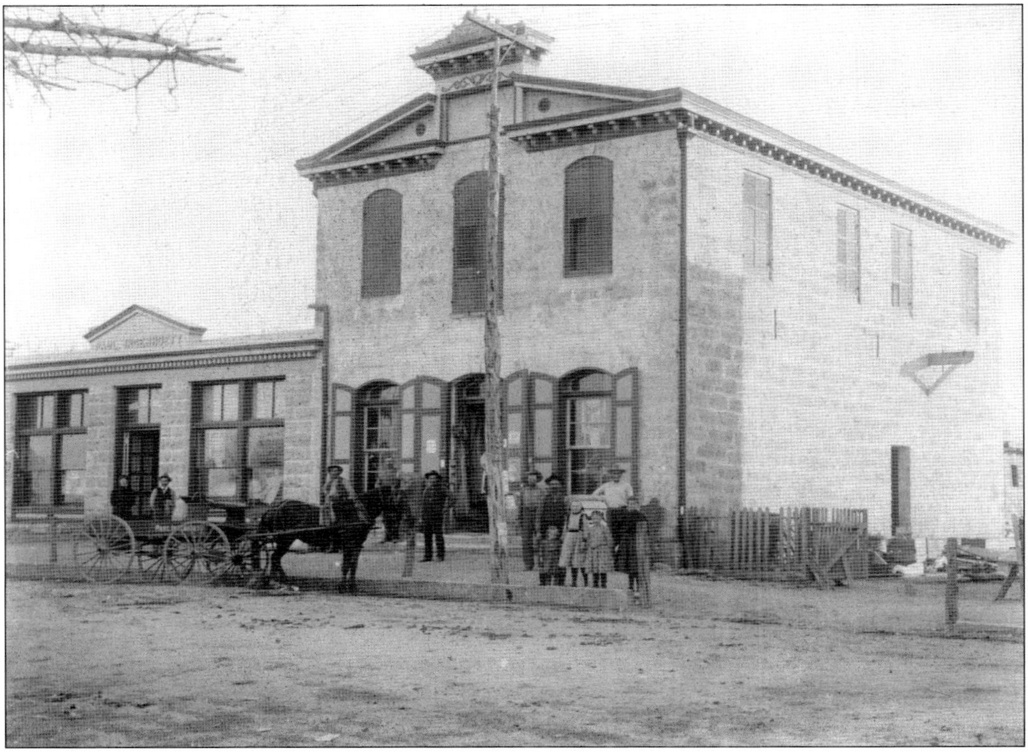

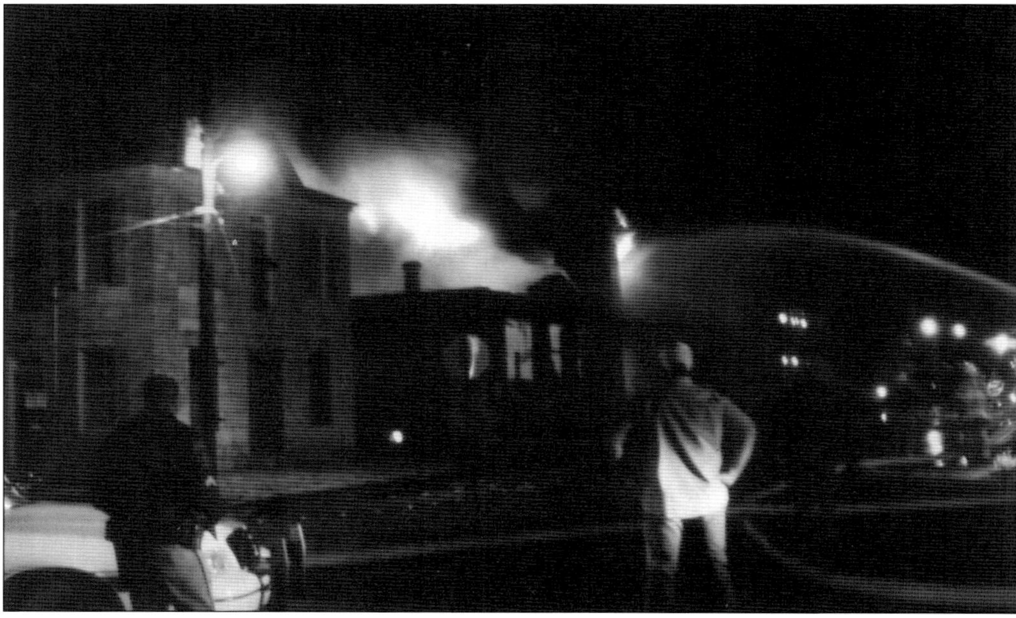

Ingenhuett Store Fire. The Ingenhuett family continued to operate the store until March 16, 2006, when fire destroyed the building. The *Boerne Star* reported that 32 firefighters from Comfort, Sisterdale, Waring, and Center Point fought the blaze for more than six hours and kept it from spreading to nearby buildings. Saddened by the loss of this landmark and grieving for the family, Comfort residents hung wreaths on the fence put up in front of the ruined structure. (Above, photograph by Frank Manitzas; below, photograph by Ruth Kiel.)

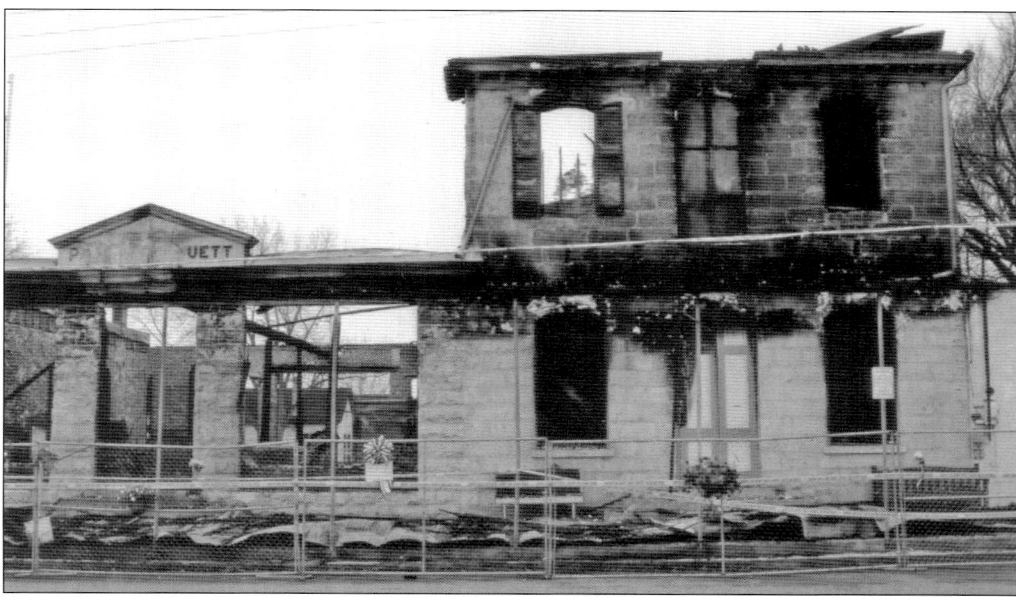

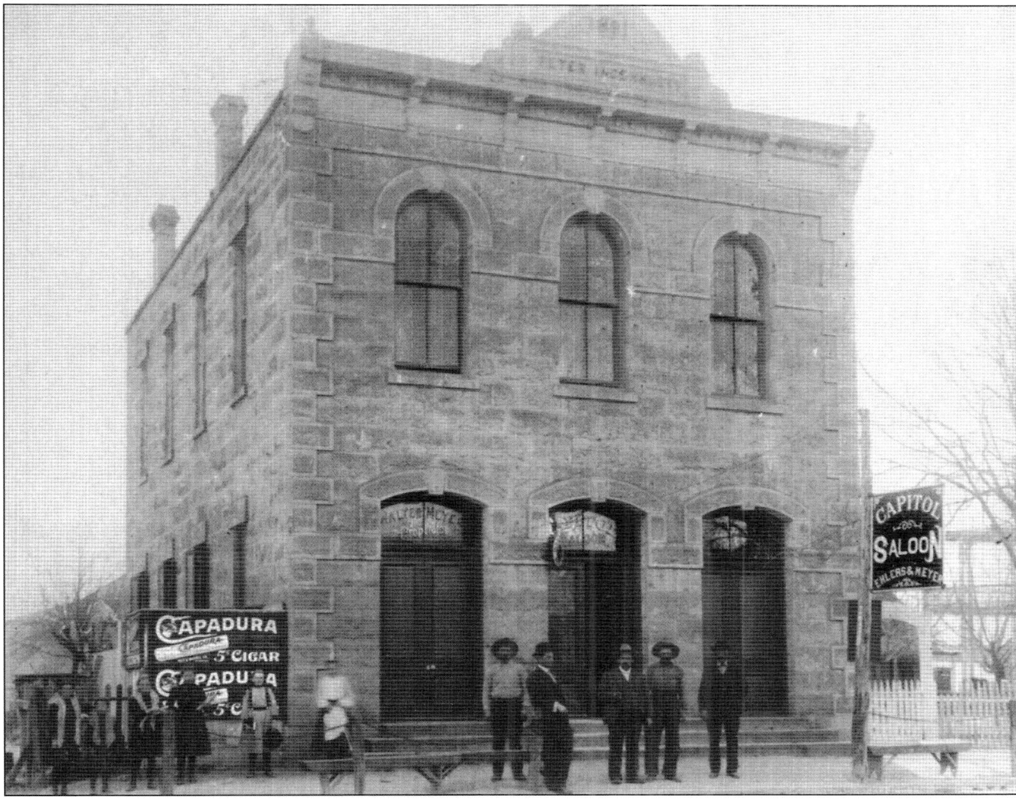

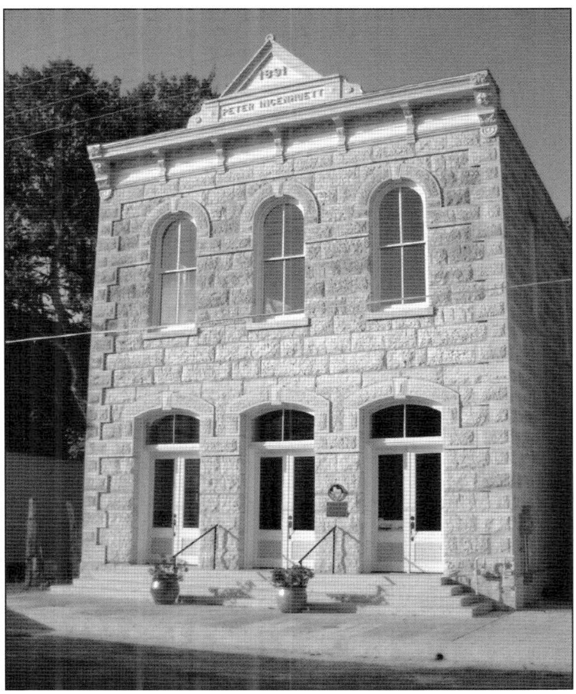

INGENHUETT-KARGER SALOON. San Antonio architect Alfred Giles designed this building for Peter Ingenhuett in 1891. Ingenhuett's son Hubert originally operated the establishment; later Ernst Karger had it. During and after Prohibition, the building served as a confectionery, a grocery, and an ice cream parlor. The pressed metal cornice has the year of construction and the original owner's name is in the pediment. On April 17, 2010, the Kendall County Historic Commission unveiled Texas Historic Building markers for both the Ingenhuett-Karger Saloon and the Karger Building. (Above, Roy Perkins collection; at right, photograph by Ruth Kiel.)

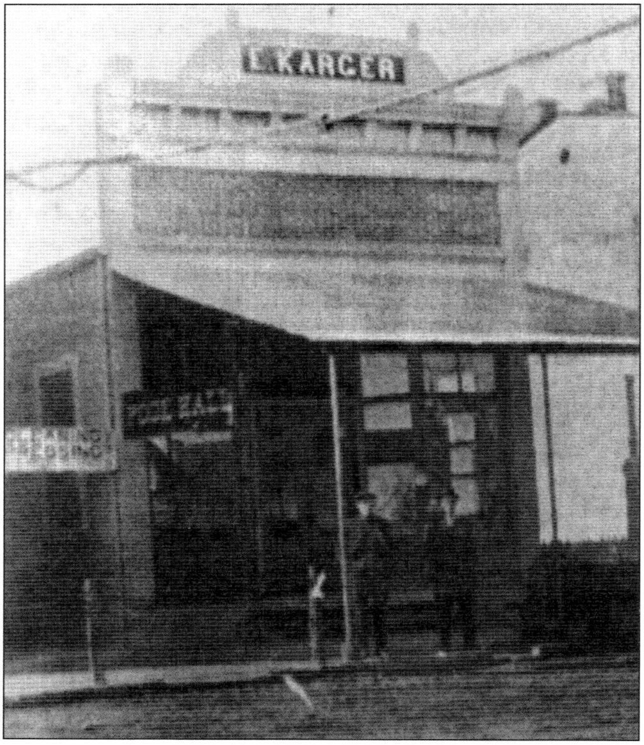

Karger Building. Ernst Karger (1861–1922), who owned and operated the saloon on the adjoining property, had this building constructed in 1913. Fritz Anderwald's pool hall was the first to occupy the building. Fred Koerlin operated a cabinetry business here after 1951. Needing a garage for his cars, he removed the original recessed entry and large windows but kept them in storage. When new owners restored the building, they reused the original entrance and windows. It is an example of the work of the George L. Mesker and Company of Evansville, Indiana. This company manufactured the building's decorative pressed metal facade, pediment, and siding. (At left, Comfort Heritage Foundation archives; below, photograph by Ruth Kiel.)

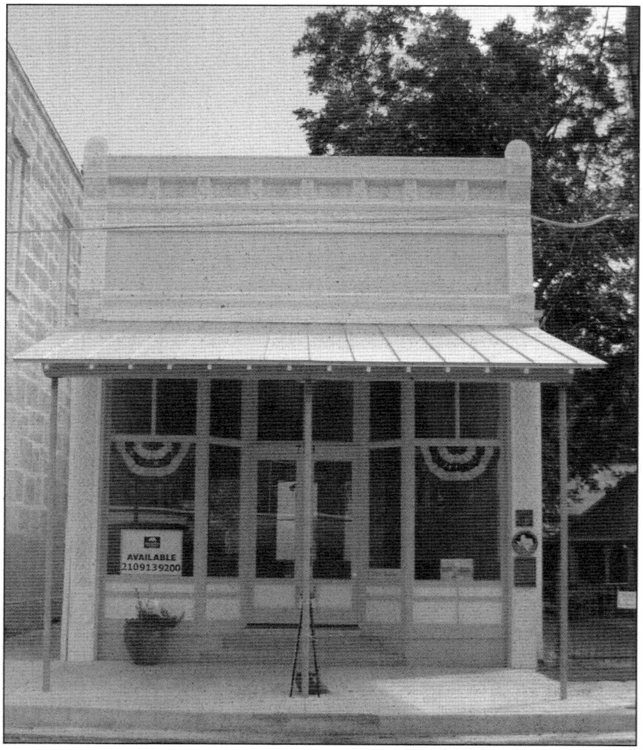

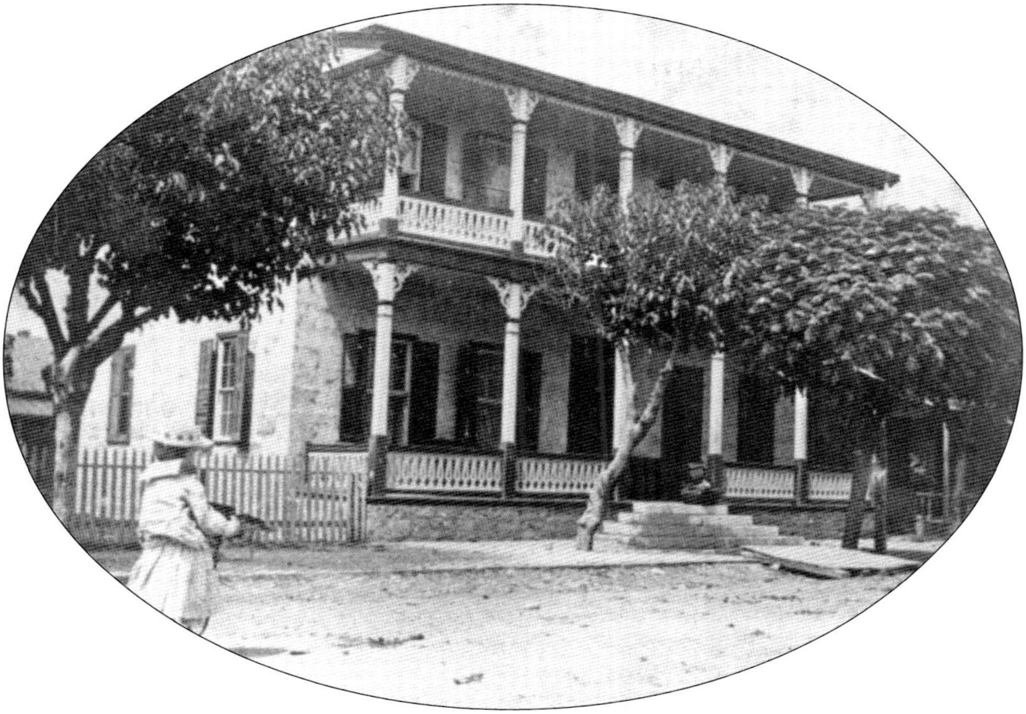

Ingenhuett-Faust Hotel. Designed by Alfred Giles, the original eight-room hotel was built in 1880–1881 for Peter Ingenhuett. His son Ernst and wife, Katie Brinkmann Ingenhuett, operated the establishment for several years. Louis and Matilda Faust purchased the hotel in 1909 and operated it until 1946. The picture below shows the adjacent 1908 post office, an atypical Alfred Giles design possibly influenced by government specifications. It has since had other uses and is now a restaurant. (Above, Roy Perkins collection; below, Comfort Heritage Foundation archives.)

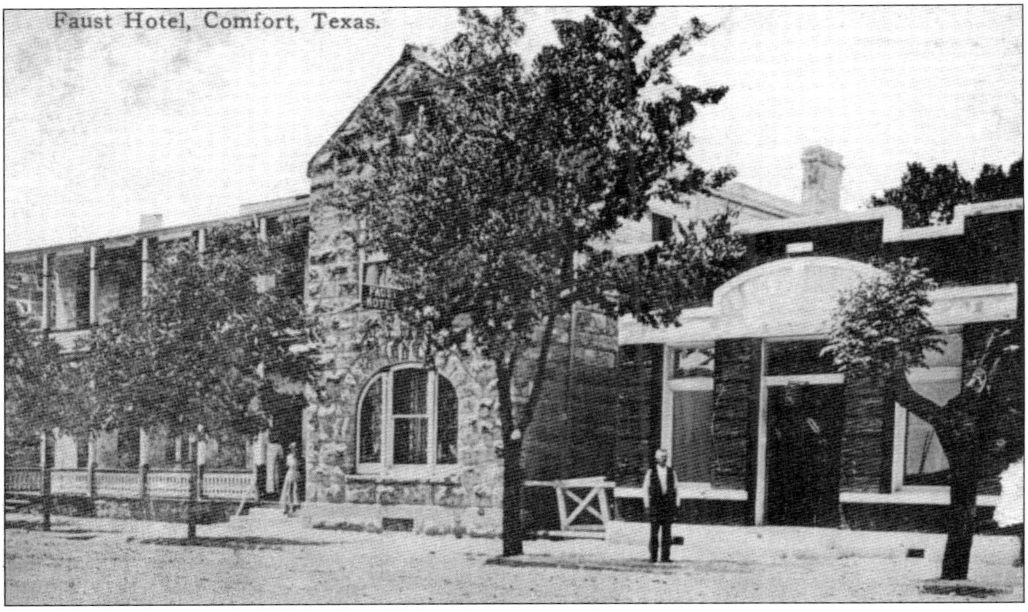

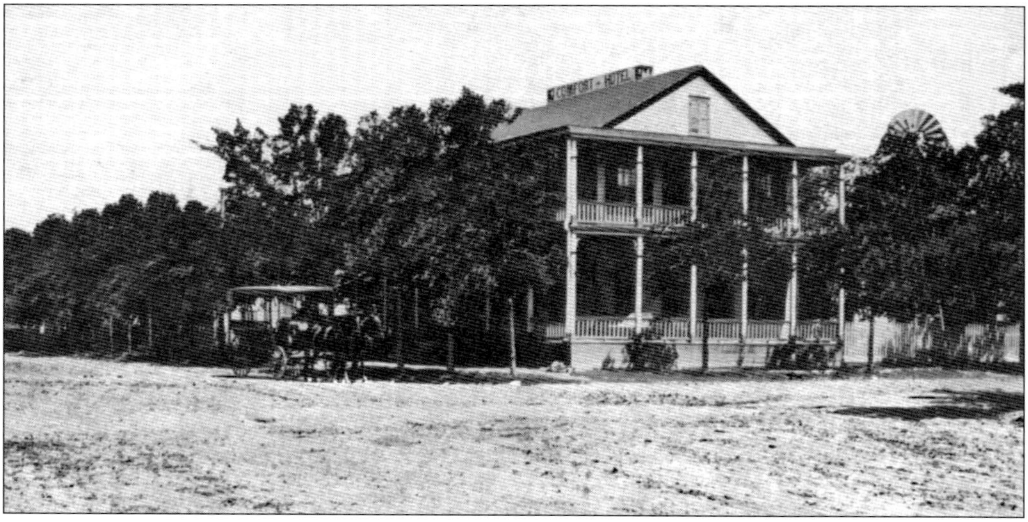

Comfort Hotel. Built by Richard Kott about 1888, it served visitors and salesmen arriving on the new railroad into Comfort. A horse-drawn buggy delivered passengers to the hotel. It was first known as the Kott Hotel and then later as the Comfort Hotel (note the sign on the roof). W. L. Surber bought the hotel about 1900 and managed it until the 1940s. It was renovated in 2006 and received the annual award for historic restoration from the Comfort Heritage Foundation. (Above, Comfort Heritage Foundation archives; below, photograph by Ruth Kiel.)

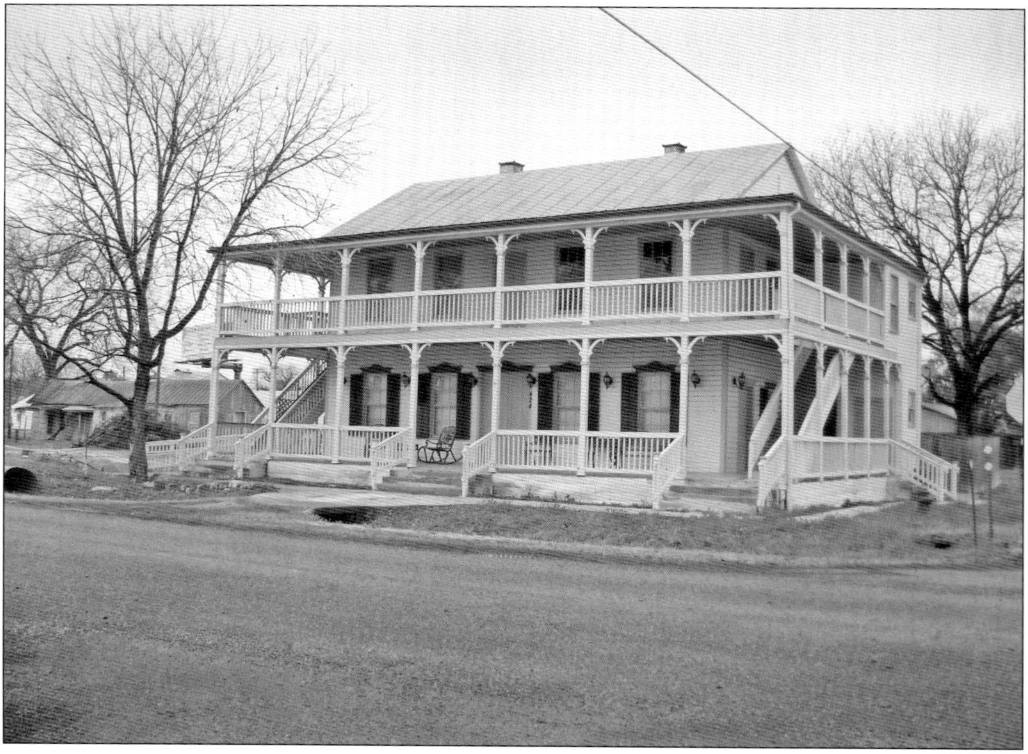

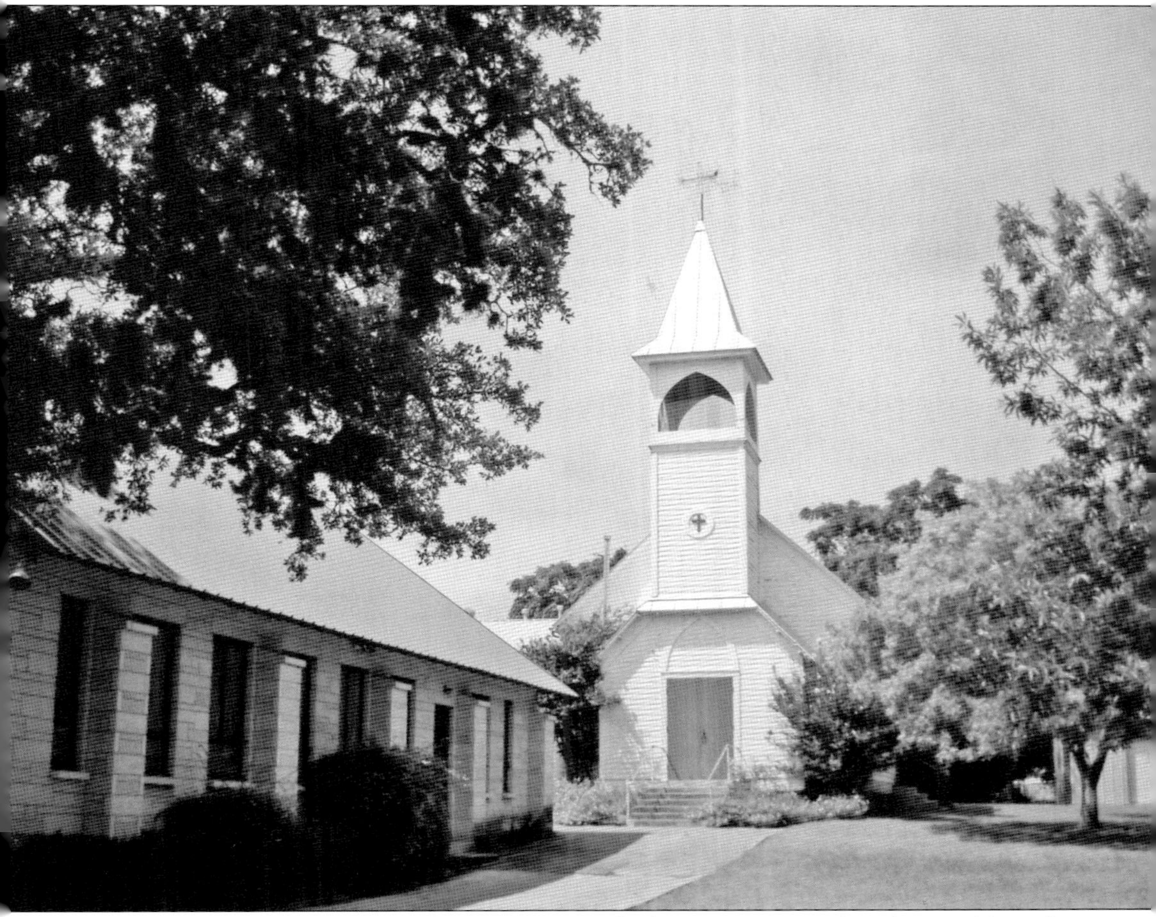

Comfort Community Church. Lutheran pastor Friedrich Bauer came to Comfort in 1891 and served until 1897. His first move was to gather a group of women who were anxious to have a church; they called themselves the Maria-Martha Verein. Initial meetings were in the railroad depot waiting room and in a local saloon. The money raised was insufficient to fund construction, but volunteer labor stepped forward to help. Dedicated in 1892, this Gothic Revival building first served the *Deutsche Evangelische gemeinde* (German Lutheran community). The bell tower was added around 1898. The Lutherans shared this building with Baptists and Methodists, and it became known as the Comfort Community Church. Immanuel Lutheran Church is seen to the left of the old church. (Photograph by Ruth Kiel.)

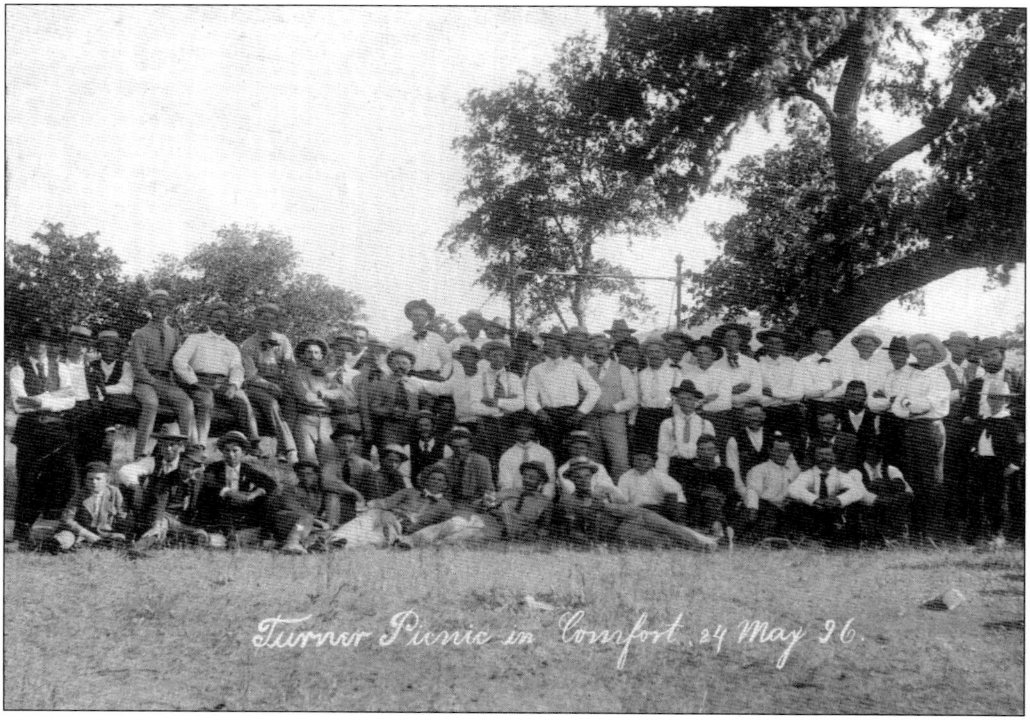

Comfort Turnverein. The Turners was a gymnastics group and the first social club in Comfort, organizing in 1860. German-language organizations encompassed many aspects of community life and included groups such as the Liedertafel Singing Society, the Maria-Martha Verein ladies circle, and the Sons of Hermann life insurance mutual aid company. The Turners built the clubhouse front part in 1870, choosing a location along Cypress Creek; it later included bowling alleys. (Above, Comfort Heritage Foundation archives; below, photograph by Ruth Kiel.)

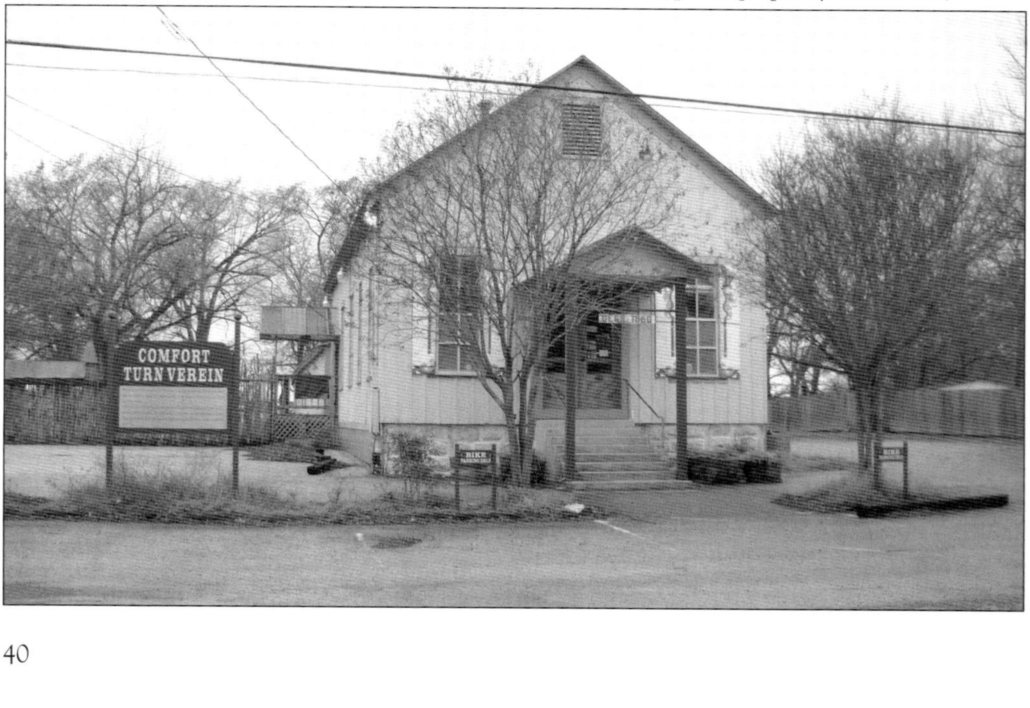

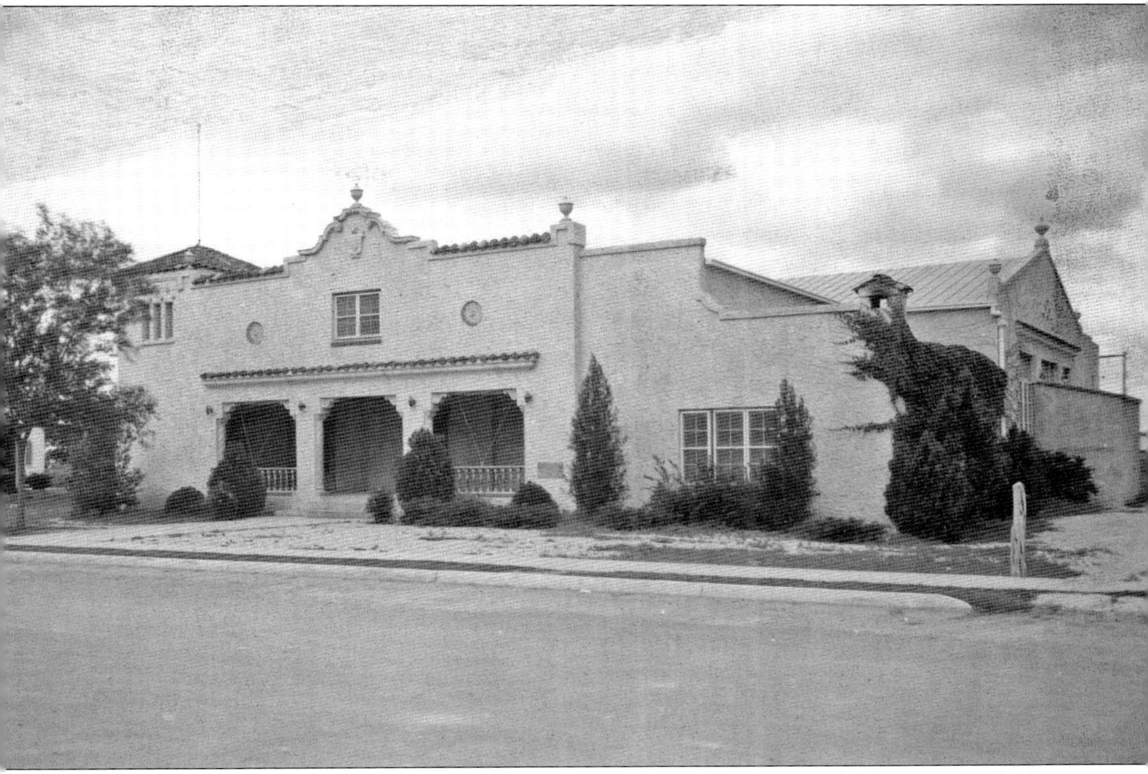

Comfort Theater. In 1929, a group gathered together, incorporated, and sold shares to build the Comfort Community Theater in 1930. The theater held dances, showed movies, and presented live stage performances. Hank Zimmermann became the manager and owner in 1945–1946. The 1948 addition converted the former porch into a new lobby. Richard and Dorothy Britt purchased the theater in 1965, and stage productions resumed. (Photograph by Ruth Kiel.)

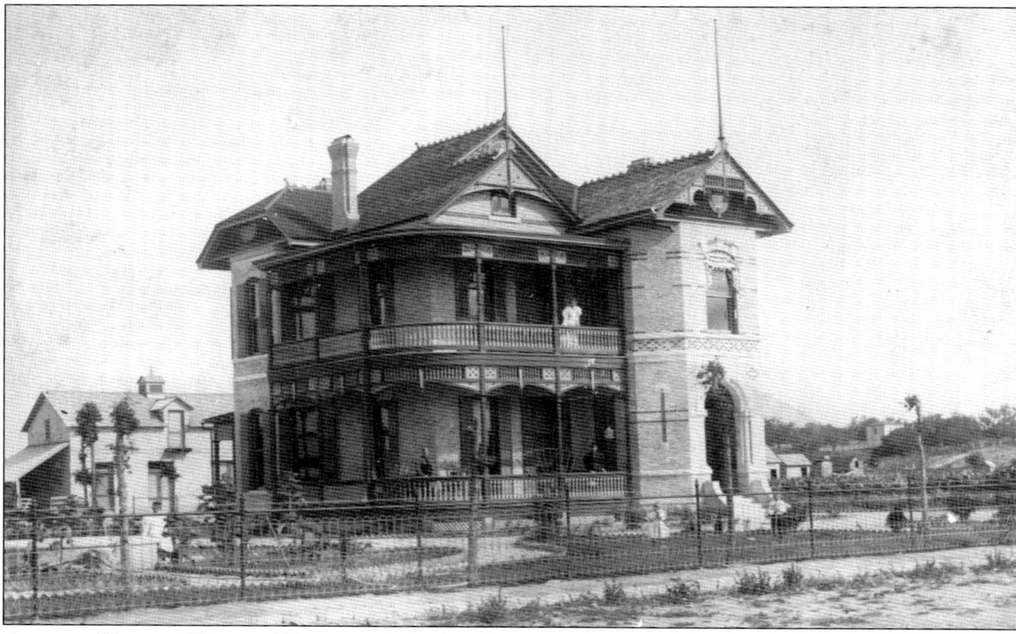

August Faltin House. This two-story brick Victorian house, designed by Albert Beckmann (son-in-law of Alfred Giles) and built in 1894, was Comfort's most elaborate and ornate home. It has an elevator, and the dining room has glass bowls, figurines, a still-life painting of fruit, a cupboard with dishes, a sewing machine, a cast-iron stove, a chandelier, and lace curtains. The grounds had a stable and water tower. (Both Tina Neumann.)

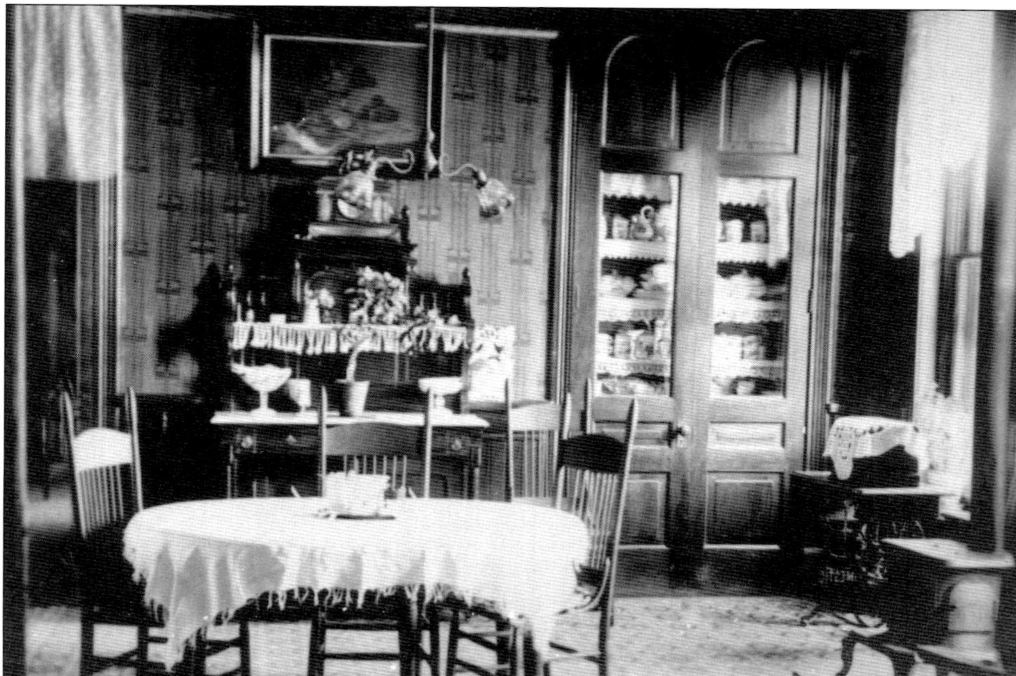

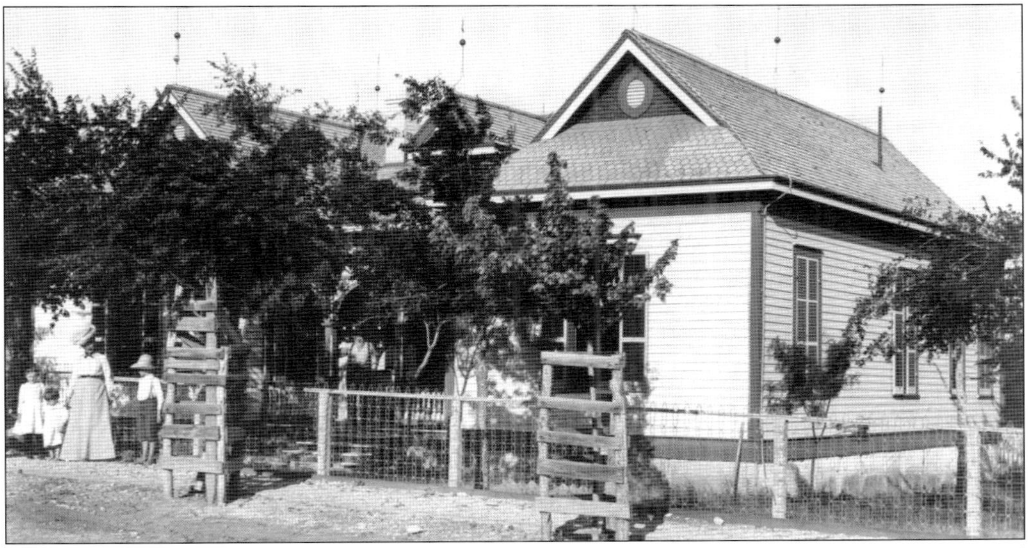

Rudolph Flach House, Third and Main Streets. Built about 1893, this is a typical H-shaped Victorian cottage. Rudolph Flach Sr. was a charter member of Pfeuffer Lodge No. 34, Order of Hermann Sons, when it organized in November 1890. The group's efforts resulted in the selection of Comfort for the site of the lodge's home for the aged. His son Rudolph "Pudel" Flach (1891–1978) was postmaster from 1915 to 1924 and was on the Comfort Independent School District Board. He served the volunteer fire department for 60 years before retiring in 1974. (Roy Perkins collection.)

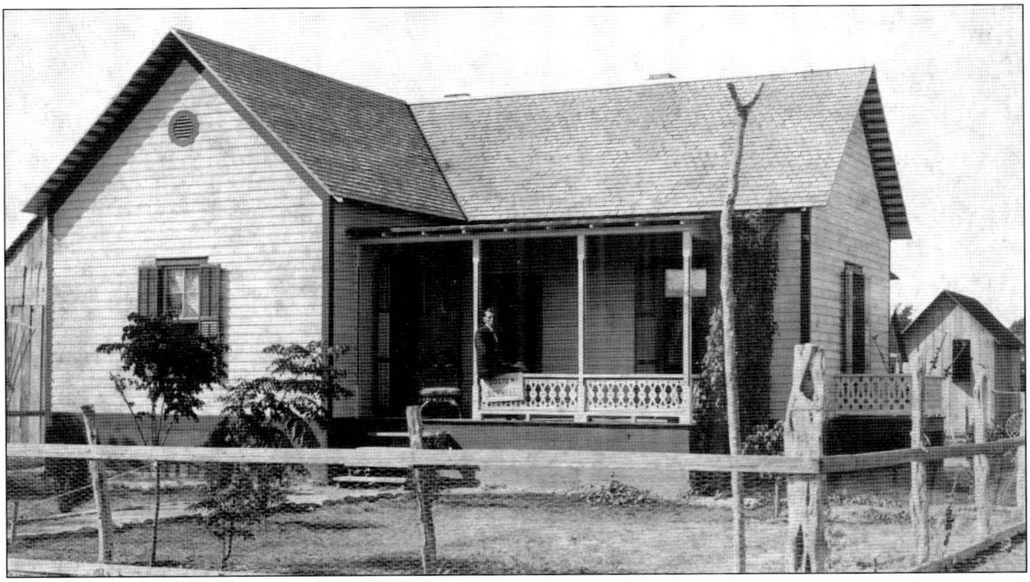

Dr. Schnell House, Sixth Street and Broadway. Constructed in 1901 by architect and builder J. F. Thompson, this was the home of Dr. Joseph H. Schnell (1850–1935). A native of Ohio, he graduated from the University of Pennsylvania Medical School in 1872. While living in Comfort, he was the local surgeon for the San Antonio and Aransas Pass Railroad and cared for the railroad employees and maintenance workers from 1893 to 1907. Afterwards he lived the rest of his with his daughter in Houston. (Comfort Heritage Foundation archives.)

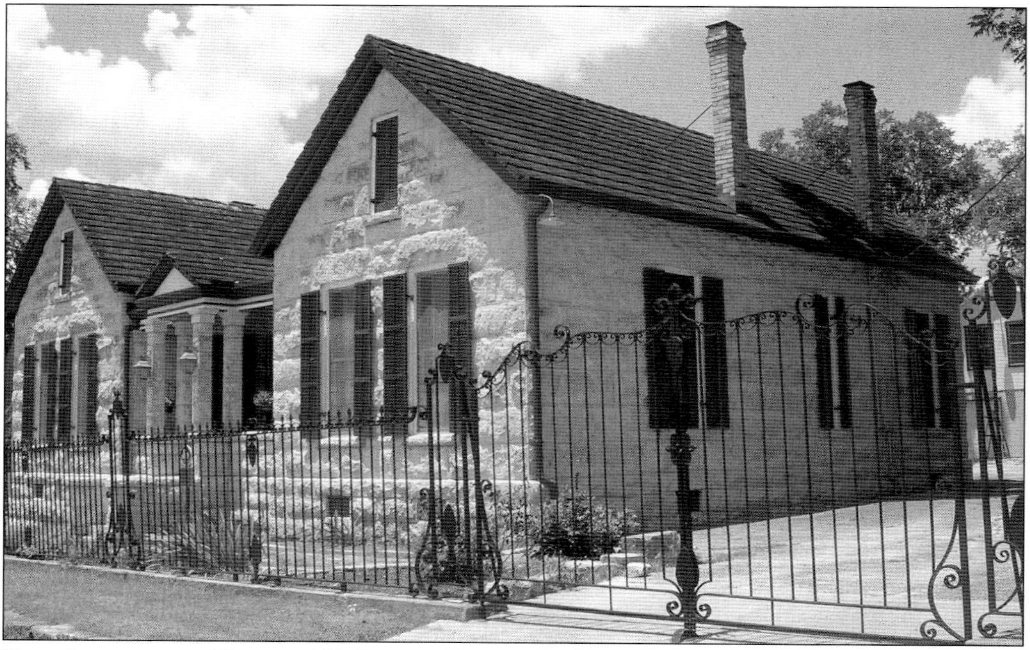

PAUL INGENHUETT HOUSE, 417 EIGHTH STREET. Built in 1895 by Bruno Schott from a design by Alfred Giles, this is an example of Giles's domestic architecture. The ironwork of the gates and fence was by Erich Riesel of Kerrville, who was originally from Magdeburg, Germany. A descendant of the Ingenhuett family lives here, using and treasuring the furnishings of his ancestors. (Photograph by Ruth Kiel.)

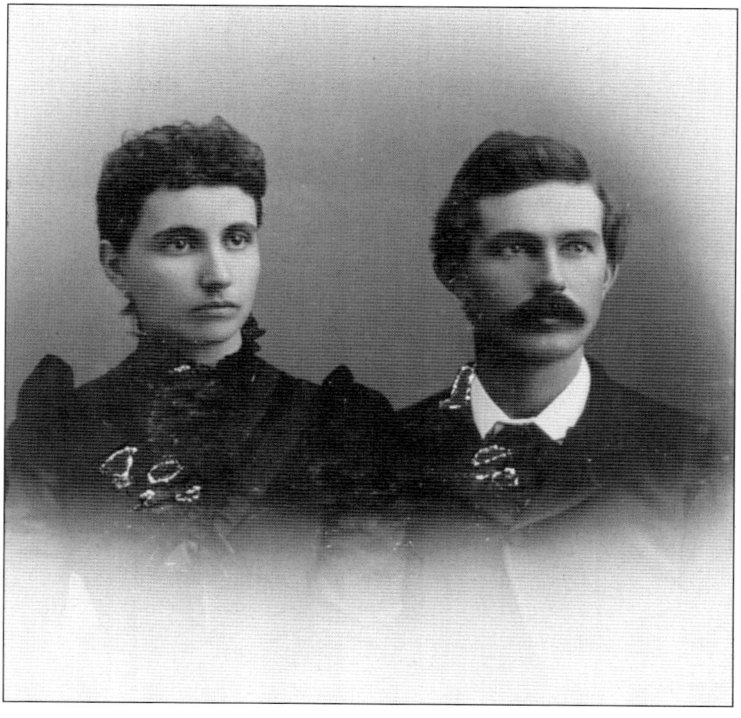

IDA FLACH INGENHUETT AND PAUL INGENHUETT. The Ingenhuetts were leaders in the community. Paul succeeded his father in the mercantile business and was a founder of the Comfort State Bank. He was also an original trustee of the Comfort Volunteer Fire Department. Ida was a member of the Literary Social Club, whose aim was to preserve the literary and cultural heritage of Comfort. (Roy Perkins collection.)

Four

Businesses

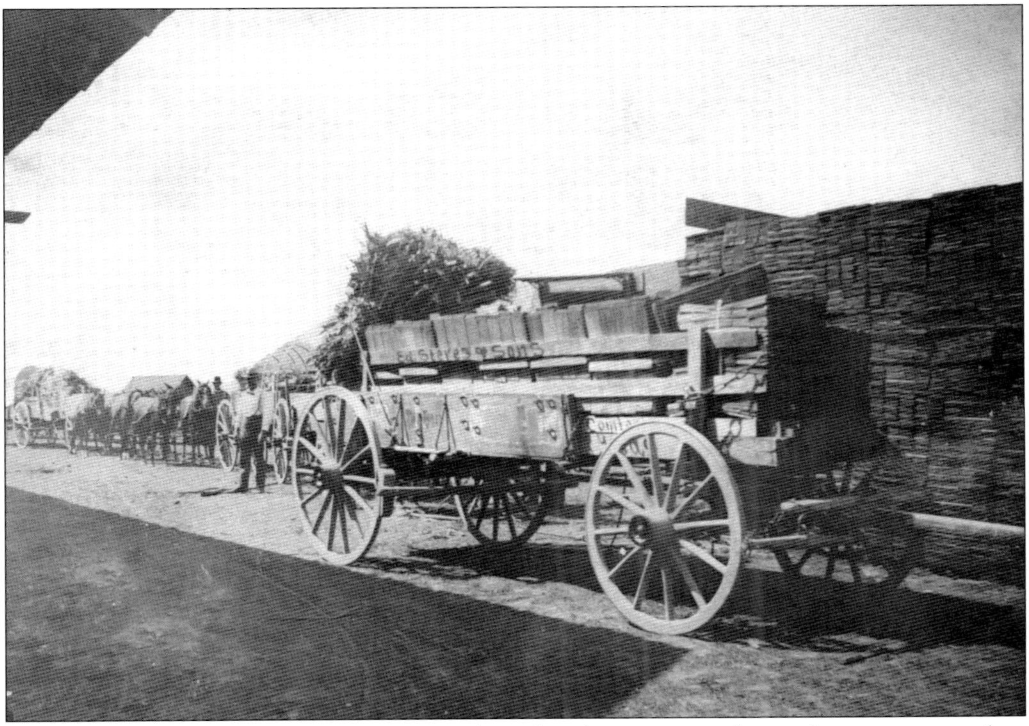

Cypress Shingles En Route to Market. These shingles were a sturdy, weather-resistant product from the tall cypress trees lining the Guadalupe River. Residential and commercial building in San Antonio and Fredericksburg created a continuing demand. Joshua Brown and his crew moved upriver from Gonzales, harvesting cypress trees at Sisterdale, Brownsboro, Comfort, and finally Kerrville, where he founded a town. (Comfort Historical Foundation archives.)

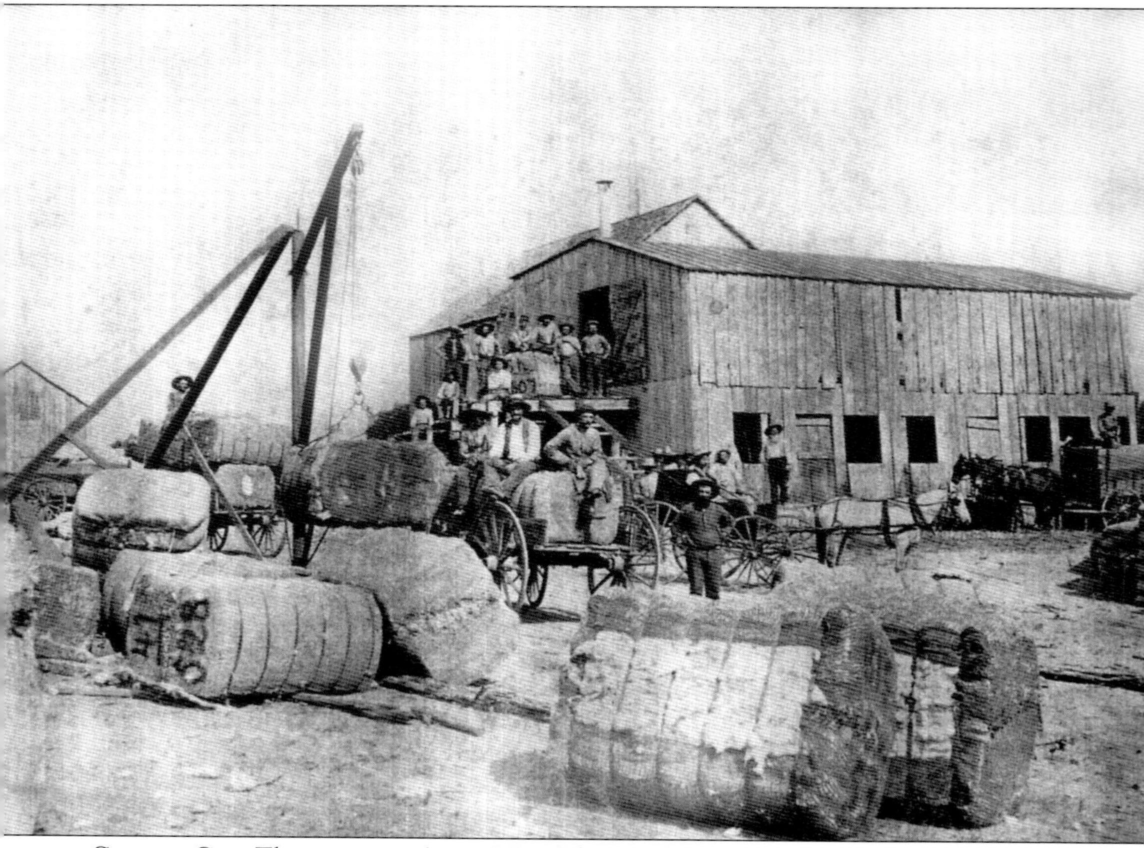

COTTON GIN. The major product of Guadalupe Valley farms was cotton, which was locally processed at the Flach cotton gin on Mill Dam Road. During ginning season, which lasted from late August through late December, the gin operated 18 to 24 hours a day. Farmers brought their handpicked cotton to the gin in wagons, often lining the roads for miles. After the cotton was ginned, farmers sold their seed to the ginner to cover ginning costs and their crop to buyers. Cotton buyers cut samples from bales and classed the cotton according to grade, staple length, color, and character (smoothness and cleanliness). Classing determined the quality, and thus the value, of the cotton. Boll weevils ruined the plants, and the gin closed in 1915. (Comfort Heritage Foundation archives.)

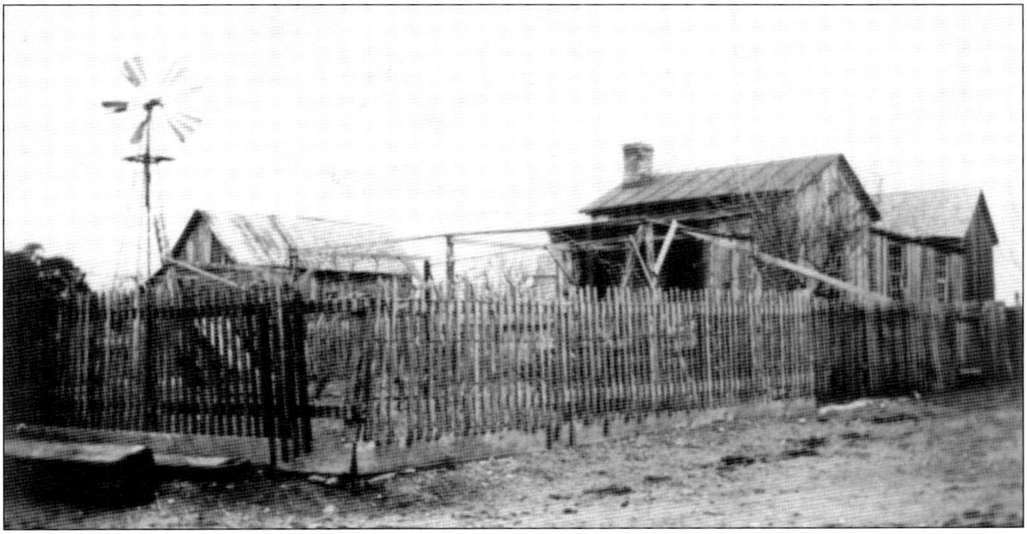

San Antonio and Aransas Pass Railroad (SA&AP), 1887–1970. The San Antonio and Aransas Pass Railway Company, chartered in 1884, had 222 miles of track between Corpus Christi and Kerrville by 1887 and then built additional lines to Waco, Rockport, Alice, and Lockhart. The Southern Pacific bought the line in 1892, and later it merged into the Texas and New Orleans Railroad Company in 1934. The 9-mile Aransas Harbor Terminal Railroad connected Harbor Island and Mustang Island with the mainland and the SA&AP Railroad, affording a sea outlet for the produce, wool, and lumber of the Hill Country. The Hill Country portion went from San Antonio, through Leon Springs, Boerne, Welfare, Waring, Comfort, and Center Point, and to Kerrville. This line helped Comfort thrive. The first depot served until construction of a larger building. (Above, Comfort Heritage Foundation archives; below, Roy Perkins collection.)

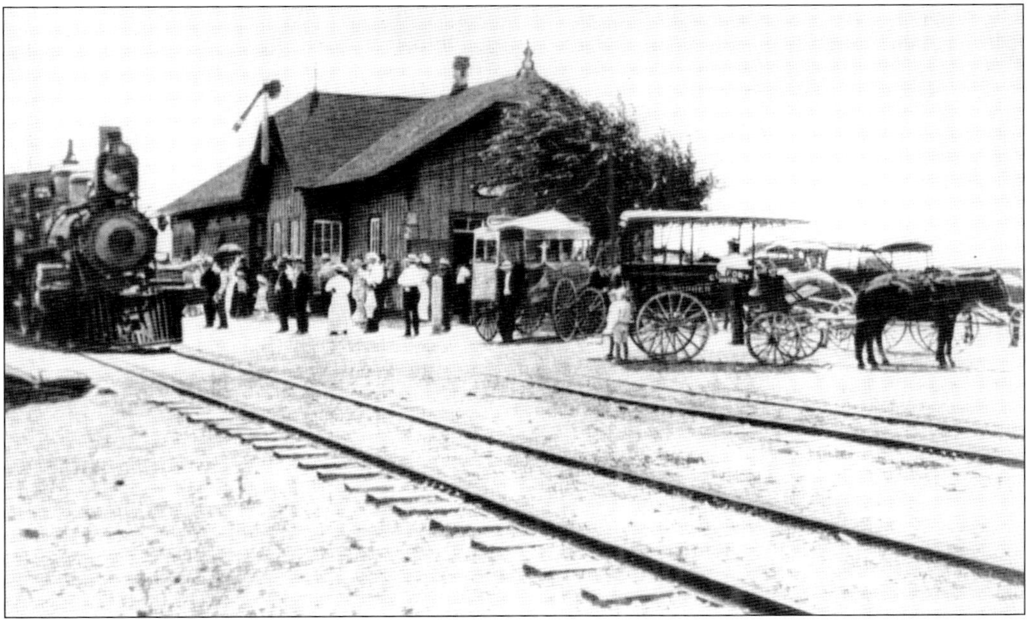

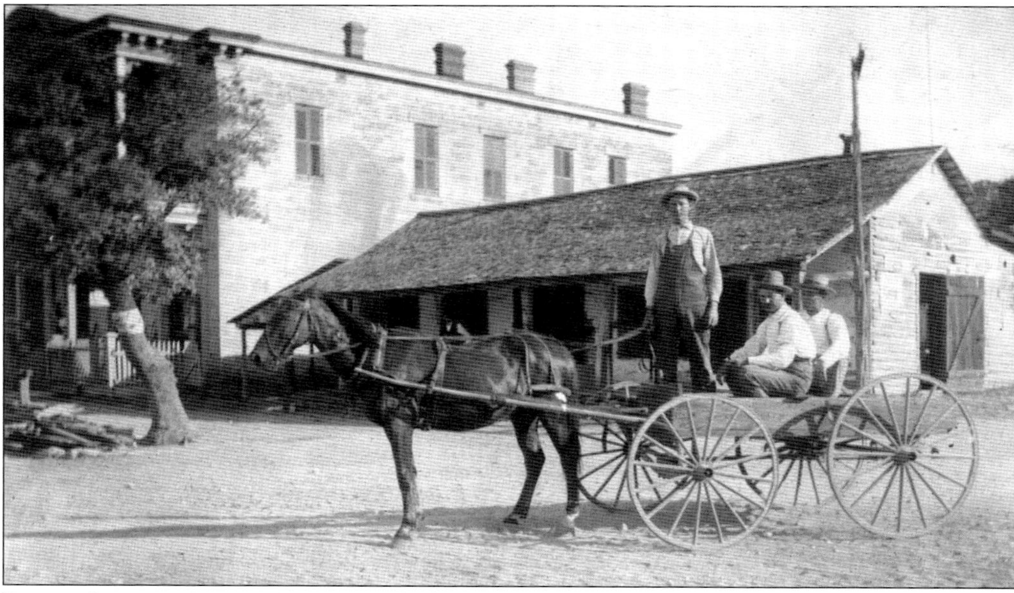

FALTIN GENERAL STORE. August Friedrich Faltin (1830–1905), from Prussia, moved to Comfort in 1856 and developed a successful general merchandise business. In the late 1870s, the business, which included banking and post office service, outgrew its original site. He had architect Alfred Giles design a new building in the Victorian Italianate style, and builder J. H. Kampmann completed it in 1879. It had two stories above a storage basement. The main level served as a general store, and the family lived on the second floor. The pictures show the structure fronting on Main Street before the 1907 addition that faces Seventh Street. In the photograph above, seated are teacher L. B. Reitzer and Alex Brinkmann, and standing in the wagon is Reinhold Ransleben. Below, Faltin is seated in front of the store wearing his customary top hat. (Both Roy Perkins collection.)

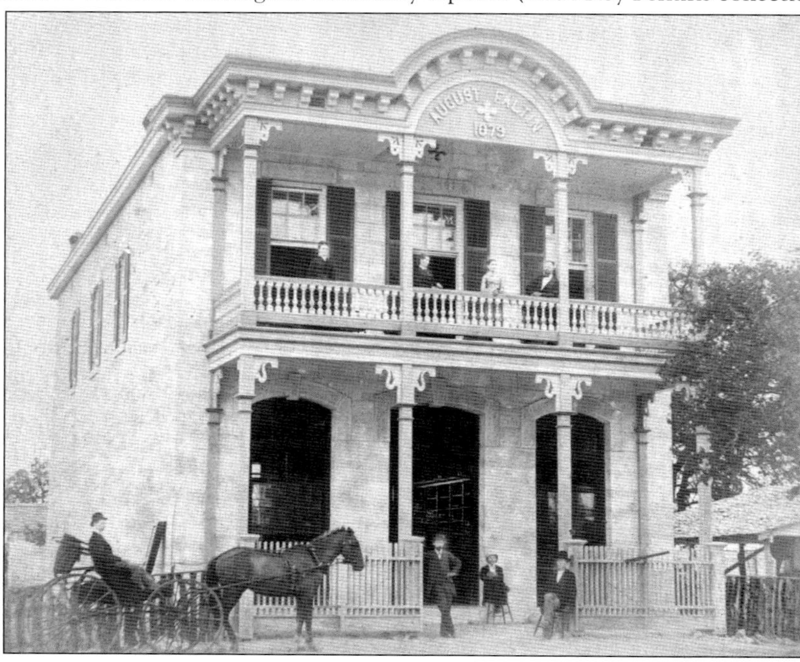

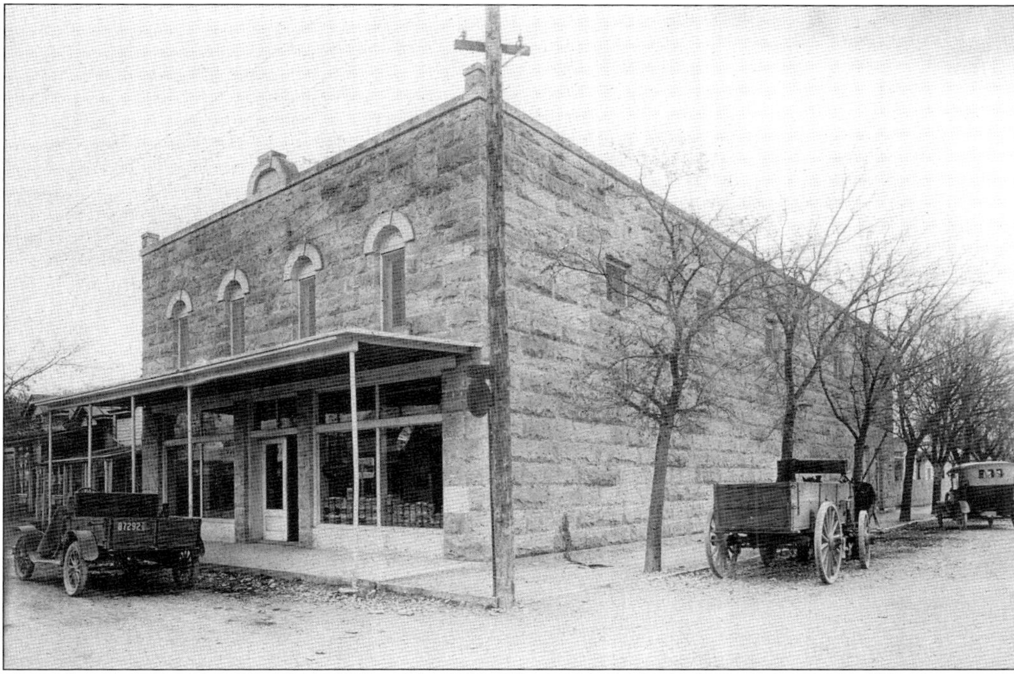

ARNO SCHWETHELM STORE. Local merchant Arno Schwethelm had this building constructed in 1916 to house his mercantile business, which included the Comfort Bottling Works. A hand-dug well supplied the water for bottling. Designed by L. Harrington of San Antonio and built by stonemason Otto Bartel, it combines the function of a 20th-century commercial structure with the details of German craftsmanship. The stone for the building was quarried from the Louis Weidenfeld farm north of town. The rocks were finished at the quarry and were so enormous that only three could be hauled at one time. (Above, A. C. Schwethelm collection; at right, photograph by Ruth Kiel.)

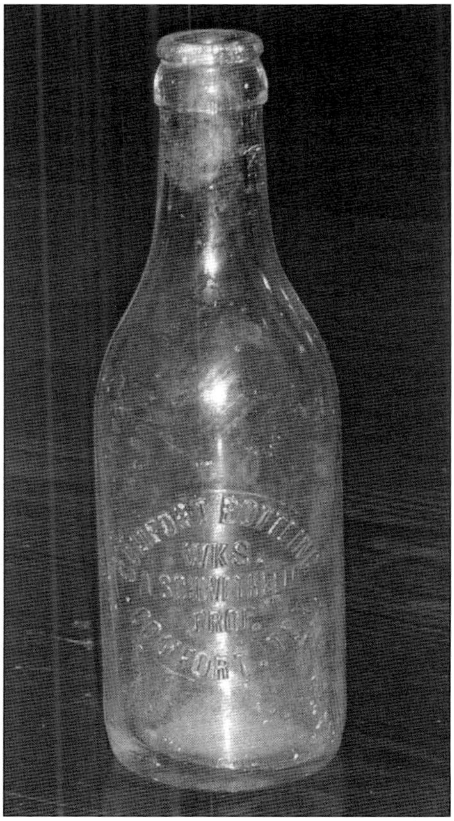

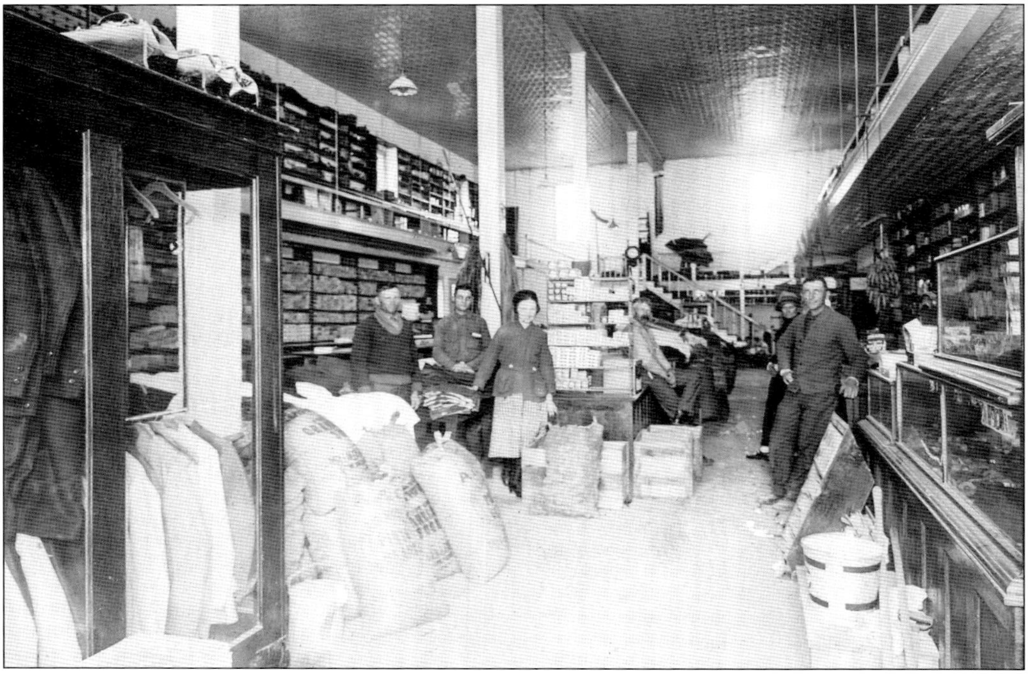

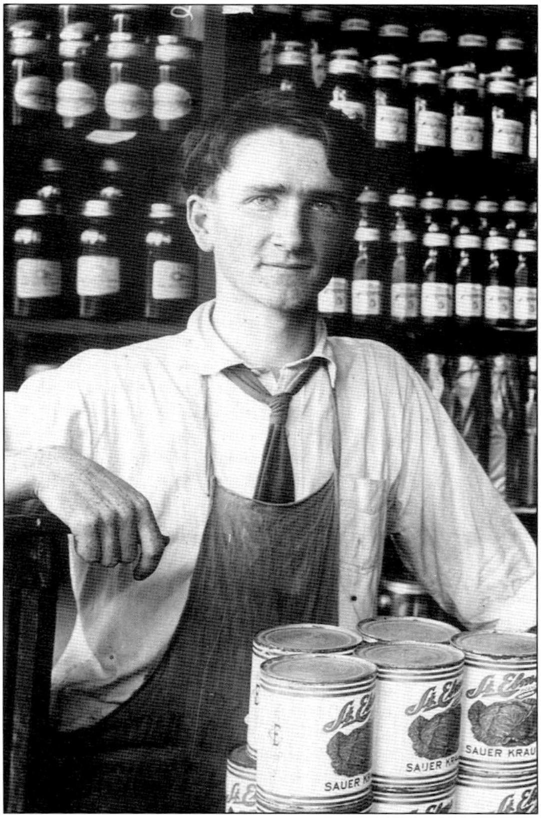

Schwethelm Store Interior. The interior offered a variety of products, from feed to clothing and canned goods, such as St. Elmo sauerkraut for the German clientele. Otto Schwethelm is shown at left tending the store. In 1981, Chester Schwethelm and his son A. C. deeded the building to the Comfort Public Library. A major renovation, including the addition of an elevator and enlargement of the mezzanine, occurred in 2000. (Both A. C. Schwethelm collection.)

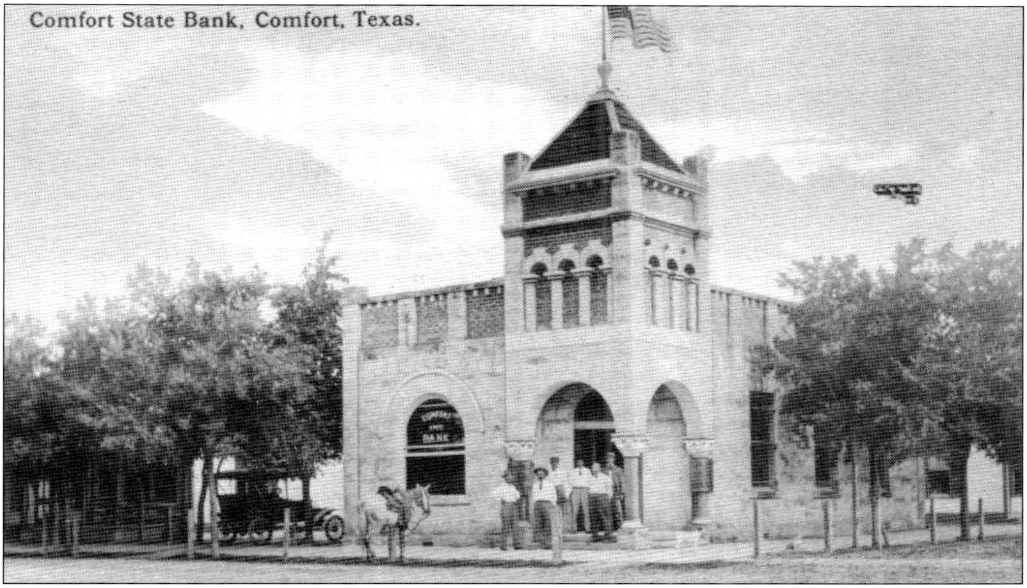

COMFORT STATE BANK, 1907–1960. Richard Doebbler, a local stonemason, built the Comfort State Bank for Alex Brinkmann in 1907. The hand-cut stone structure features a modified Richardsonian Romanesque style with polished red granite pillars flanking the entrance, a round-headed window, and a blind arcade in the tower. A 1914 picture of the bank (above) shows the car of Dr. Charles Clinton Jones, parked between his office and the bank, and a horse tied to the hitching post. For this postcard, an artist added a biplane overhead and a flag and flagpole. Directors in the entrance are T. O. Codrington, August Faltin, Alex Brinkmann, Albert Faltin, William Wiedenfeld, and Dr. Jones. The Comfort Public Library occupied the building from 1961 to 1982. Currently it houses the Comfort Heritage Foundation museum and archives. (Above, Roy Perkins collection; below, Comfort Heritage Foundation archives.)

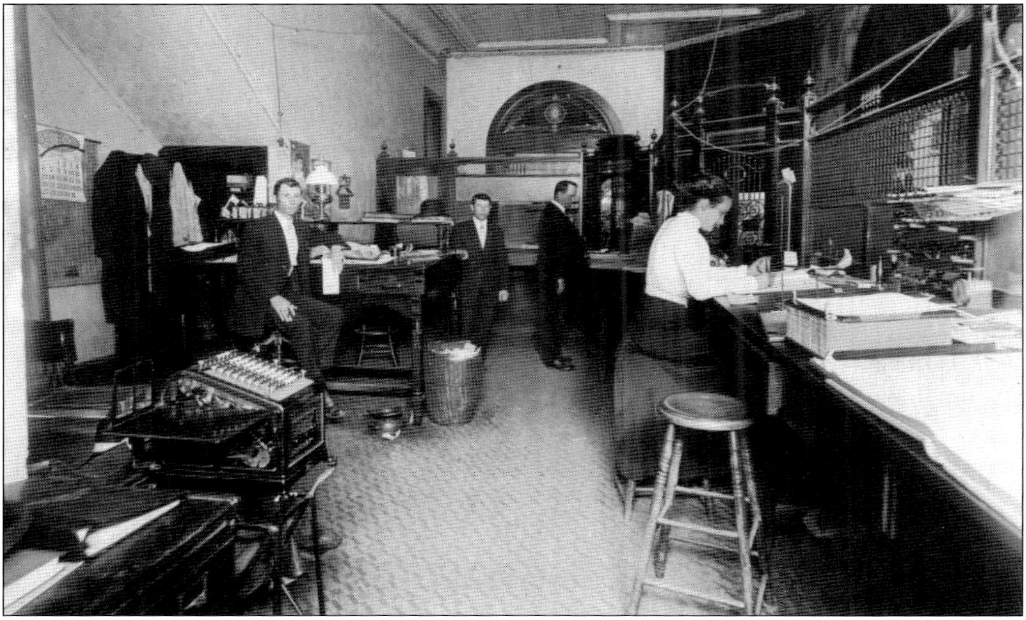

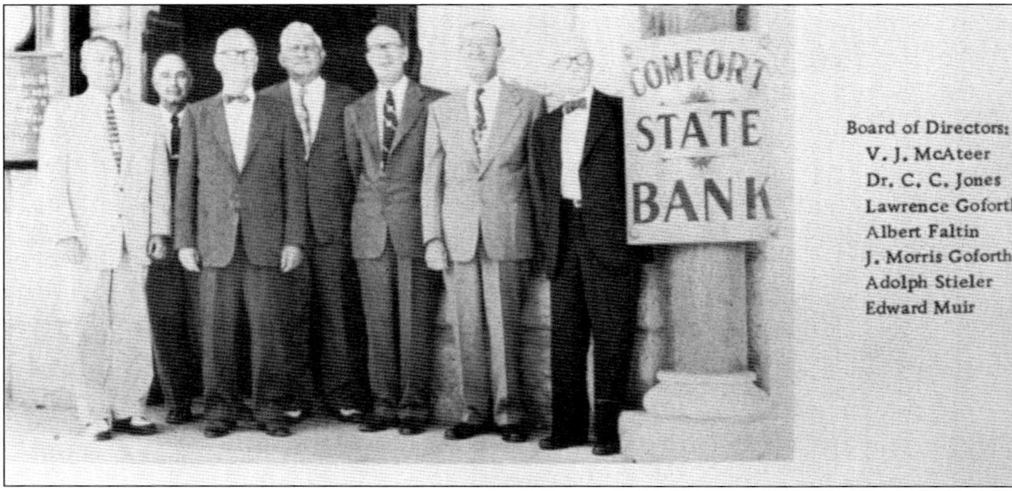

Directors of Comfort State Bank. The 1905 State Bank Law created a new system of local banks. Two years later, community leaders organized the Comfort State Bank. State banks accepted real estate as collateral, while national banks did not. By the 1920s, the main loans were for automobiles and oil production. A 1940s board of directors poses in the entrance in the above photograph. Below, a 1954 picture shows Lawrence "Lefty" Goforth, Dr. Charles Clinton Jones Sr., Charlotte Belsey, Morris Goforth, Albert Faltin, and Dr. R. O. Perkins Jr. perhaps going for refreshments at the confectionery across the street. Dr. Jones came to Comfort in 1904 at the age of 29. He graduated from the University of Texas Medical Branch at Galveston in 1898. In addition to caring for the sick and delivering babies, he owned a Ford agency and was a director of the Comfort State Bank. He passed away in 1960. (Both Roy Perkins collection.)

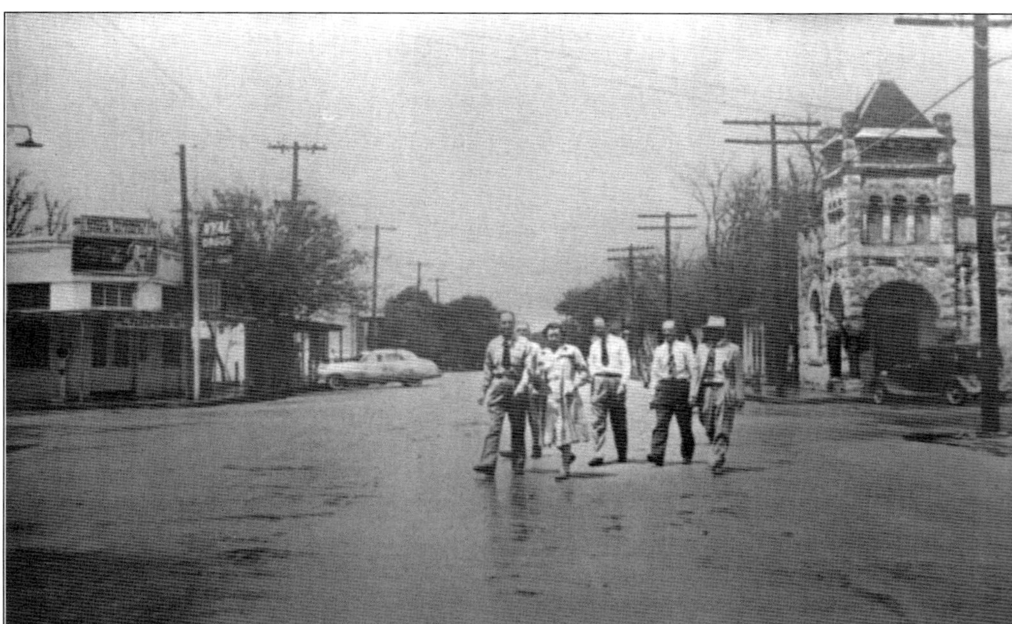

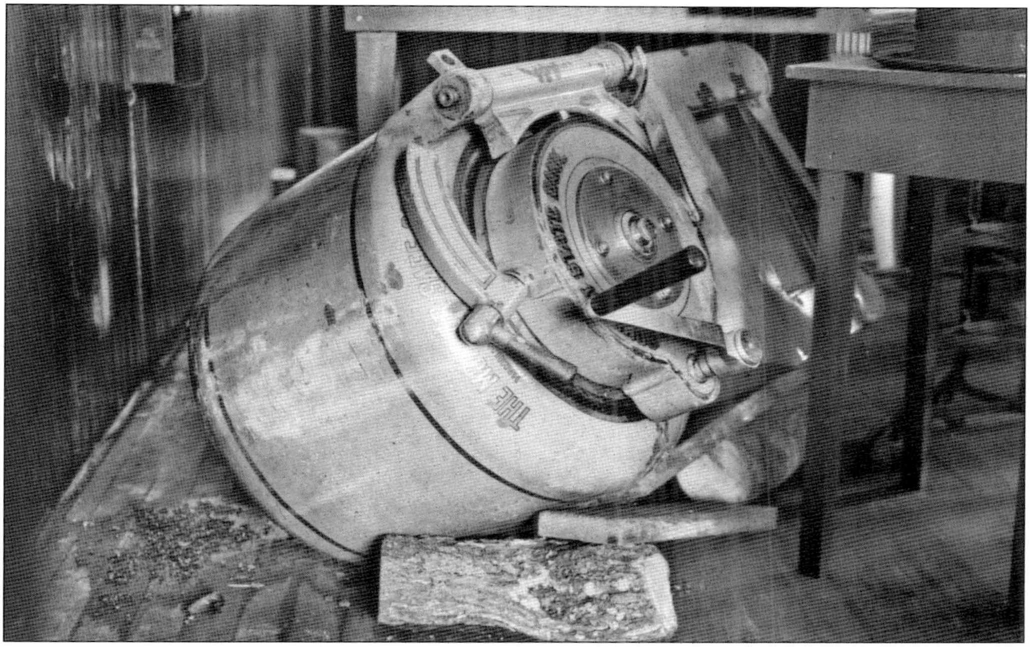

Great Bank Robbery of 1925. On February 26, 1925, sometime after midnight when power to the streetlight was off, a gang of safe robbers jimmied the entrance to the bank. The 1,500-pound safe on the west wall was toppled and, using an acetylene torch, the leader bored a 3-inch hole in the manganese wall of the safe. The leader became known as "Torch Man." After introduction of water to cool the interior, he enlarged the hole enough to reach in and take $9,700, of which $6,000 was in gold coins. The gang fled north in two cars. These pictures show the toppled safe and Kendall County Sheriff Edward Bierschwale surveying the scene. Police arrested six men on April 17, 1925, in Galveston, where they were planning their next robbery. (Both University of Texas Institute of Texan Cultures at San Antonio.)

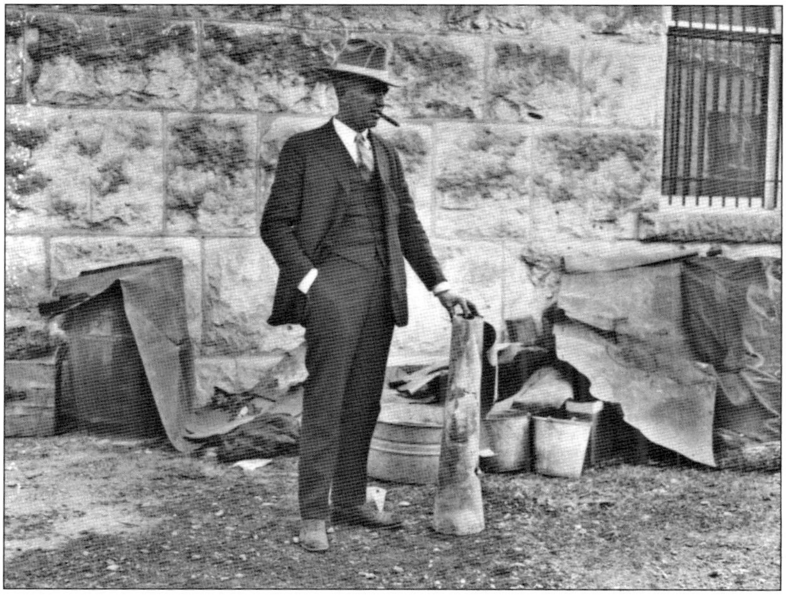

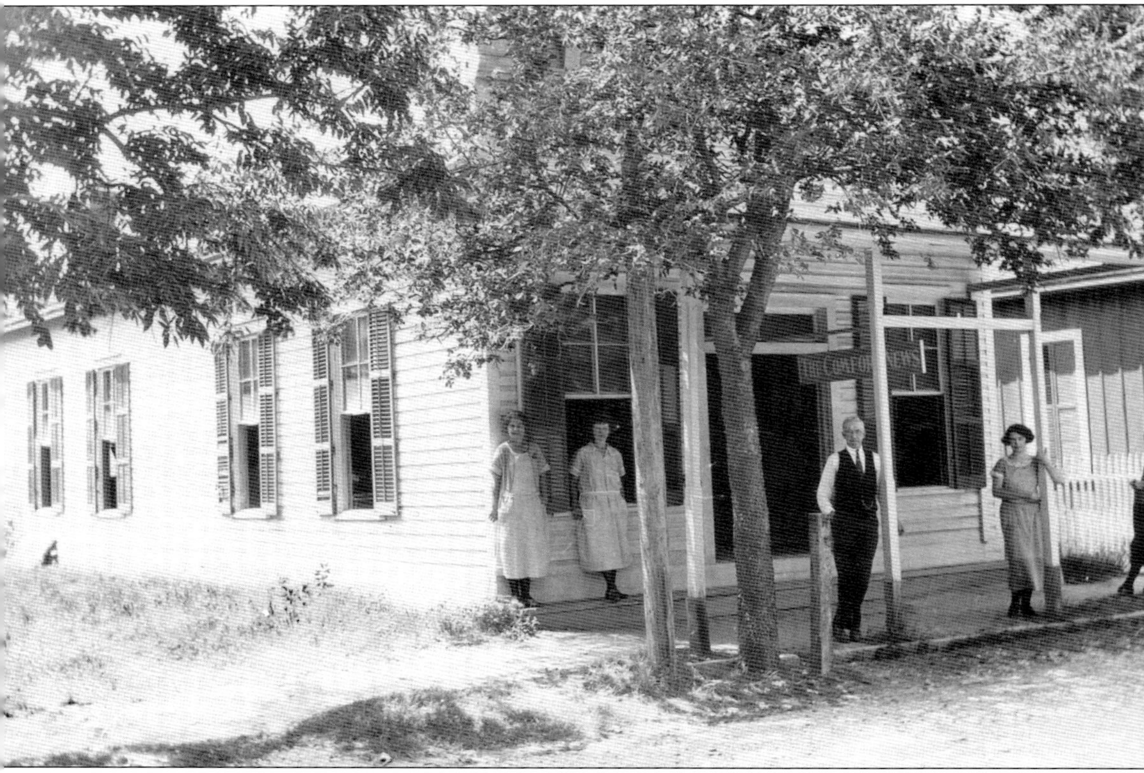

The Comfort News. On the masthead it proclaimed "Serving the Comfort community since 1904, including the Cypress Creek community, Sisterdale, Kendalia, Waring, Welfare, Grapetown, Center Point, the Holiday area, Luckenbach, Lindendale, Block Creek, Lane Valley, and the Comfort Independent School District, and towns and communities in the counties of the central Texas Hill Country including Kendall, Gillespie, Kerr, Bandera, Blanco and Bexar." This newspaper followed the *West Texas Independent Courier,* which provided news for the community from 1900 to 1904. Vincent J. McAteer (1869–1966) came from Louisville, Kentucky, to Comfort in 1902. Town leader Alex Brinkmann persuaded him in 1904 to start a publication with more local coverage. The newspaper succeeded, and McAteer remained the editor for 19 years. Active in the community, he was one of the original Comfort State Bank directors (1907), developer of Hill Crest Addition residential subdivision (1907), one of organizers of the Comfort Business Men's Association (1908), and one of organizers of Comfort Electric Light and Power Company (1923). (Comfort Heritage Foundation archives.)

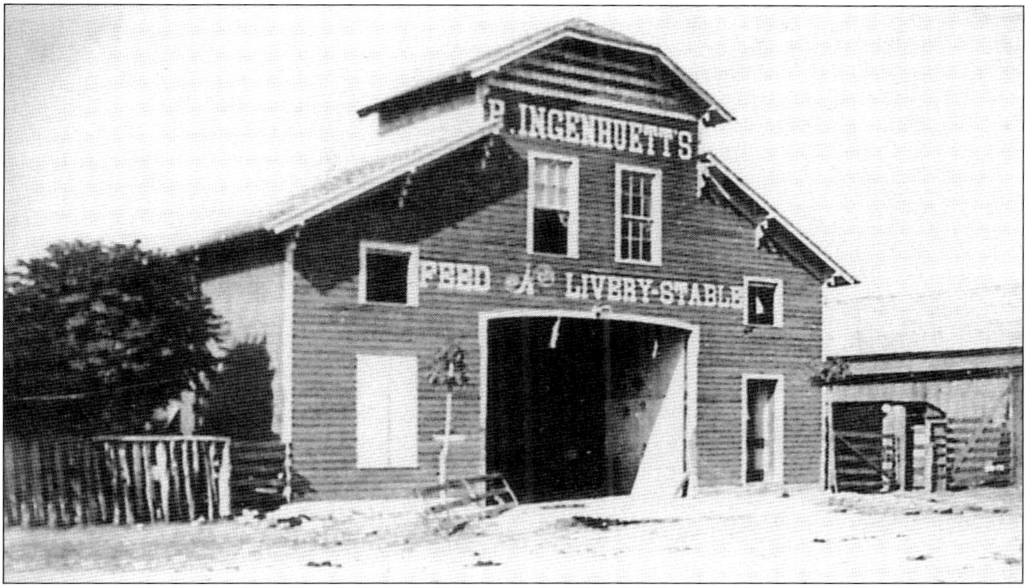

Comfort Garage. Originally a livery stable and part of the Ingenhuett complex, it became an automobile garage. The Faust Motor Company window advertises Dodge Brothers Motor Cars, filtered gasoline, and operating oils and greases. In the image below, the vehicle on the left resembles a 1918–1920 Dodge Roadster, while the one on the right with the elevated rear seat resembles a 1920 Dodge touring car. By 1926, according to the *Comfort News,* Comfort had three car dealers—Faust Motor Company that sold Dodge cars and Fisk tires, Holekamp Motor Company that sold Chevrolet, Buick, and Oakland cars, and the Comfort Auto Company (formerly Doebbler Motor Company) that sold Ford cars and Goodyear tires. Prices for a Ford were as follows: runabout, $260; touring car, $290; coupe, $520; Tudor sedan, $580; and Fordor sedan, $660. For comparison, prices for a Chevrolet were as follows: Roadster, $510; touring car, $510; coupe, $645; coach, $645; sedan, $735; and landau, $765. (Both Comfort Heritage Foundation archives.)

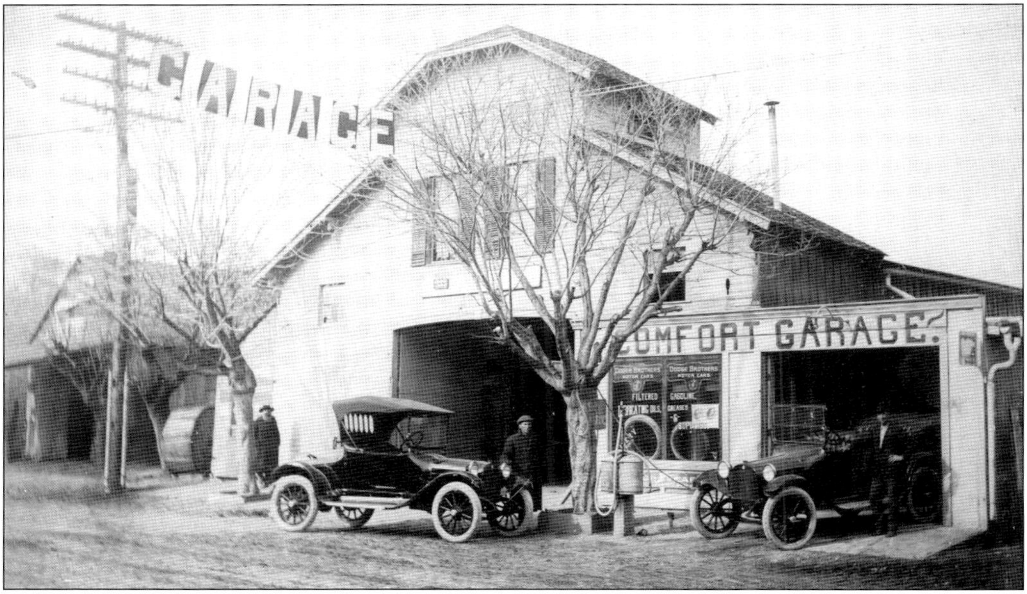

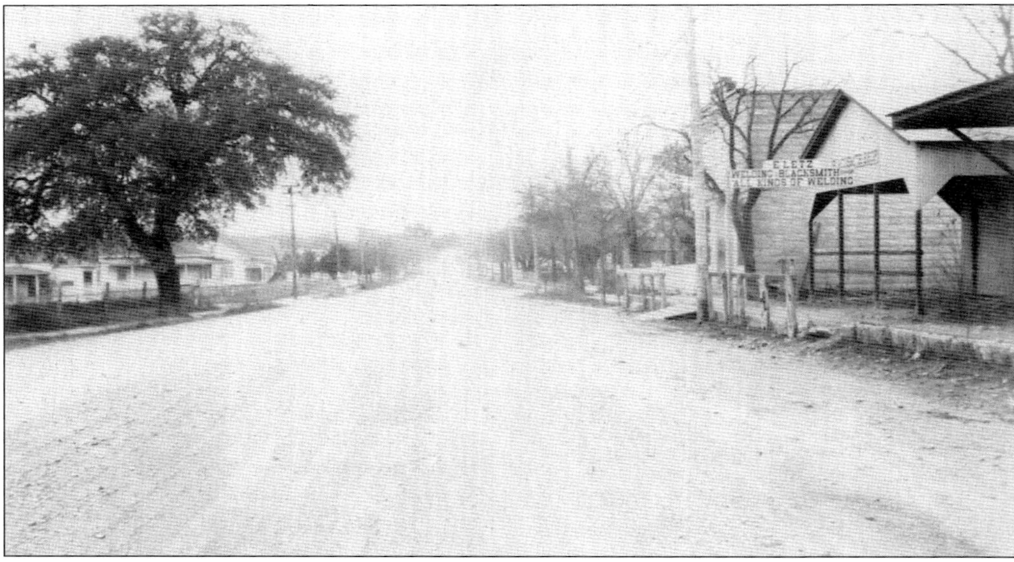

LETZ BLACKSMITH SHOP. Ferdinand Pfeiffer constructed this building at 608 (or 612) High Street in 1921 for Ernst Letz (1865–1948) and his son Udo (1898–1987), who operated a smithy there until 1925 when they moved to a larger building one block east on High Street. A hitching post for horses was in front. His sign (above) reads, "E. Letz—Welding Blacksmith—All Kinds of Welding." The interior shows Ernst Letz standing beside his workstations, with the sun streaming in through the doorway in the back and a water trough for dowsing hot metal in the foreground. (Above, Comfort Heritage Foundation archives; below, Jonathan Letz collection.)

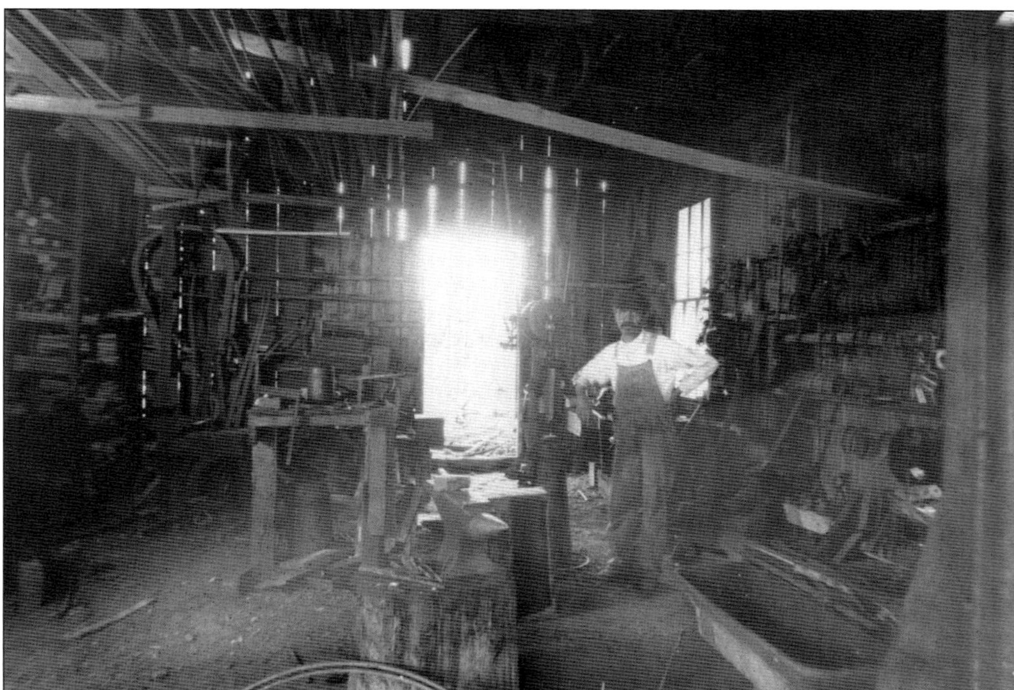

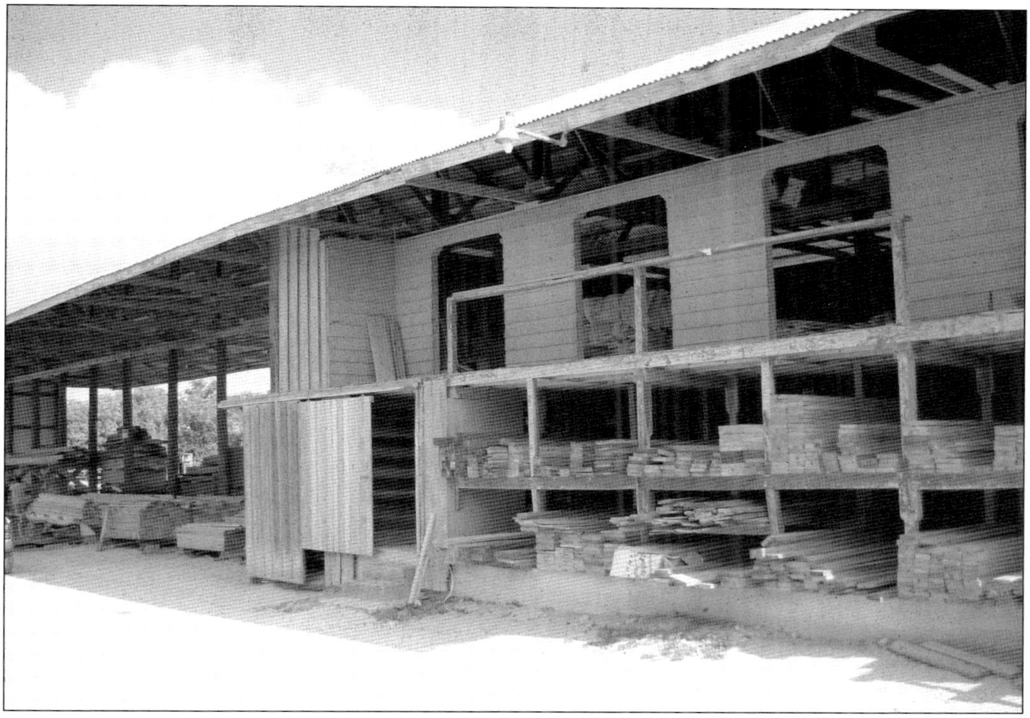

Bohnert's Lumber and Milling. Edward "Ed" Steves opened a lumberyard in Comfort in 1888. He combined a hardware business with the lumber business in 1947 and opened a store on Front Street (Texas Highway 27). In 1973, he built a larger establishment on Texas Highway 87, which he sold in 1983 to Randolph (below left) and Steven Bohnert (below right), the present owners. (Both photographs by Ruth Kiel.)

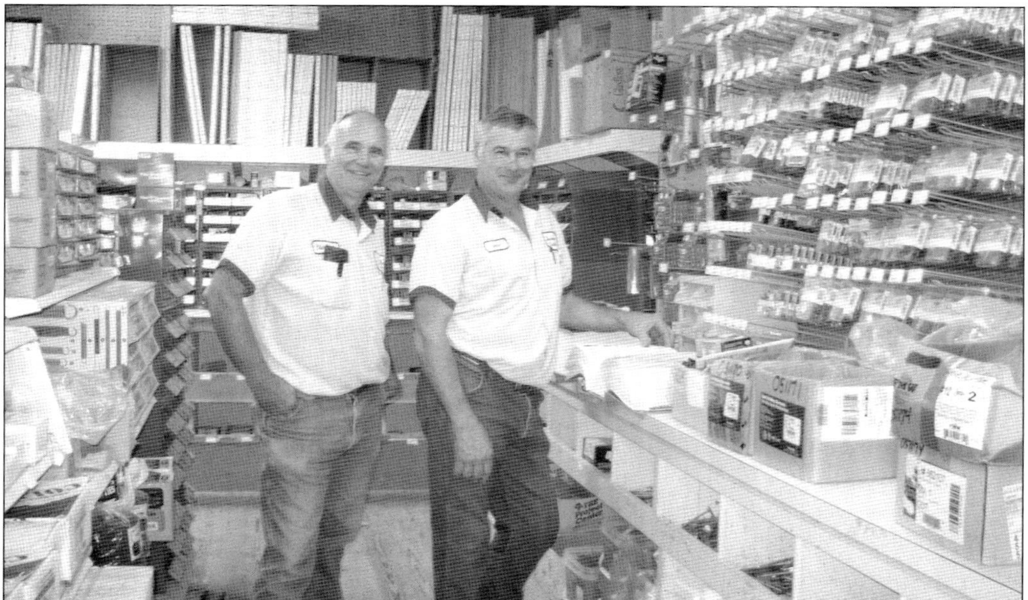

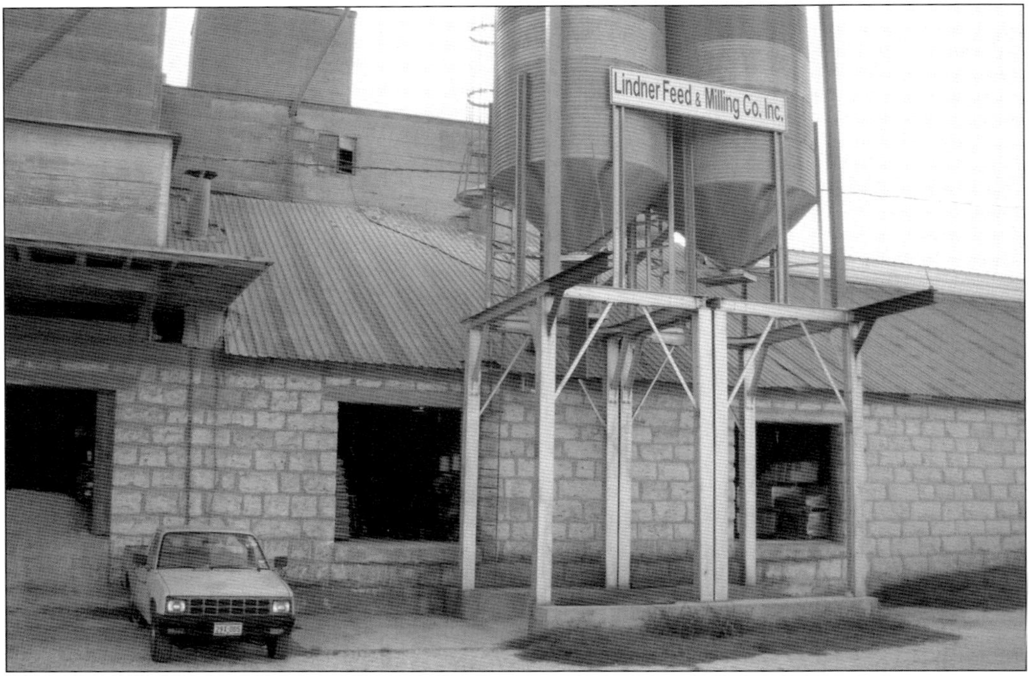

Lindner Feed and Milling Company, Inc. Julius Lindner Jr. (1899–1940) started the business in 1938, buying and selling bulk grains and fertilizer. After his death, his older brother Michael Lindner succeeded him and built the first part of the current building using limestone from the defunct Handy Stop Dance Hall at Grapetown. A family enterprise, Percy Lindner, Ralph Lindner, Ruth Lindner Zoeller, and Kay Lindner all were active in the operation. The latest improvement is a robotic system that permits faster production for shipment to a multistate area. Ralph Lindner and his son Jason pose in front of that system. (Both photographs by Ruth Kiel.)

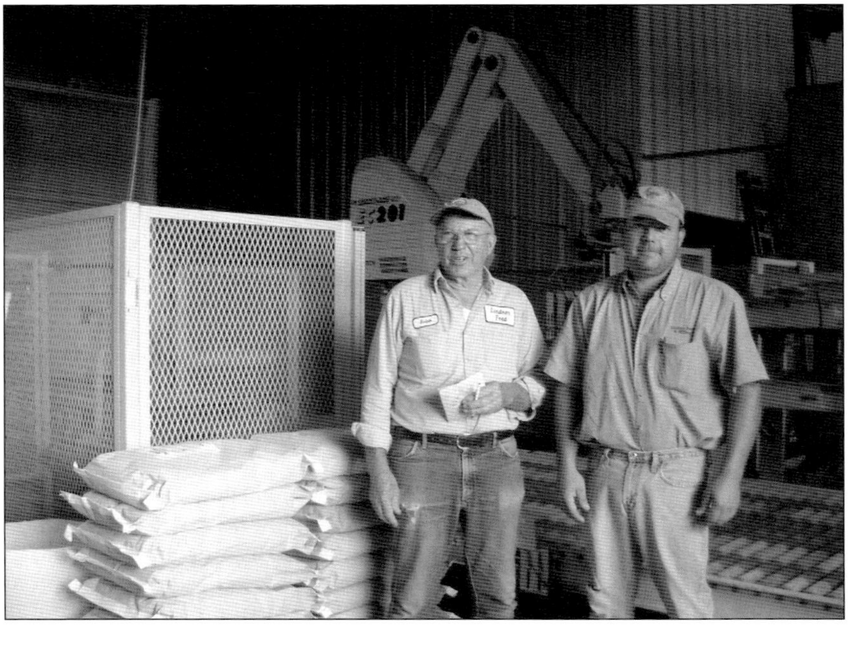

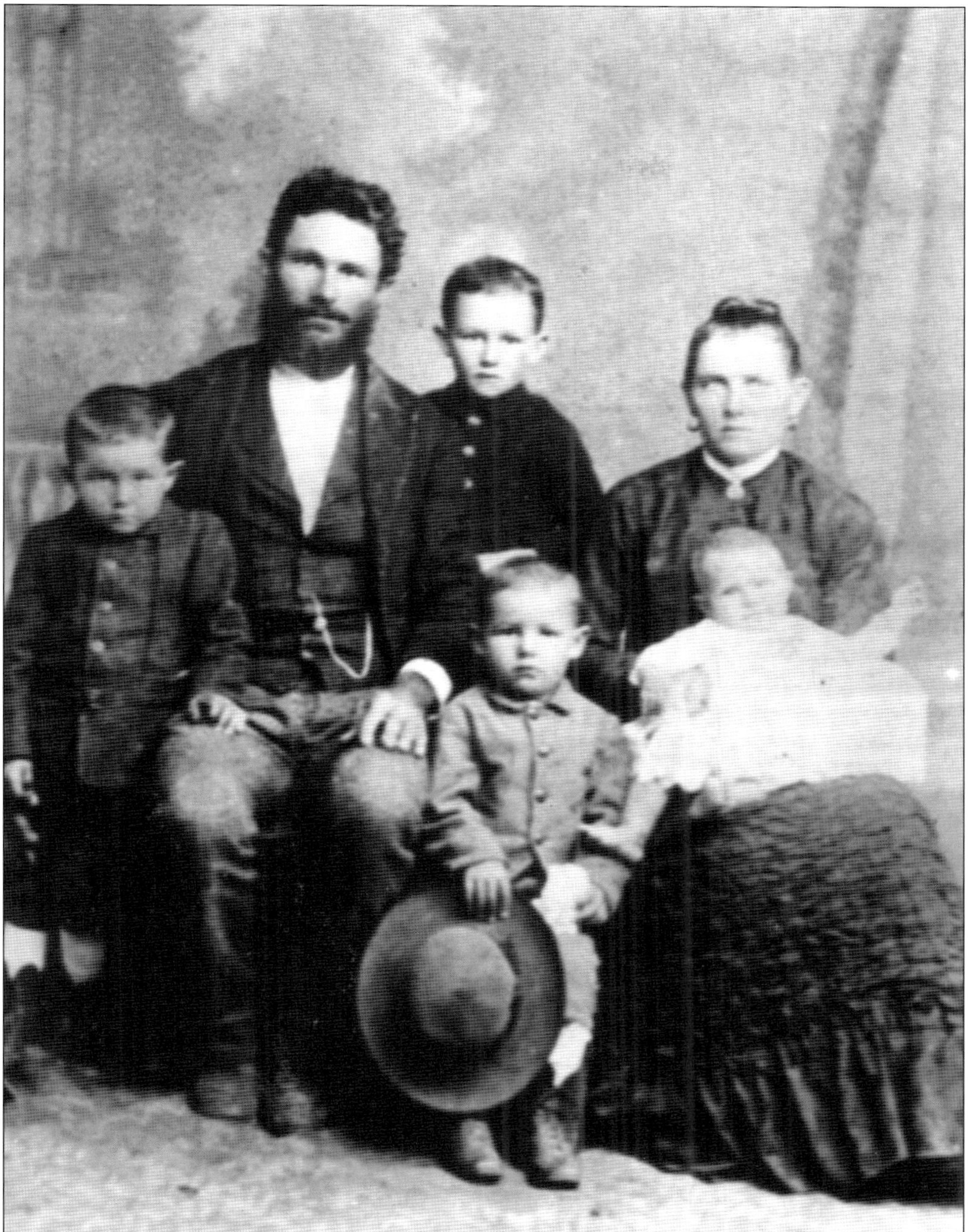

The Julius Lindner Family. Julius Lindner, the son of immigrants Michael Lindner (1820–1878) and Margarethe Seigner Lindner (1829–1910), was born on September 30, 1854, as the first white child to be born in the town site of Comfort. He died in 1934. Shown here, from left to right, are (first row) Willy (born 1886), and Gretchen on her mother's lap (born 1888); (second row) Michael (born 1883), father Julius, Otto (born 1881), and mother Emma (1862–1941). The picture was probably taken in 1889 before the birth of Rudolph in 1890. (Ruth Lindner Zoeller collection.)

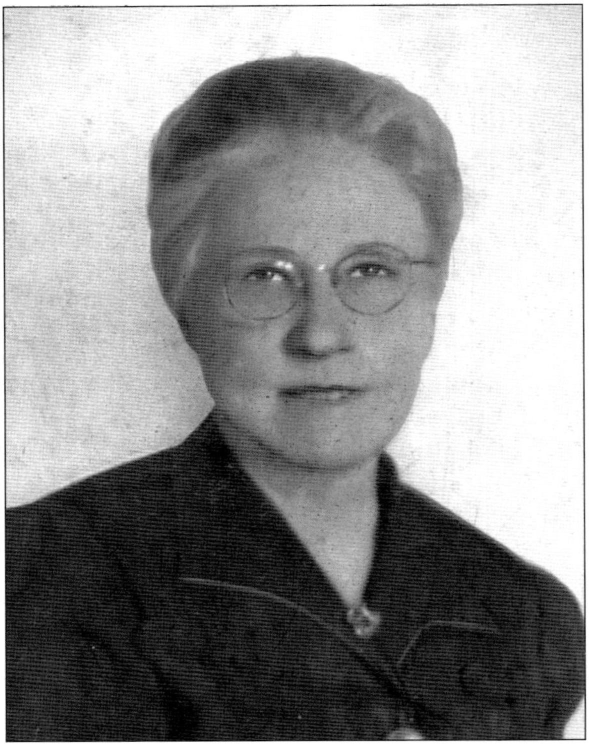

Emilie Allerkamp Lindner and Michael Lindner. Michael (1883–1979), part of the third generation of the family in Comfort, was a 1908 graduate of Texas A&M University. After graduating, he went to Mexico where he worked on the railroad until he became ill. Returning to San Antonio, he worked at Friedrichs Air Conditioning Company. In 1912, he married Emilie Allerkamp (1888–1984) of Comfort. Their only child, Percy, was born in 1914 and died in 2001. After returning to Comfort, Michael operated a welding shop on High Street. Emilie belonged to the Comfort Garden Club, but her primary interest was her home and family. According to her granddaughter Ruth Lindner Zoeller, meals were served promptly at the same time each day. (Both Ruth Lindner Zoeller collection.)

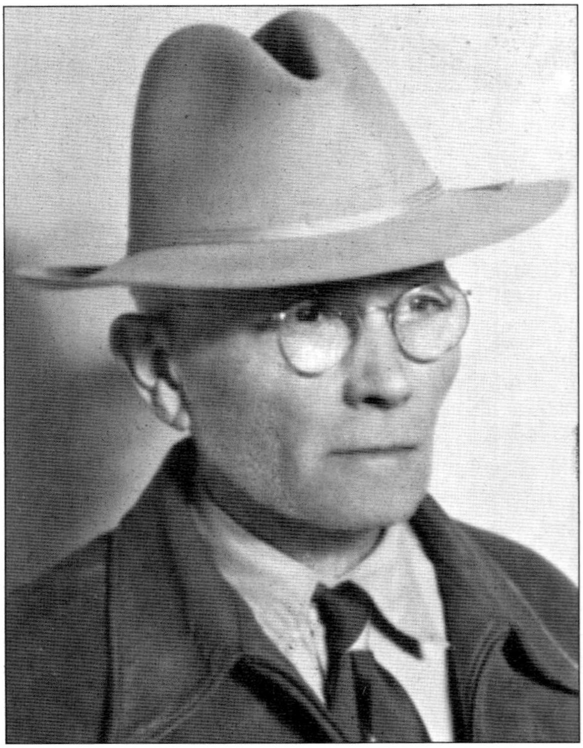

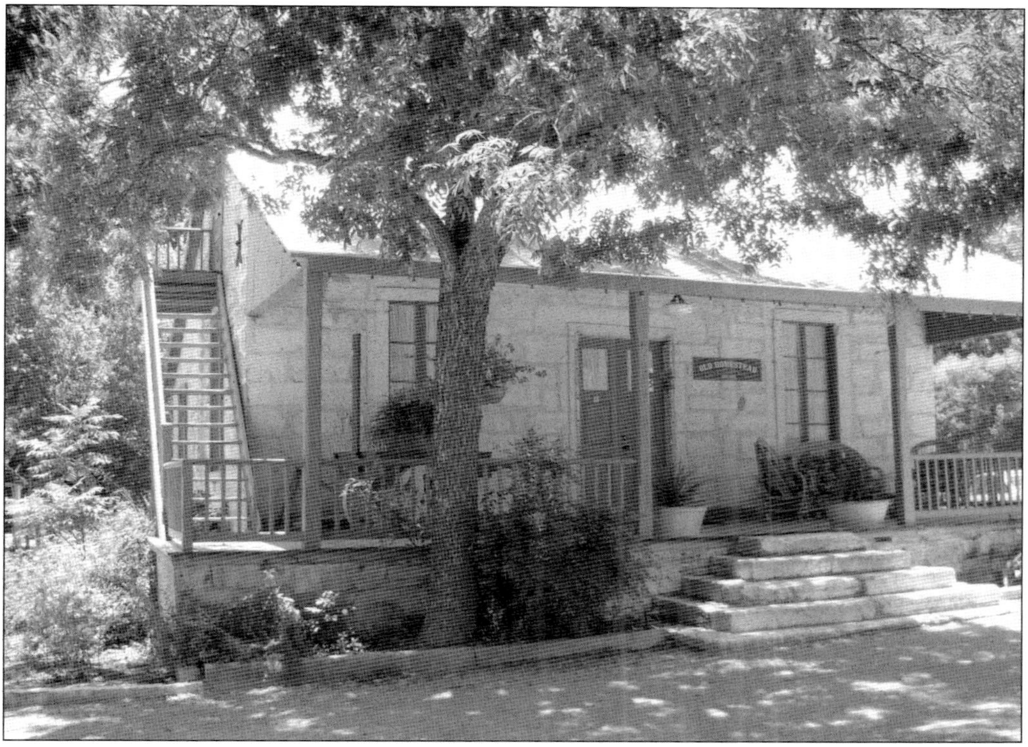

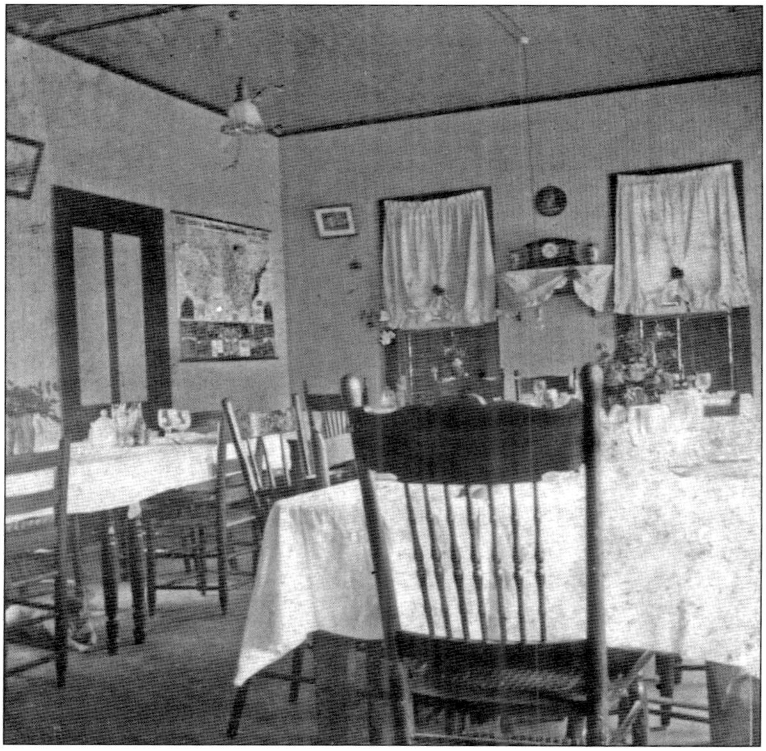

Gast Haus. Friedrich Christian Meyer came to Comfort in 1862 and established a stagecoach stop. The old homestead, constructed of locally quarried limestone, was a classic German-Texan house. In 1887, when the railroad came to Comfort, Meyer added more buildings to serve as a hotel. Set alongside the scenic Cypress Creek that soon joins the Guadalupe River, it continues to attract visitors. (Above photograph by Ruth Kiel; at right, Tina Neumann.)

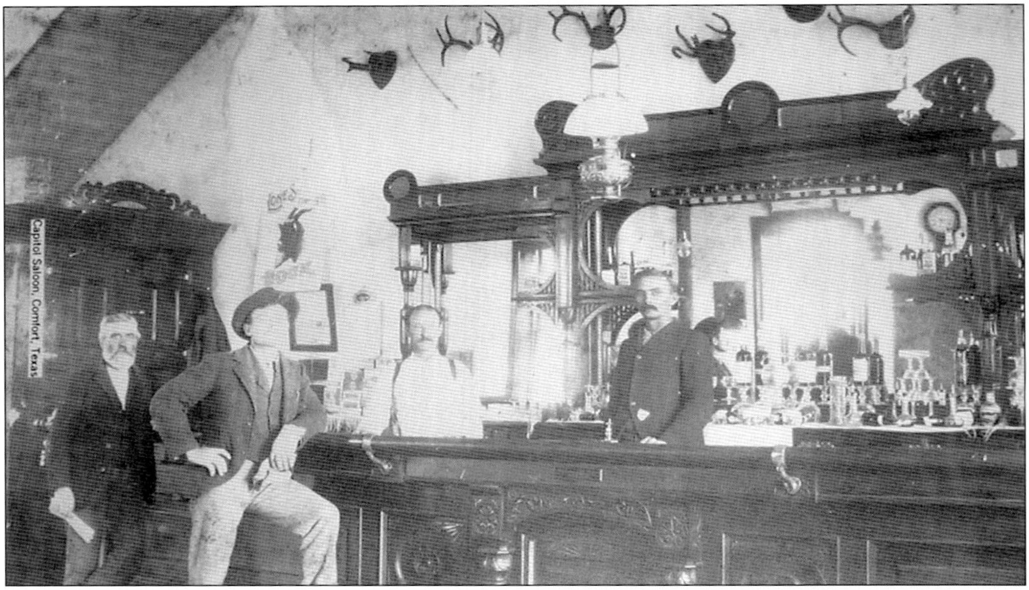

CAPITOL SALOON. The Ingenhuett Saloon (above) derived its name from Peter Ingenhuett (1833–1923). Later it was owned by Ehlers and Meyer and later still by Ernst Karger, who operated it as the Capitol Saloon until Prohibition. Note the designation "Capitol Saloon, Comfort, Texas" on the left edge of the picture postcard. It served beer imported from San Antonio. The phonograph behind the bartender may have provided music. The Holekamp Saloon (below) was the Capitol Saloon's competition. (Above, Comfort Heritage Foundation archives; below, Roy Perkins collection.)

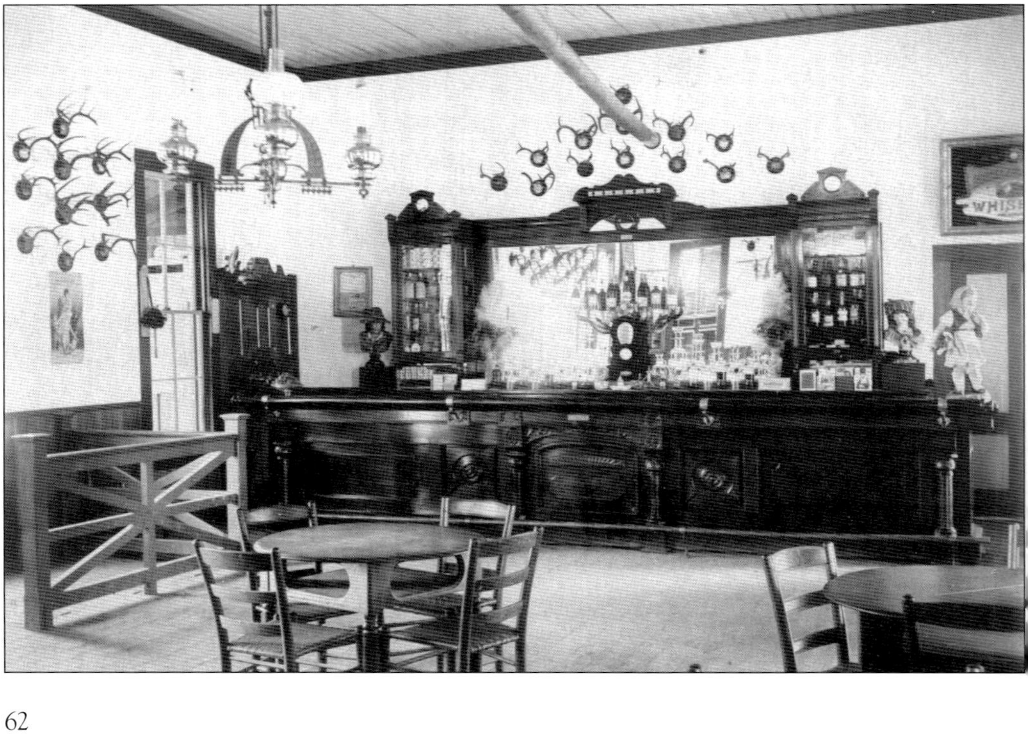

Five

Celebrations

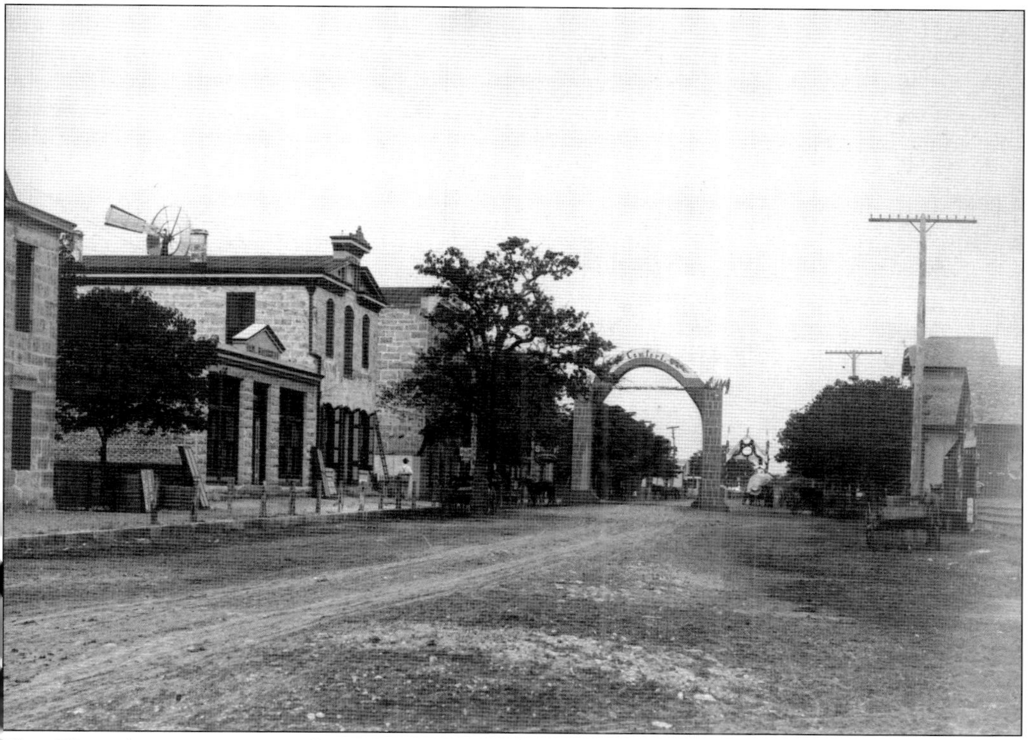

The 50th Anniversary of Comfort, 1904. The archway was erected on High Street between Seventh and Eighth Streets for parade participants. In the left foreground are the Gass blacksmith shop, Ingenhuett store, and Ingenhuett-Karger saloon. In the right foreground is the livery stable. Utility poles line the street, hitching posts are in front of the stores, and a windmill rises behind the store. (Comfort Heritage Foundation archives.)

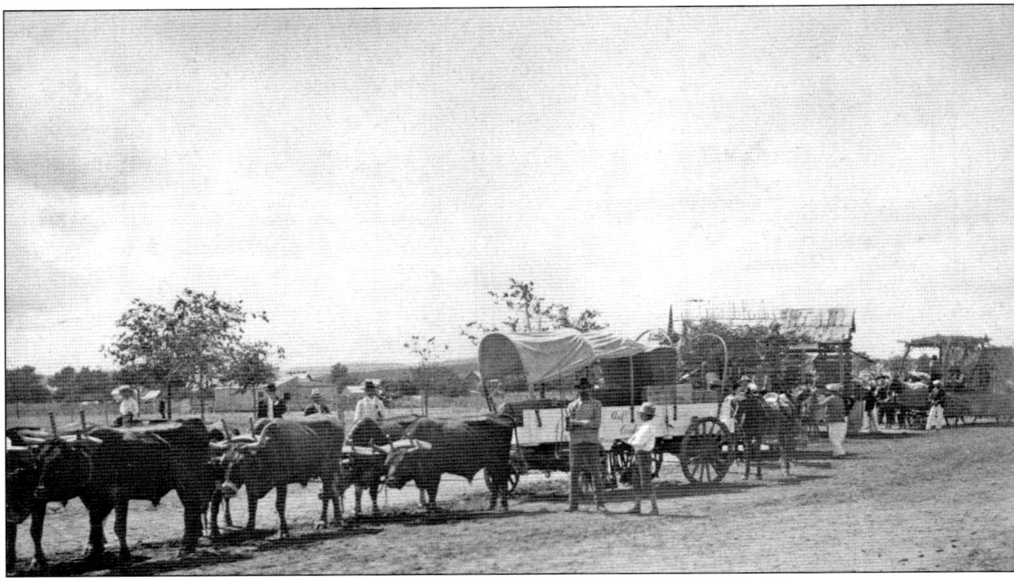

Transportation Models, 1904. Early travel is represented here by an immigrant wagon pulled by a team of six oxen. Henry Hamilton drove this Black Angus team owned by Alfred Giles in the historical parades of both 1904 and 1929. According to Guido Ransleben, Giles "had the last team of oxen to tread the streets of Comfort, hauling wool, mohair, and grain to local merchants for shipment to distant markets." Flower-festooned surreys drawn by two horses carried honored guests. (Both Comfort Heritage Foundation archives.)

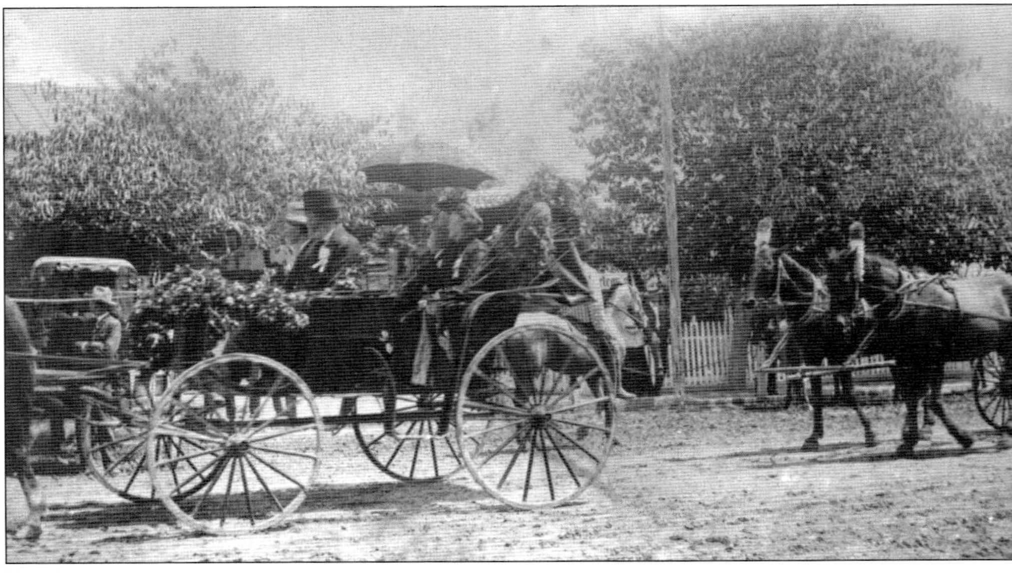

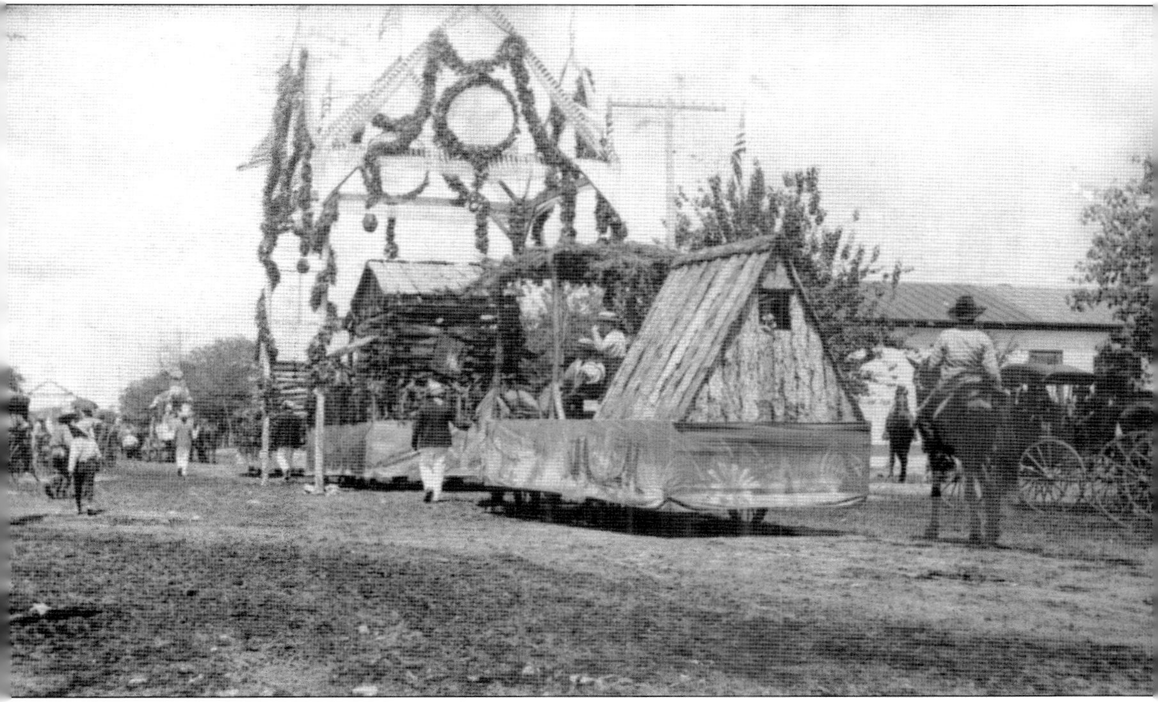

First School in Comfort, 1904. A replica of the first Comfort schoolhouse was on the float shown entering another archway farther west on High Street. The original 1856 school location was on Main Street between Fifth and Sixth Streets. The Comfort School Association incorporated on May 2, 1880, with Robert Steves as president; the directors were Thomas Ingenhuett, Emil Serger, Richard Kott, and Heinrich Boerner. Article 3 of the Bylaws stated that the following subjects would be taught: reading, writing, grammar, arithmetic, geography, history, natural history, composition, German, singing, and gymnastics. Article 12 stated that no open religion is to be taught, and no dance shall be held in the schoolhouse. (Comfort Heritage Foundation archives.)

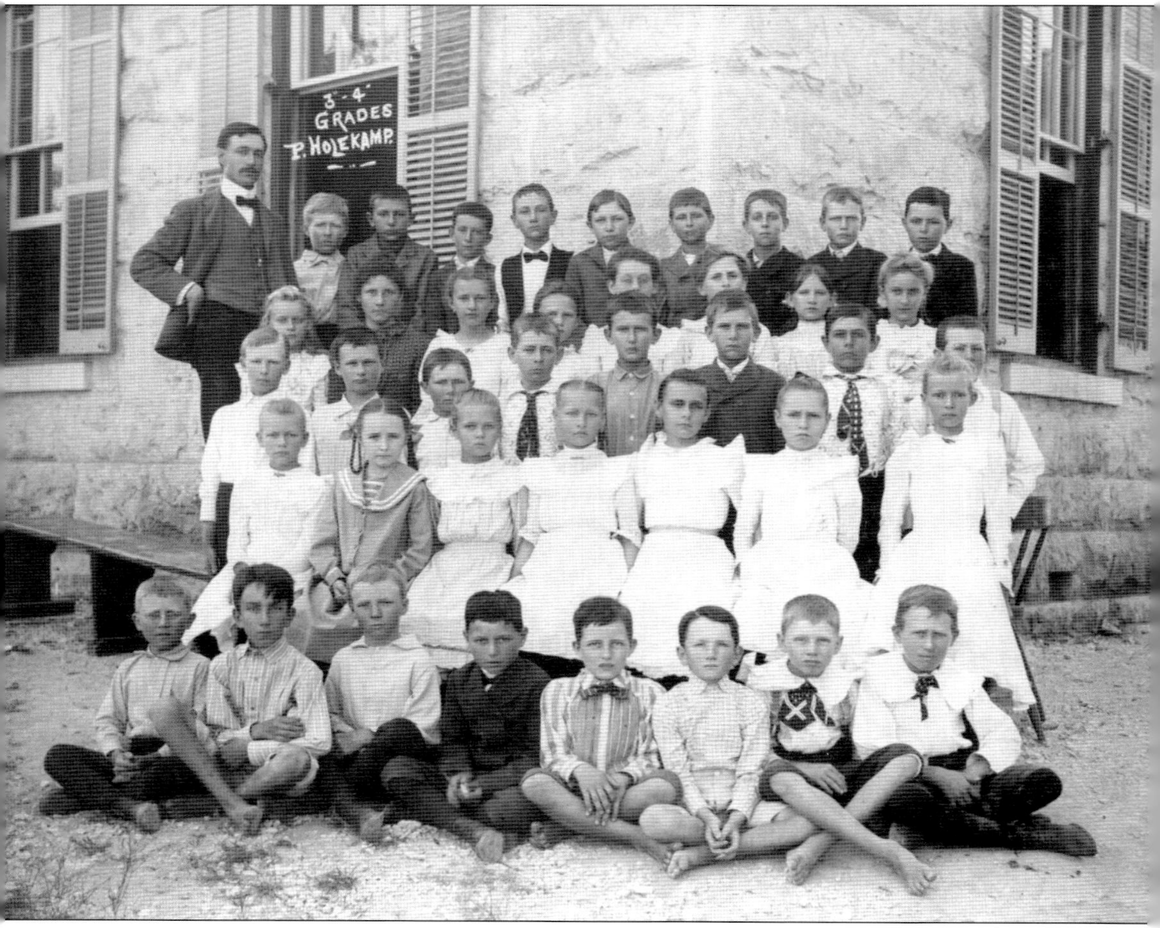

SCHOOL PICTURE. Paul Holekamp was the teacher of the 1901 third- and fourth-grade classes. The rock school with a bell tower was built in 1893, which was the third school to be built in this small, progressive community. The students are, from left to right, (first row) Theodore Schroeder, Charles Schwethelm, Oscar Neunhoeffer, Rudolph Flach Jr., Peter Ingenhuett, Otto Schwethelm, Carl Biermann, and Edgar Wiedenfeld; (second row) Erna Spenrath, Katy Flach, Emilie Karger, Hedwig Herbst, Bertha Spenrath, Helene Herbst, and Ella Spenrath; (third row) Louis Karger, ? Weiss, Rudolph Lindner, Martin Spenrath, Louis Koehne, Hermann Boerner, Daniel Spenrath, and ? Weiss; (fourth row) Betsy Faust, Alma Schmidt, Ida Lindemann, Ellie Fellbaum, Meta Keller, Elizabeth Boerner, Josephine Ransleben, and Gretchen Faust; (fifth row) Robert Schladoer, Eddie Ransleben, Charles Burrow, August Rusch, Albert Schreiber, Otto Brinkmann, Henry Herbst, Otto Flach Jr., and unidentified. (Comfort Heritage Foundation archives.)

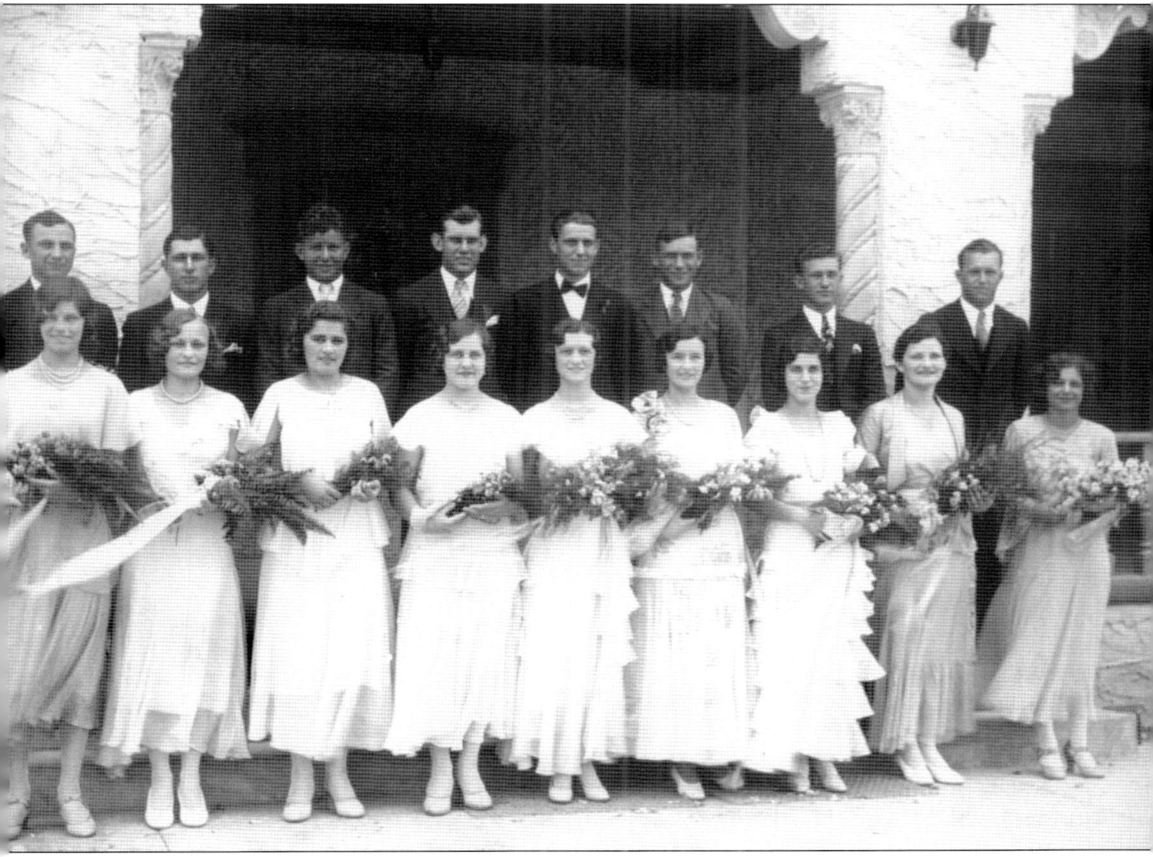

GRADUATION. High school graduation pictures were taken in front of the Comfort Theater on Seventh Street. The 1931 class included, from left to right, (first row) Lydia Meyer, Anna Rusch, Helen Gass, Edna Stieler, Adelaide Heinen, Kathryn Schuetz, Mildred Main, Ruby Flach, and Carmen Schoenewolf; (second row) Arno Flach, Kenneth Saylor, Leo Tomlinson, Herbert Lindemann, Arthur Flach, S. P. Tomlinson, Christie Lindemann, and unidentified. (Comfort Heritage Foundation archives.)

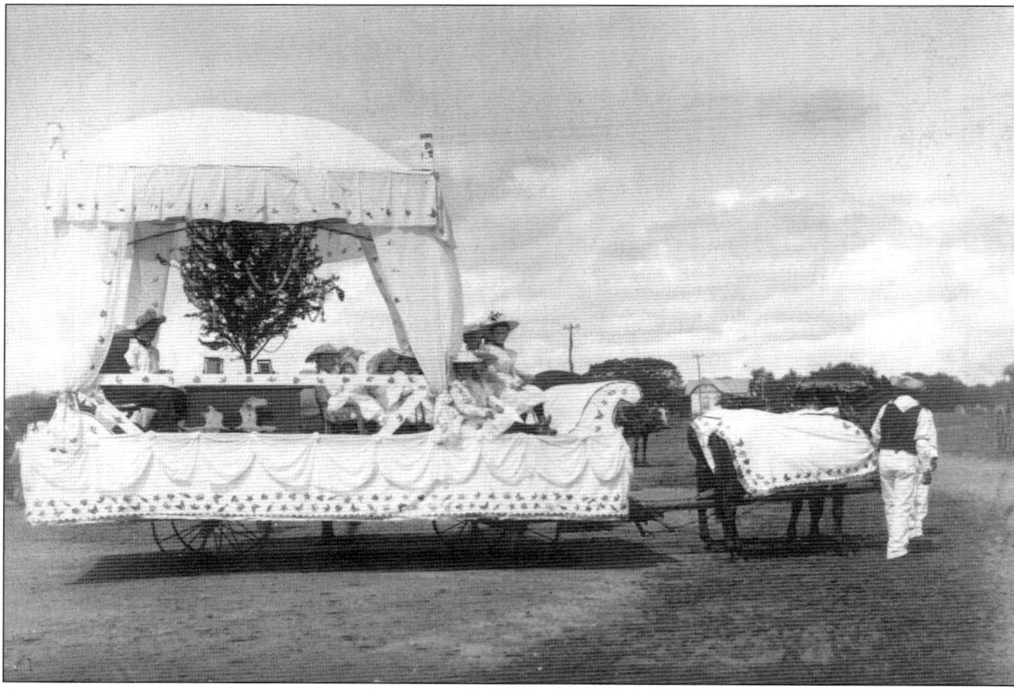

Social Organizations, 1904. The Maria Martha Verein tented float held a Christian ladies organization founded by Lutheran pastor Friedrich Bauer in 1891. Its name derives from the biblical story of Jesus visiting the home of sisters Martha and Mary and their brother Lazarus. The club raised money to support the needy, to maintain the cemetery, and to improve the church. The Comfort Liedertafel was a men's singing group that performed at anniversaries and sang at funerals. The singers were Emil Karger (director), Walter Brinkmann, Otto Ingenhuett, ? Rusch, ? Ritzer, Emil Habecker, and Fritz Fisher. The Comfort Park gazebo is in the background of the image below. (Both Comfort Heritage Foundation archives.)

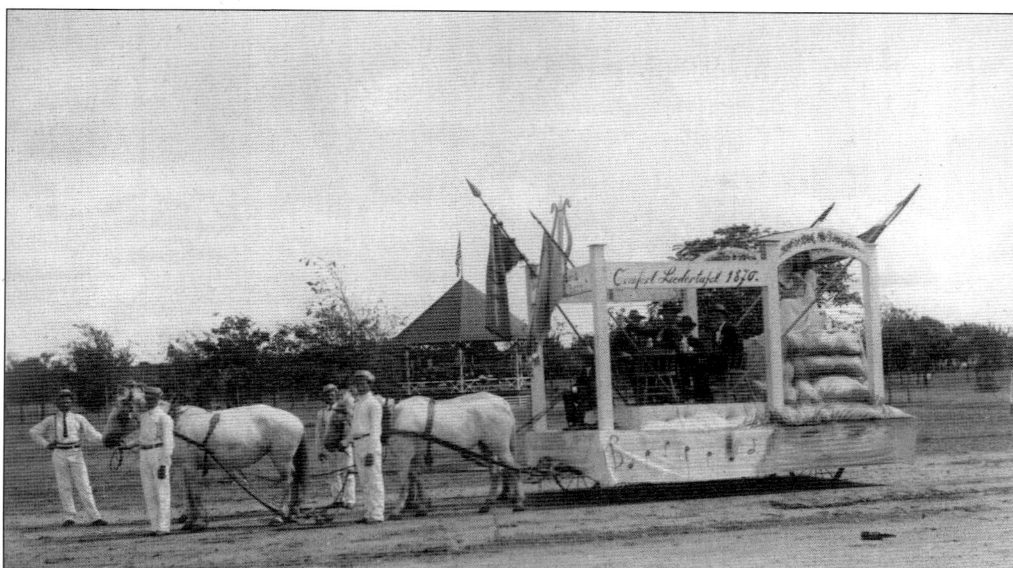

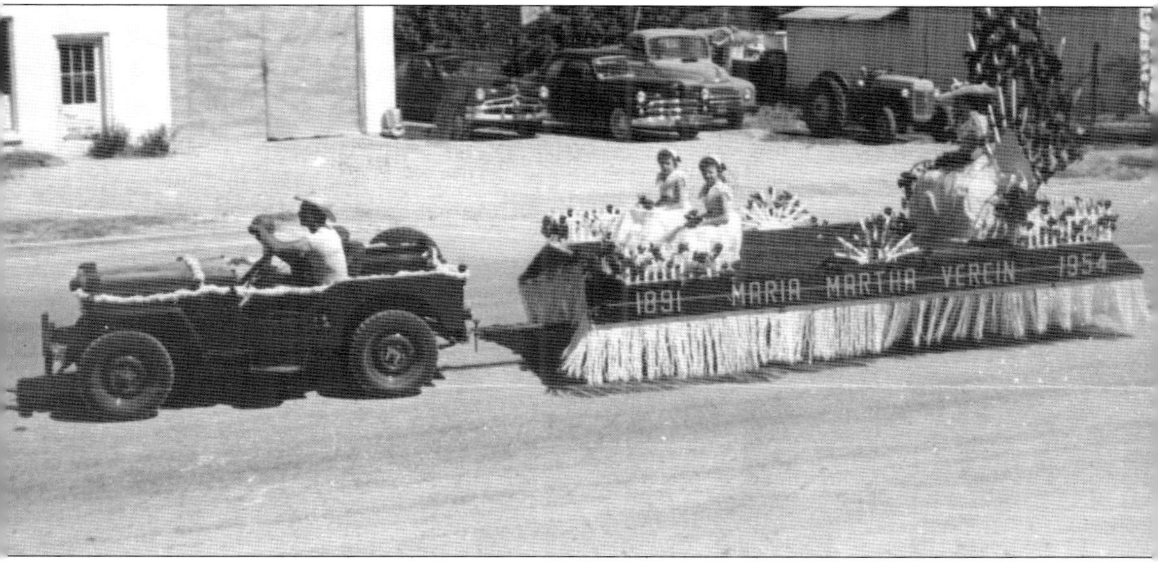

THE 100TH ANNIVERSARY OF COMFORT, 1954. The centennial brought forth many organizations. A Marine Corps color guard and the Comfort High School band led the way. After the parade, Brooke Army Medical Center troops gave a battlefield first-aid demonstration before enjoying a barbecue sausage meal. A pageant about the history of Comfort occurred in the evening, as did street dancing. The Maria Martha Verein proclaimed its 93 years of existence. Perry Lich is driving the jeep, while Jean Lois Karger and May and Fay Lindner ride on the float. (Comfort Heritage Foundation archives.)

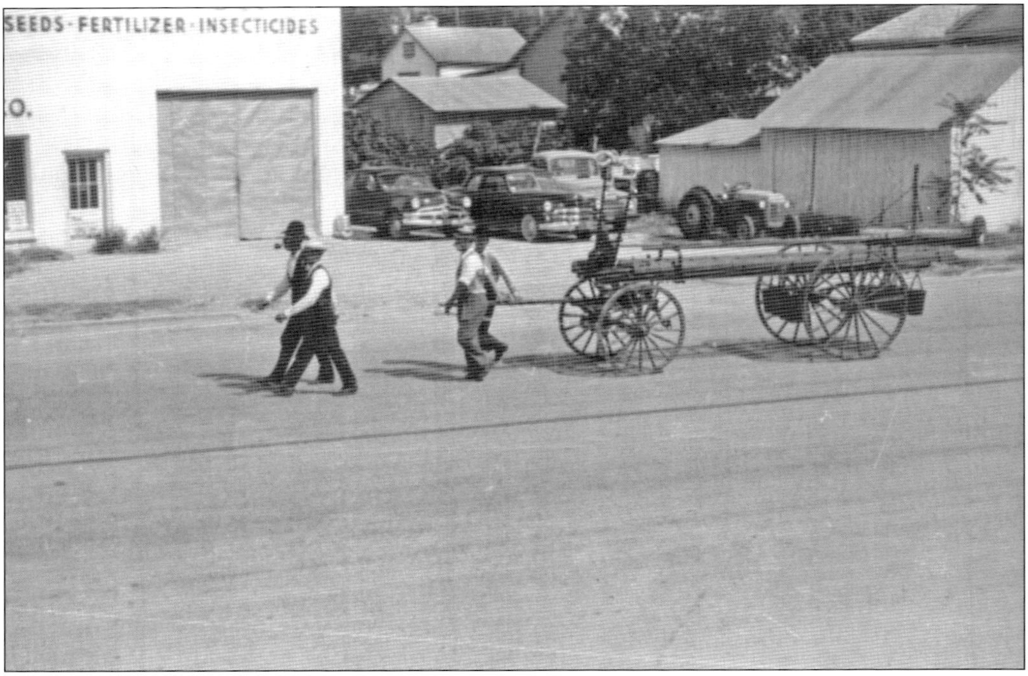

VOLUNTEER FIRE DEPARTMENT, 1954. The 50-year-old ladder truck with suspended buckets was the first piece of fire-fighting equipment. Pictured here pulling the ladder truck are Melvin Pankratz, Lee Jung, Chester Kirchhoff, and Jack Simon. As seen below, the new fire truck enhanced emergency capability. Kurt Biermann is driving, while Clarence Schaefer and Alex Spenrath ride on the side. (Both Comfort Volunteer Fire Department collection.)

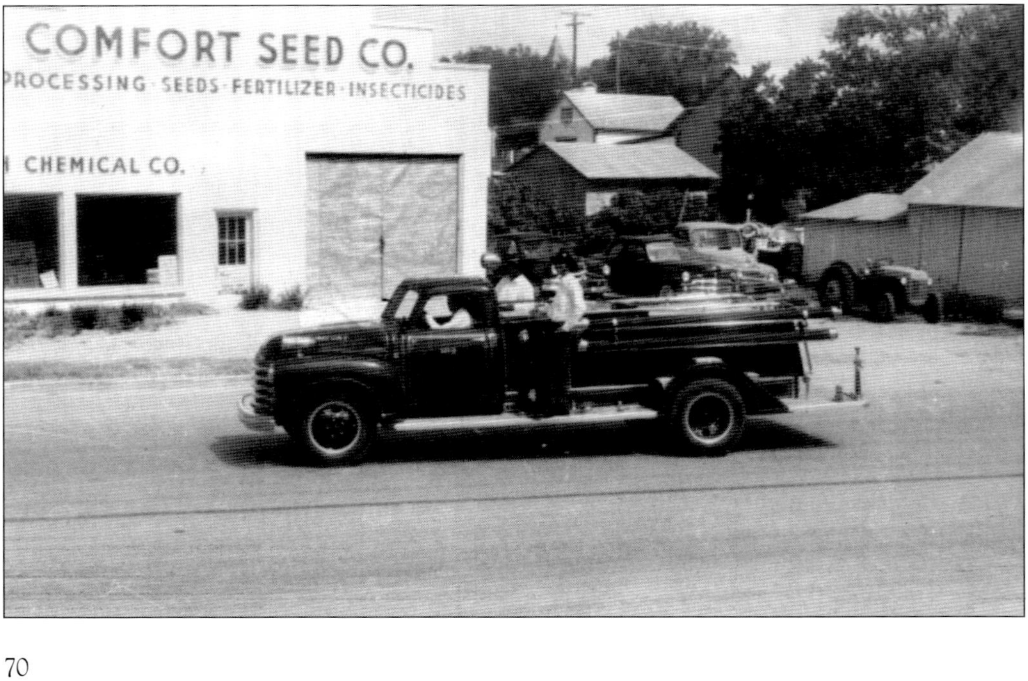

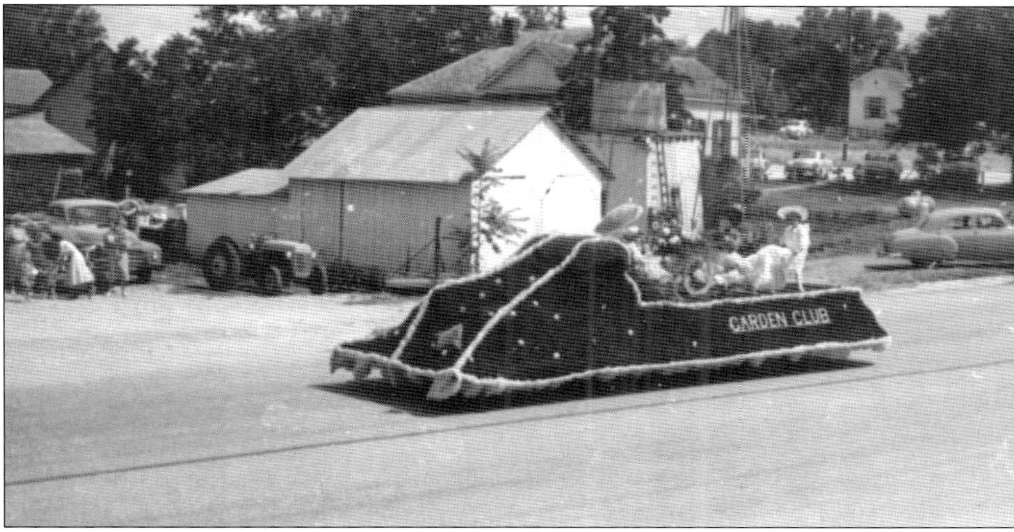

Social Organizations, 1954. The Comfort Garden Club is promoting decorative yards in the image above. Anna Chamberlain, Katherine Goforth, and Hilda Elstner Poth are riding on the float. The Literary Social Club, seen below, used a traditional horse-drawn carriage. (Both Comfort Heritage Foundation archives.)

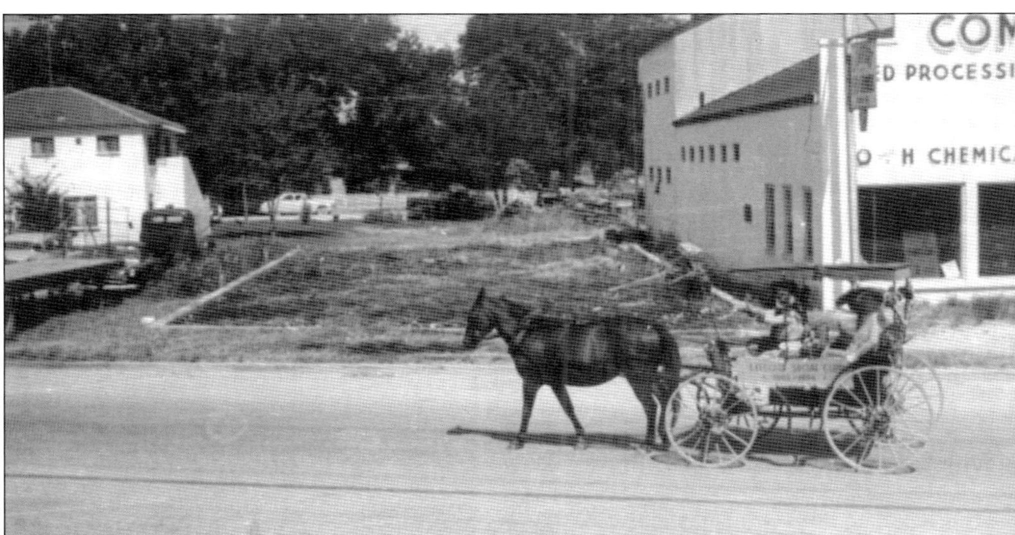

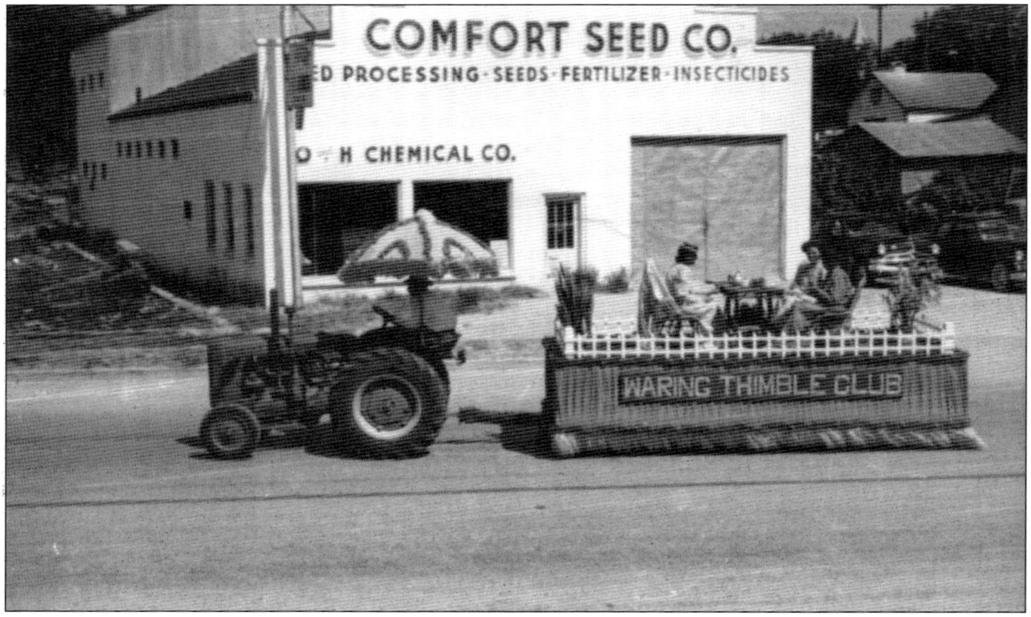

WARING THIMBLE CLUB AND FAIRYLAND, 1954. Above, members are depicting a meeting of the club in bygone days. Herbert Treiber is driving the tractor, while Myrtle Blaschke, Lema Steubing Treiber, and Marie Moreau are riding on the float. The building in the background, which was constructed in the 1930s on Texas Highway 27, housed the Comfort Seed Growers Association seed-cleaning enterprise, but its main business was selling seeds and fertilizer. Fairyland, a popular ballroom west of Comfort on Texas Highway 27, featured bands and beverages. Walls could be retracted for additional space and the evening breeze. In 1952, Denny Beckner's orchestra gave a charity performance there to benefit the Comfort Broncos baseball team. (Both Comfort Heritage Foundation archives.)

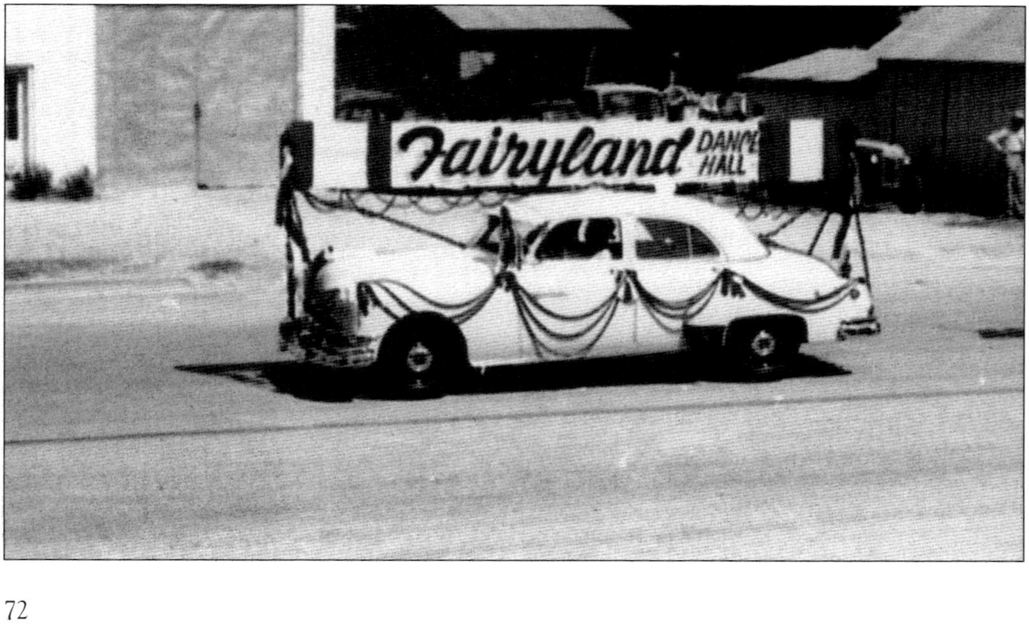

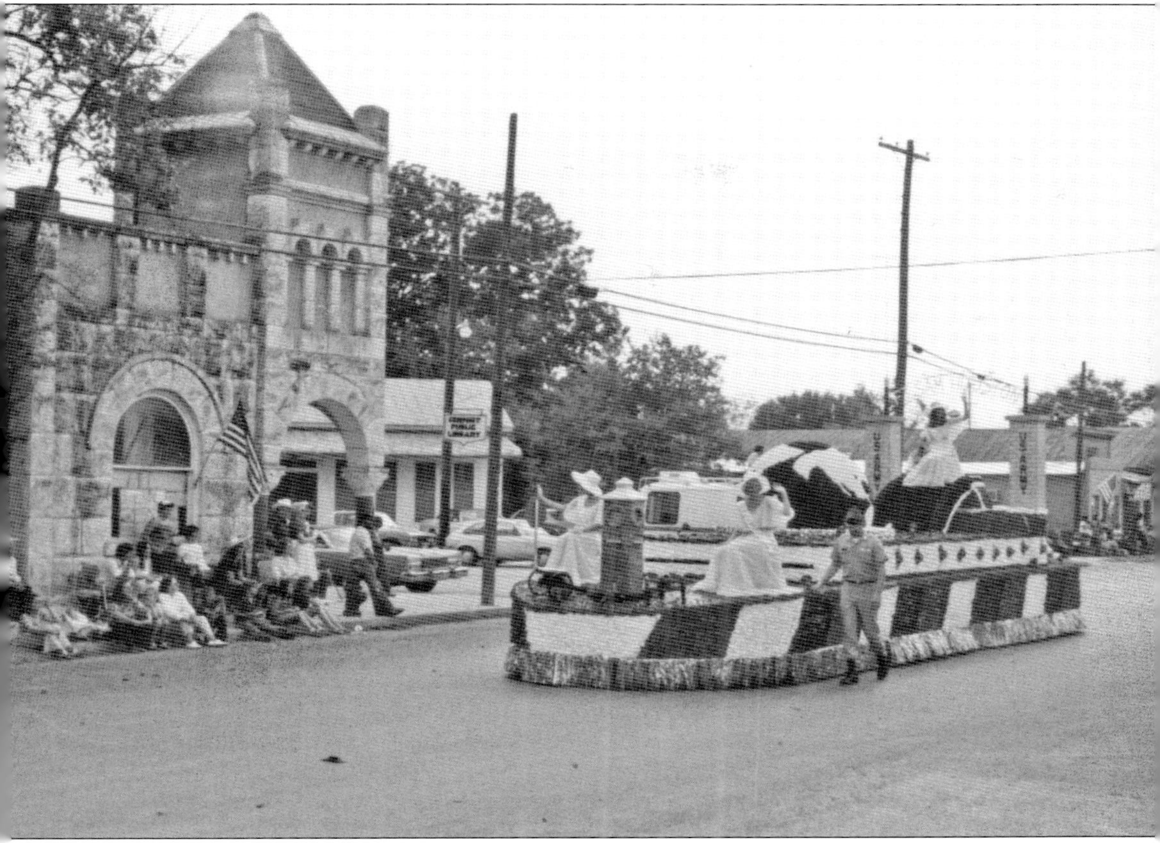

The 125th Anniversary of Comfort, 1979. The U.S. Army Band played that year, and the Beethoven Maennerchor and Damenchor of San Antonio sang. The Comfort Hermann Sons School of Dancing danced and won second prize in the organization category. The Cypress Creek School celebrated 100 years as well. Old Comfort State Bank, at that time home of the Comfort Public Library, is on left. (Comfort Heritage Foundation archives.)

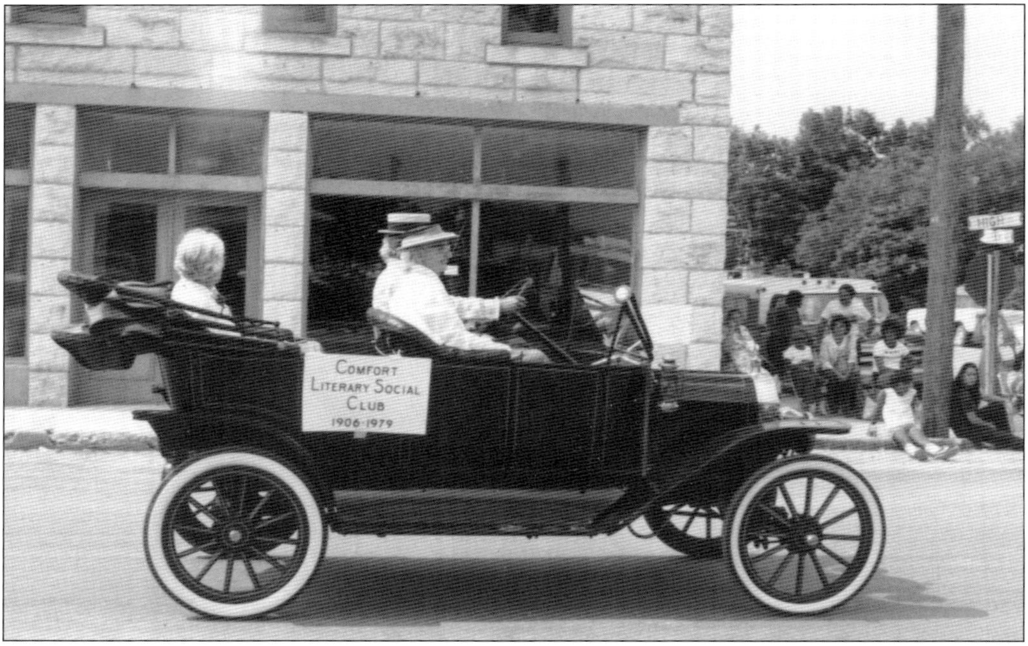

OLD CARS, 1979. The Comfort Literary Social Club proclaimed its 73 years of existence and won the prize for Most Decorated Car. Below, the Comfort Historical Society offered tours of the town; this group operated the Comfort Museum. Roy Perkins is driving the 1920 Ford Model T touring car for the historical society, with his mother, Ida Ingenhuett Perkins, in the front seat with him; Mildred Main and Minnie Bergmann are in the back seat. (Above, Comfort Historical Foundation archives; below, Roy Perkins collection.)

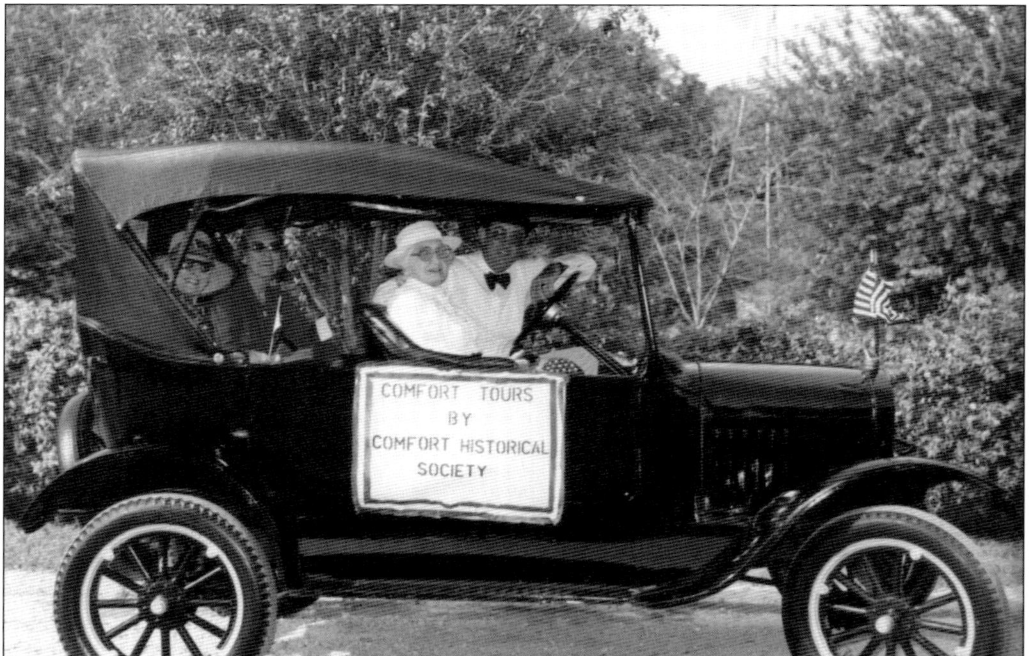

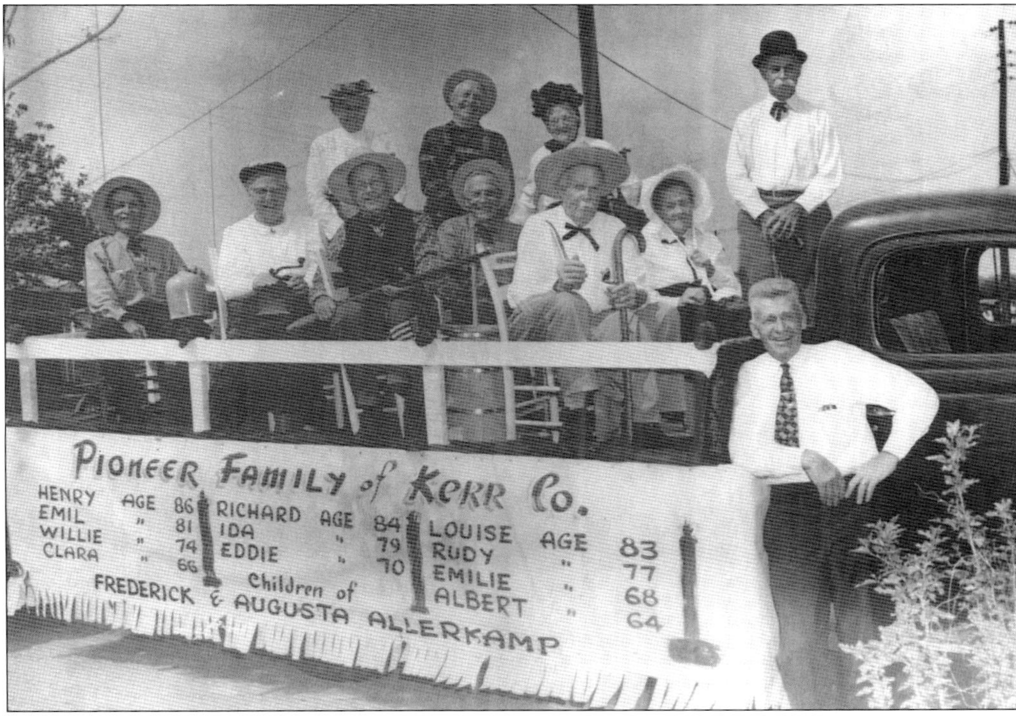

FAMILY FLOATS, 1979. Some of the original families in the area held family reunions at this time and assembled on floats to announce their long heritage. The Allerkamp family and the Faltin family are represented here. (Both Comfort Heritage Foundation archives.)

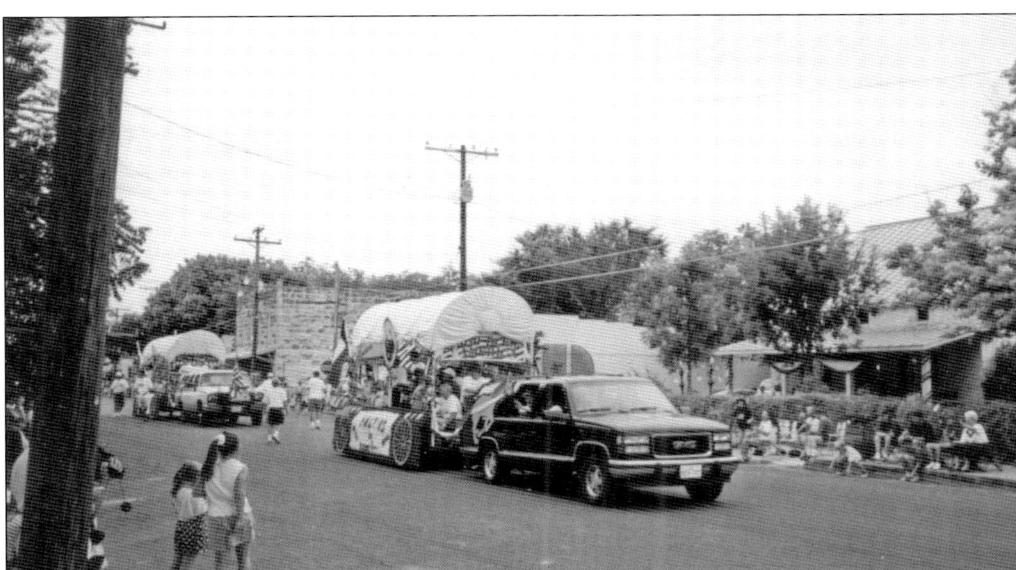

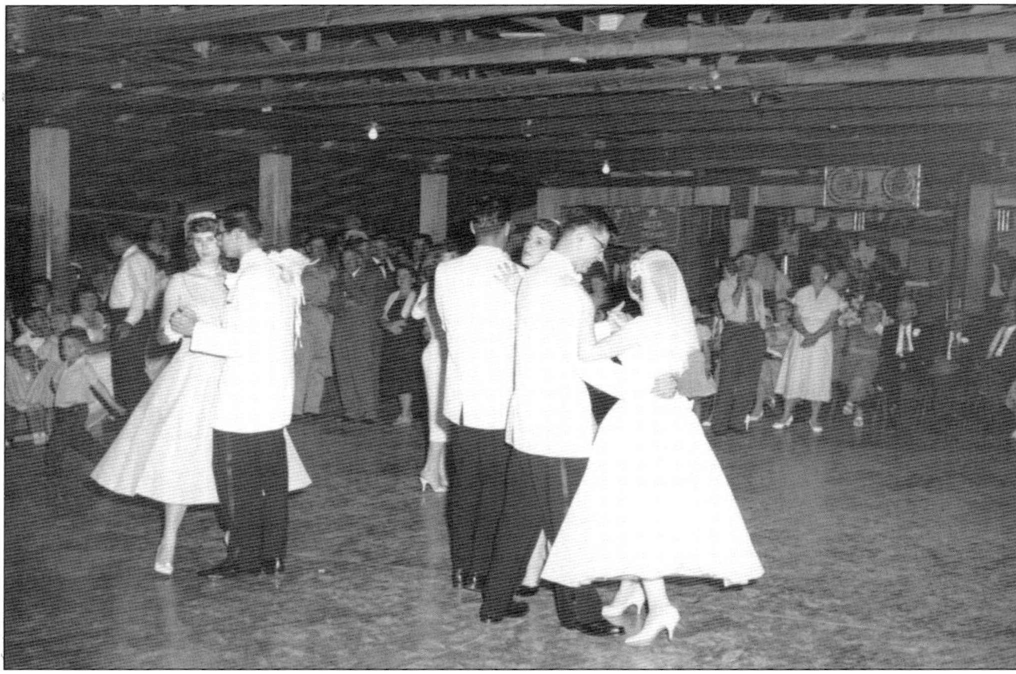

Wedding, 1958. Lois Albrecht Haufler and R. C. Haufler had their wedding reception at Fairyland Dance Hall on May 10, 1958. The grand march, led by Walter and Odiele Lux, was a traditional element of the celebration. The children who participated were Kirby Holekamp and Patty Waite. R. C. is known for his restoration of Oliver tractors and equipment, for which he received a Comfort Heritage Foundation award in 2009. Lois is the daughter of Lydia and Walter Albrecht, recipients of a Texas One Hundred Year Ranch certificate. She is a past president of the Comfort Heritage Foundation. (Both Lois Haufler collection.)

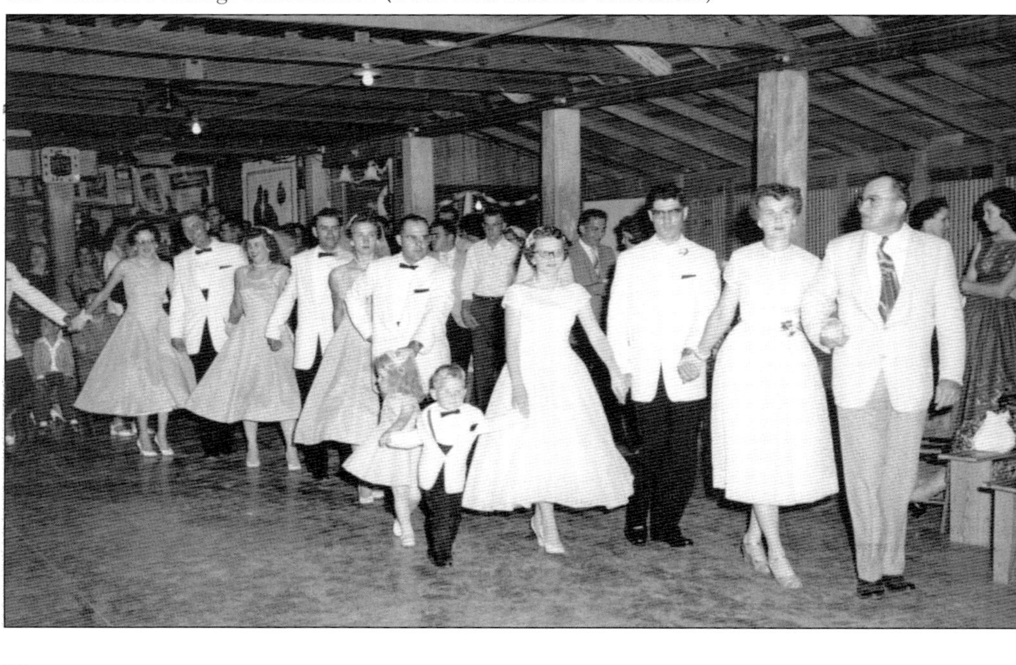

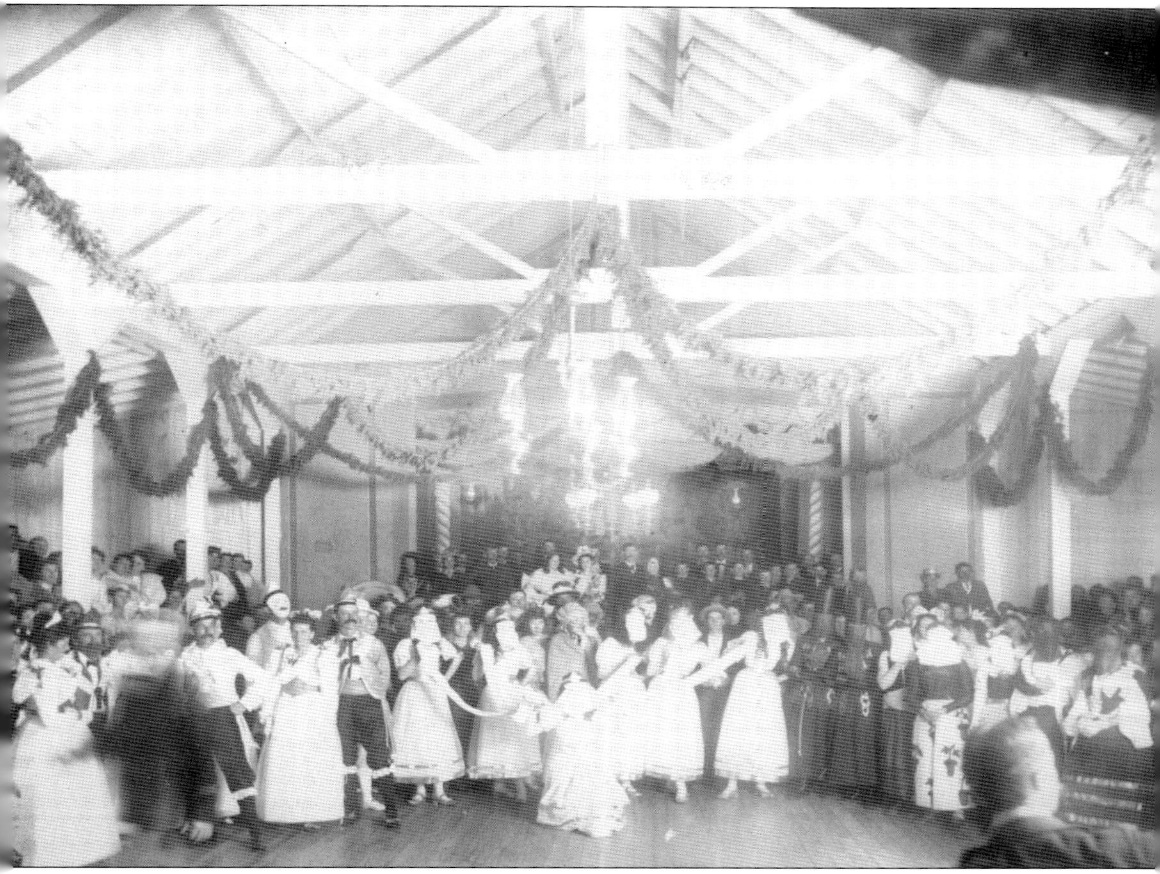

CARNIVAL BALL. The limestone opera house behind the Ingenhuett store was the site of formal balls, masquerades, and vaudeville shows. German costumes in this picture suggest Fasching, the annual pre-Lent festival week when people often dressed up or masqueraded during the celebration. (Roy Perkins collection.)

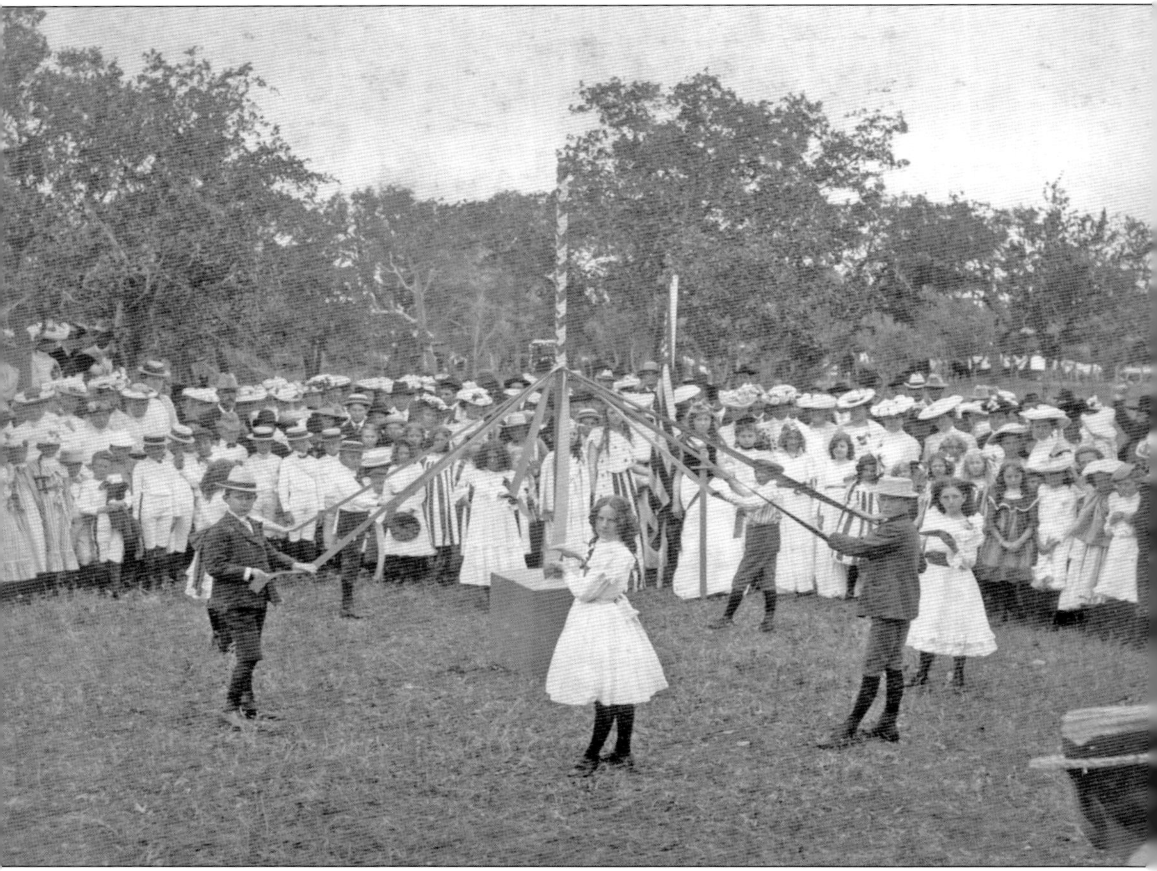

MAYPOLE. To celebrate May Day, this traditional event at the school picnic at Camp Laf-a-Lot on North Creek Road involved circling a tall wooden pole to which were attached long colored ribbons. This photograph was taken about 1902. Guido Ransleben identified participants, going clockwise and beginning with the girl in the immediate front, as Josephine Ransleben, Carl Fischer, Clara Moehring, August Steves, Rosa Wertheim, Theodore Schroeder, Katy Below, and Kurt Flach. (Tina Neumann collection.)

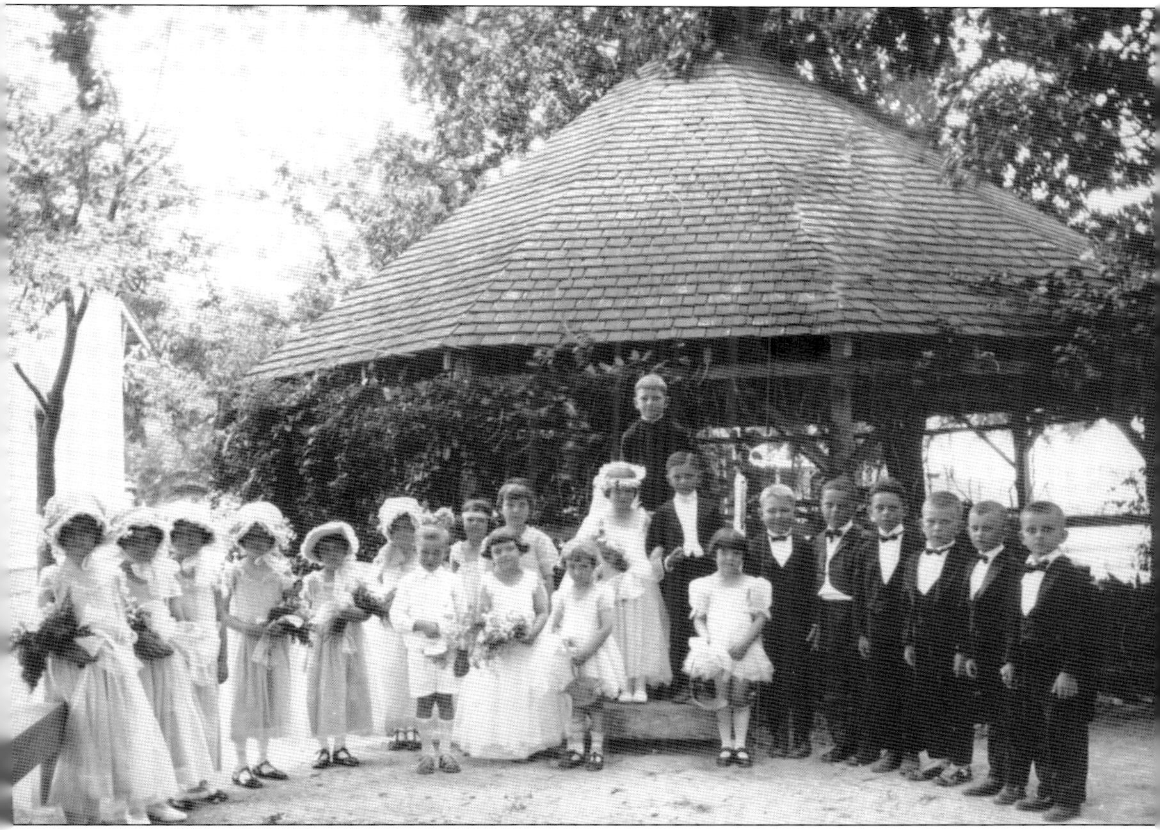

Tom Thumb Wedding. Tom Thumb weddings were a fad in the 1920s, with the name deriving from the tiny hero of a 16th-century nursery tale. This was part of a school benefit program. The wedding pageant itself derived from the actual wedding of Charles Stratton (stage name General Tom Thumb) to Lavinia Warren in 1863. (Tina Neumann collection.)

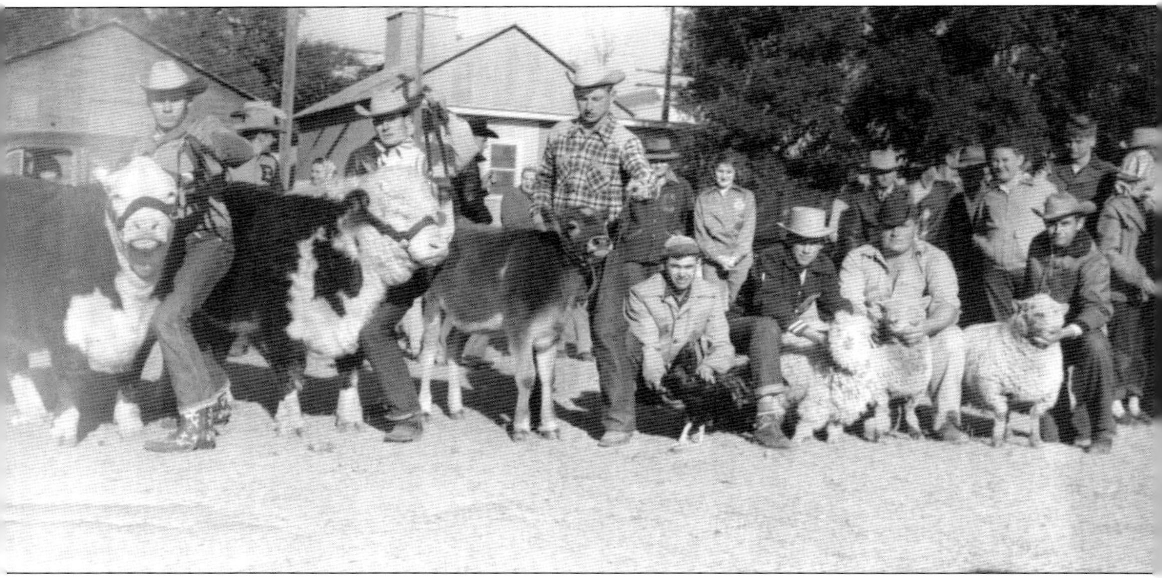

Stock Show. Animal showing as a community or a school event occurred regularly, as in this depiction of cattle and sheep. In the background is Comfort's first fire station at Seventh and Main Streets. (Comfort Heritage Foundation archives.)

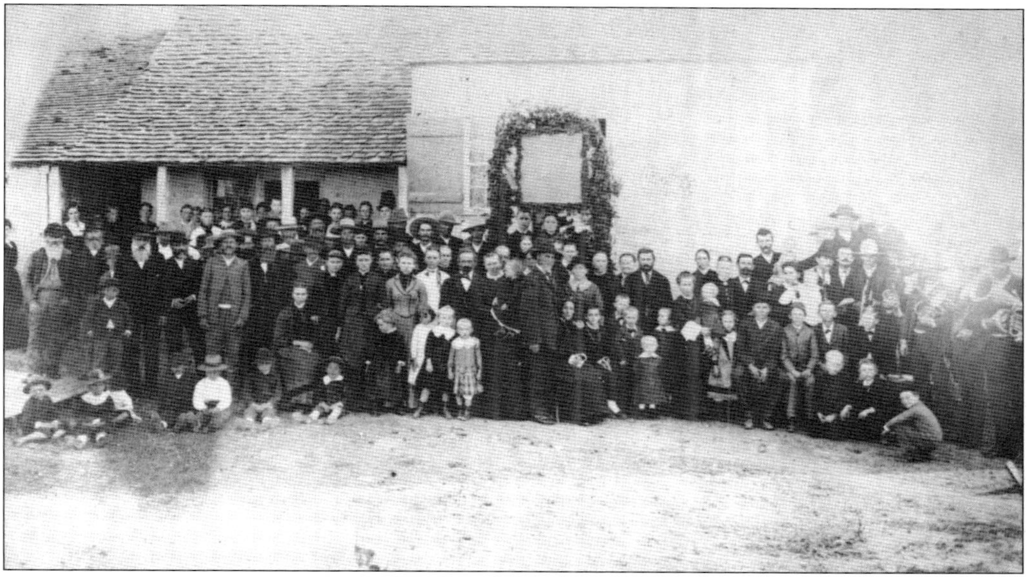

Family Anniversaries. Burgeoning families, by the time of the 50th wedding anniversary of the Heinen patriarch and matriarch (above), could gather up to 85 people, young and old, for the occasion. The Allerkamp family gathering was smaller, centering around a large punch bowl on a linen tablecloth. (Above, Roy Perkins collection; below, Ruth Lindner Zoeller collection.)

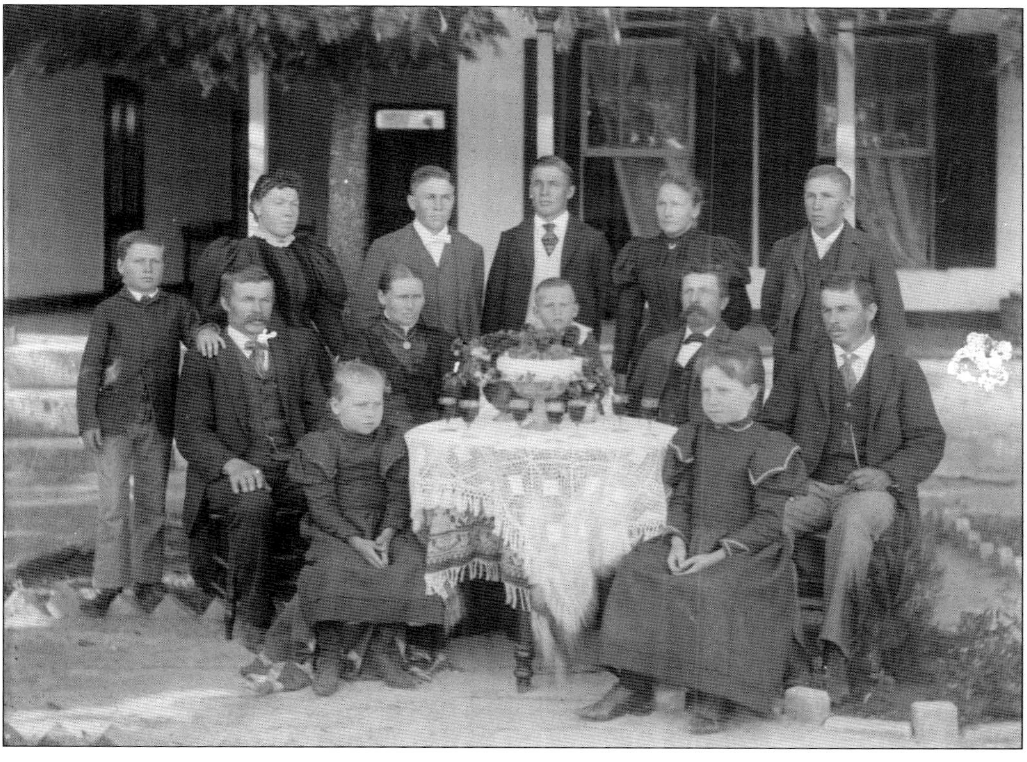

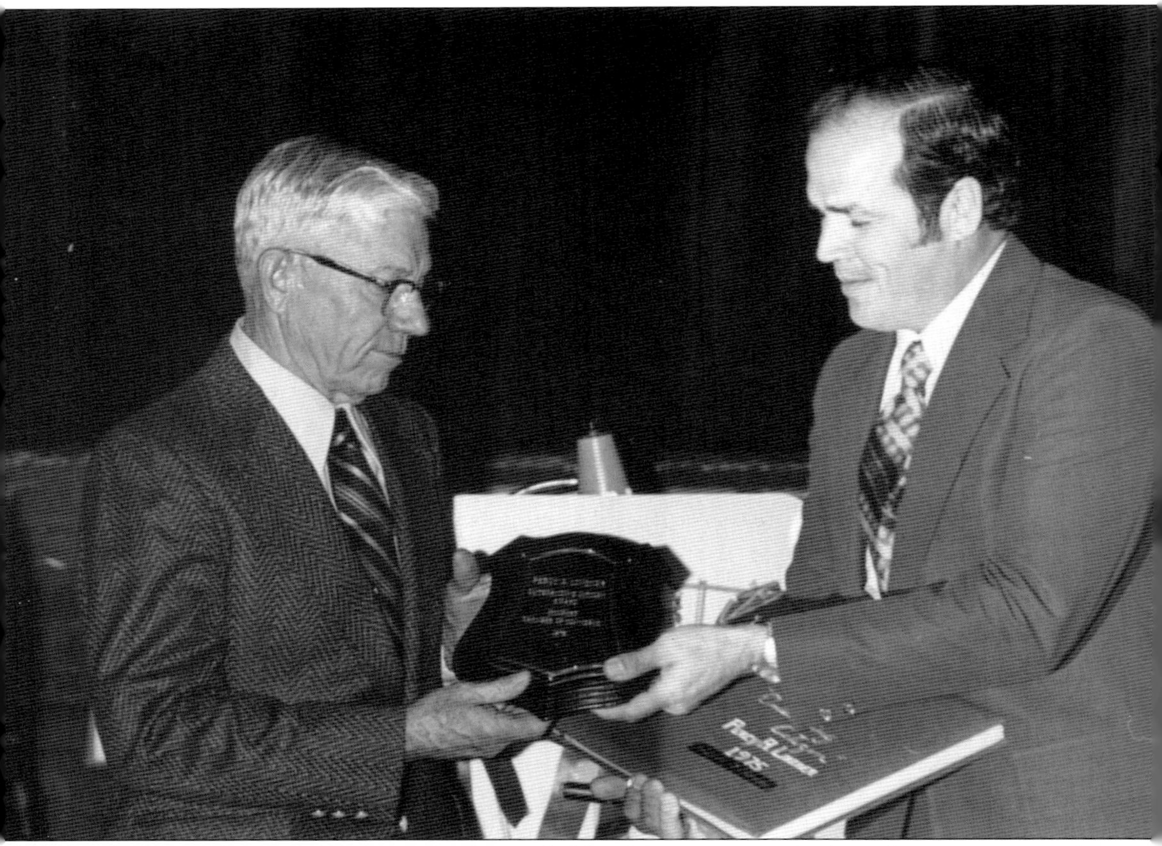

Annual Honors. Civic organizations held celebrations at which an honoree received an award. Here David Biermann, president of the Comfort Chamber of Commerce, presents the 1975 Citizen of the Year award to Percy Lindner for his service to the community. Tributes were made by JoEllen Biermann on behalf of the Comfort Hospital, by Eugene Pankratz on behalf of Lindner's farm and business interests, and by Presley Arhelger, the general manager of Hill Country Telephone Cooperative. Special mention was made of the fact that Lindner annually donated Christmas trees to be sold as a chamber of commerce fund-raiser and that he was currently working to secure a nursing home for the community. Lindner thanked his wife, Viola, his parents, Michael and Mrs. Lindner, his children, and other family members for their help. (Ruth Lindner Zoeller collection.)

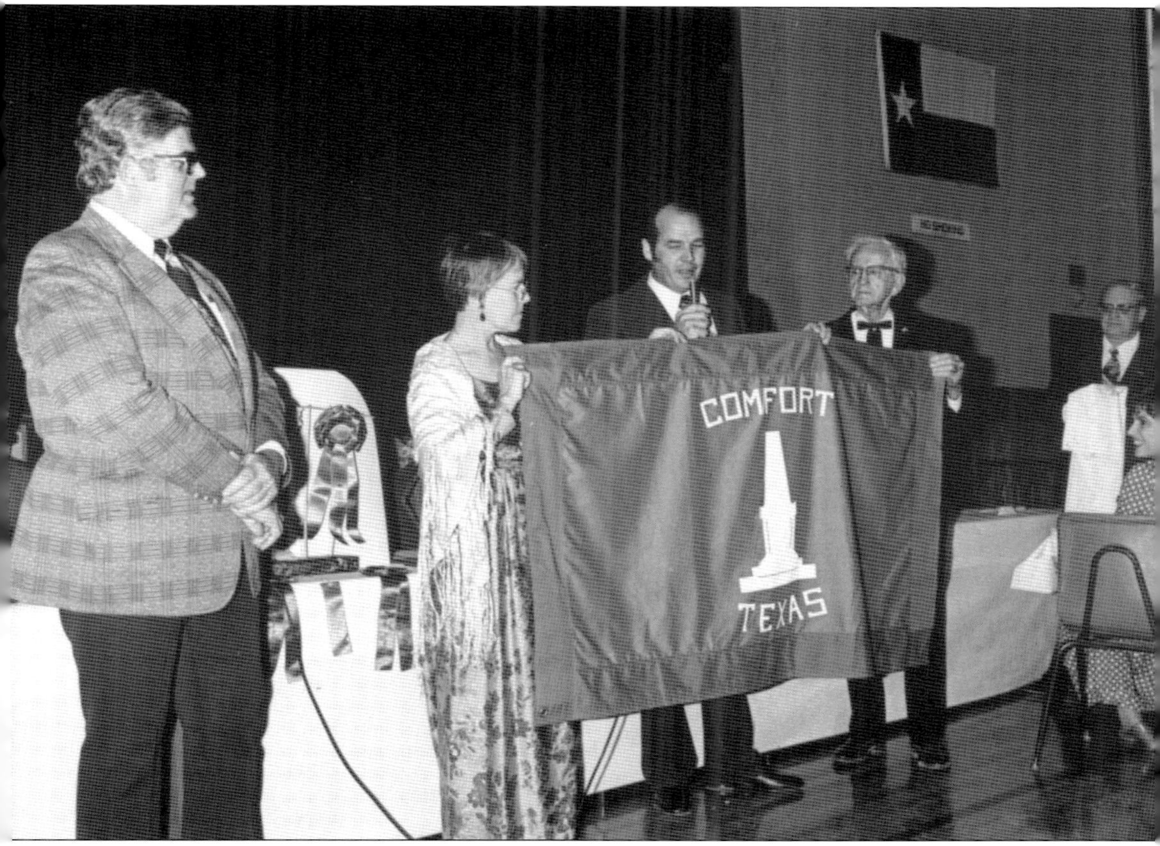

Comfort's Official Flag. Also at the 1976 Comfort Chamber of Commerce banquet, Charles "Chuck" Snyder looks on as, from left to right, Esther Wiedenfeld, David Biermann, and Guido Ransleben display the new official flag of Comfort: a red, white, and blue banner made by JoEllen Biermann, Betty Ross Murphy, and Kit Nelson. To the right are Eugene C. Burow, a previous Citizen of the Year, and Judy Lindner. Snyder, of the San Antonio Bicentennial Committee, presented two certificates in designation of Comfort as both a state and a national Bicentennial City. Accepting the awards for the Comfort Bicentennial Committee were general chairman Guido Ransleben and co-chairman Esther Wiedenfeld. Snyder noted that the certificates made Comfort one of 8,000 bicentennial communities in the nation. Special Awards of Merit went to Eugene Pankratz for his work on the city park and float and to Esther Wiedenfeld for her bicentennial activities. A. C. Schwethelm, in the far left corner of the photograph, served as master of ceremonies at the banquet. (Ruth Lindner Zoeller collection.)

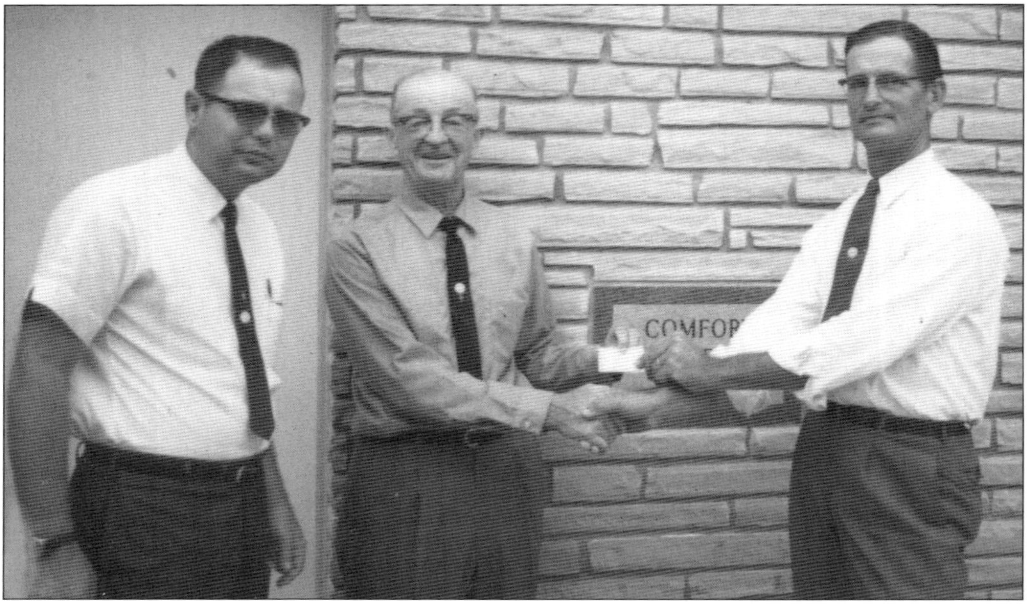

Retirement Honors. Albert Faltin served as secretary of the Comfort Volunteer Fire Department for 53 years. Chief C. B. Chenault presented his honorary card, assisted by Melvin Pankratz. Many members of the family remained in Comfort and continued to serve the community. Both Helen Faltin Martin and Frances Faltin Chamberlain were library volunteers and also members of the Friends of the Library and the Comfort Heritage Foundation. "Fanny's" son Frank Chamberlain returned to Comfort with his family and is a leader in the Gaddis Methodist Church. (Above, Comfort Volunteer Fire Department collection; below, Tina Neumann collection.)

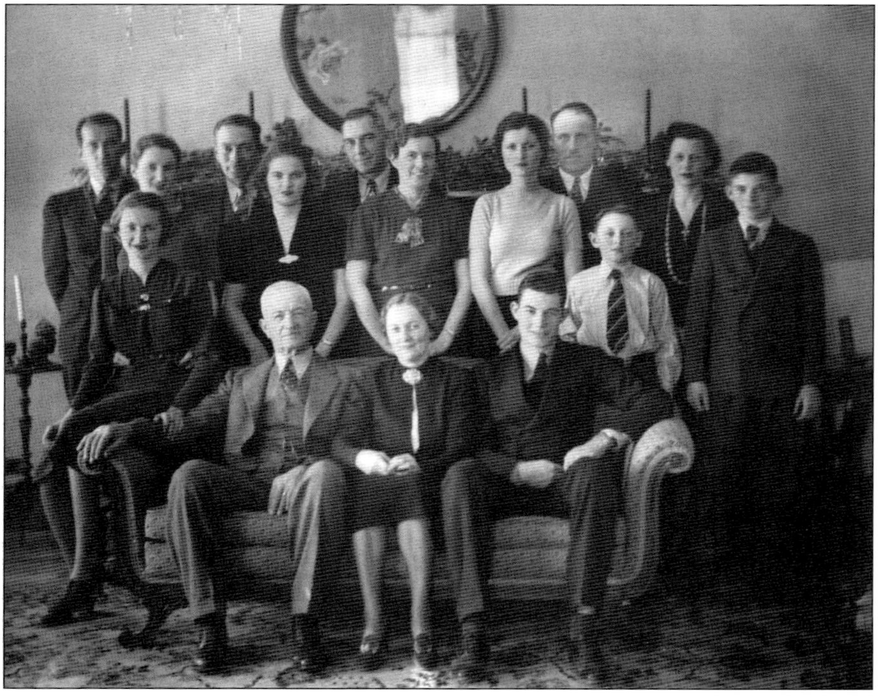

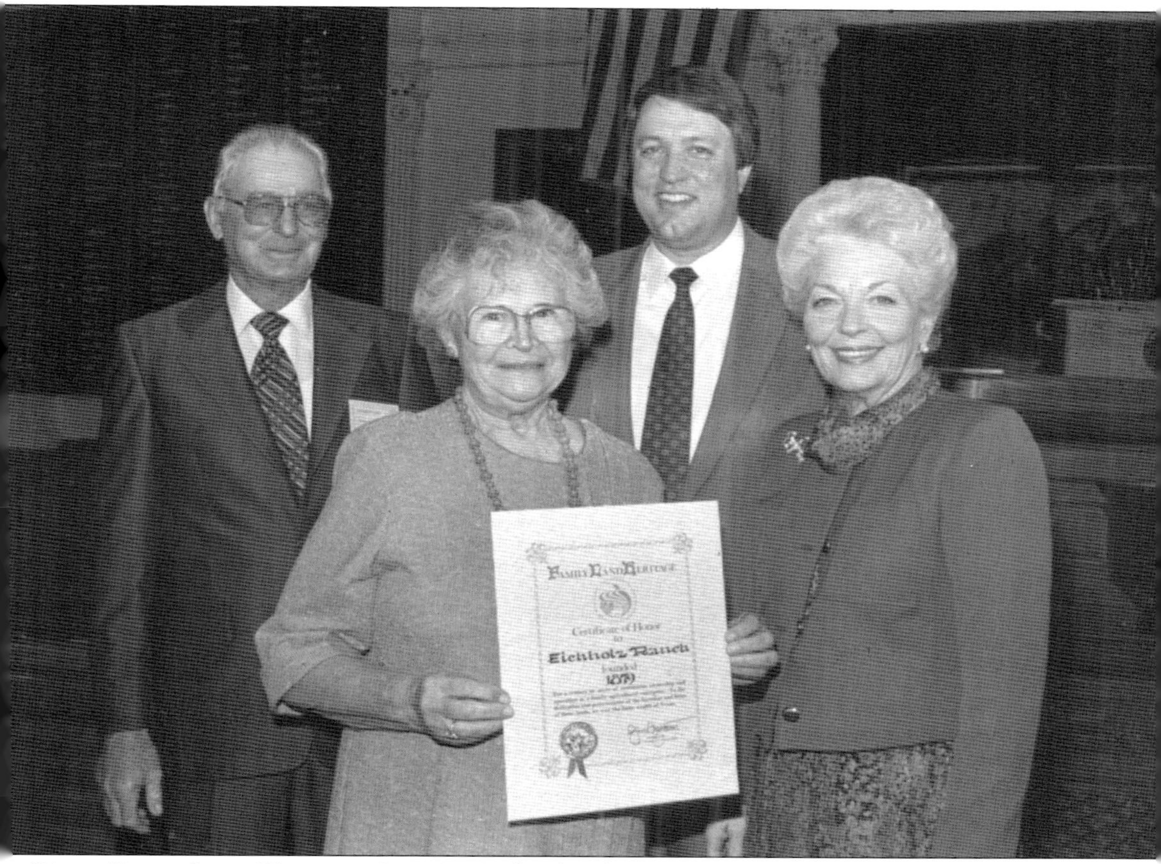

Texas Family Land Heritage. In 1989, Gerhard and Ruby Lu Seidensticker Eichholz accepted the Texas Family Land Heritage certificate for the Eichholz Ranch on Texas Route 473 in Kendall County from deputy state agriculture commissioner Michael Moeller and state treasurer Ann Richards during ceremonies at the Texas capitol. This program honors properties that have been in continuous agricultural production for 100 years by the same family. The family must also reside in Texas and actively manage daily operations. The land cannot have been leased to someone outside of the family. S.Sgt. Eichholz was absent only during World War II when he served with Company L, 3rd Battalion, 351st Infantry Regiment, 88th Infantry Division in Italy. His battalion earned the Distinguished Unit Citation, and he earned the Silver Star for gallantry. (Comfort Heritage Foundation archives.)

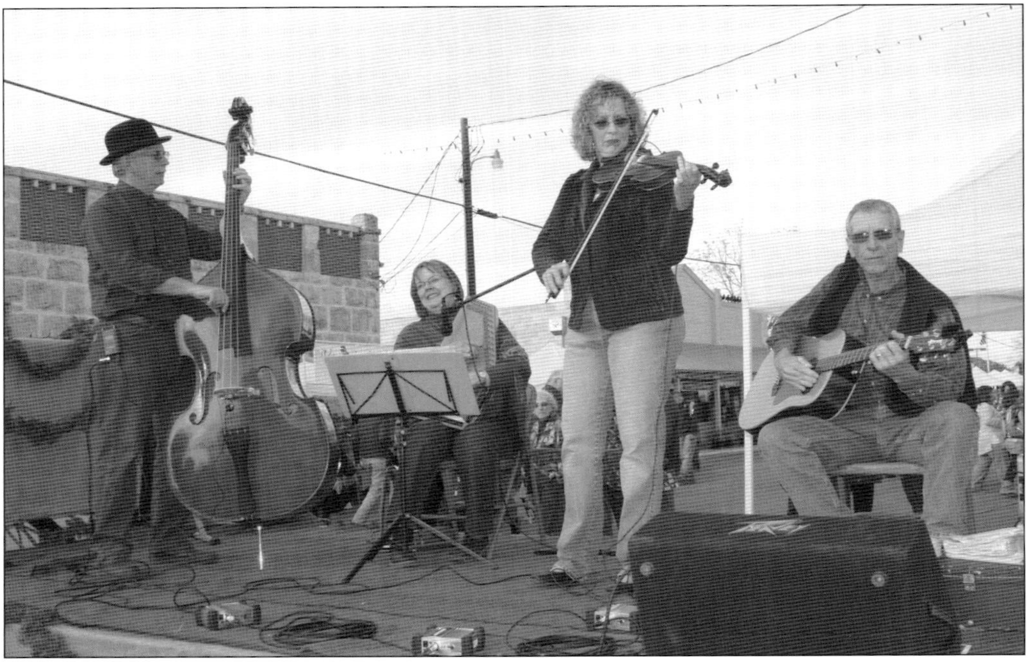

Christmas in Comfort. Christmas in Comfort is an annual event that takes place on the Saturday after Thanksgiving. Vendors from throughout the state line the historic district with booths selling artwork, crafts, furniture, and food. The post office issues a special pictorial postmark that is approved by the U.S. Postal Service. Sponsored by the Comfort Chamber of Commerce, this community celebration began in 1986. In 1989, a new tradition began with the Weinachten Lichter Parade (the Christmas Lights Parade), when Santa comes with over 100 floats. At the parade on November 22, 1997, Denise McCurdy, the "Fiddle Chick," is at the center of town at the corner of Seventh and High Streets to provide the music with Cliff Moses playing bass, Mary Moses playing the autoharp, and John McCurdy playing the guitar. (Both photographs by William "Bill" Terry of the *Comfort News*.)

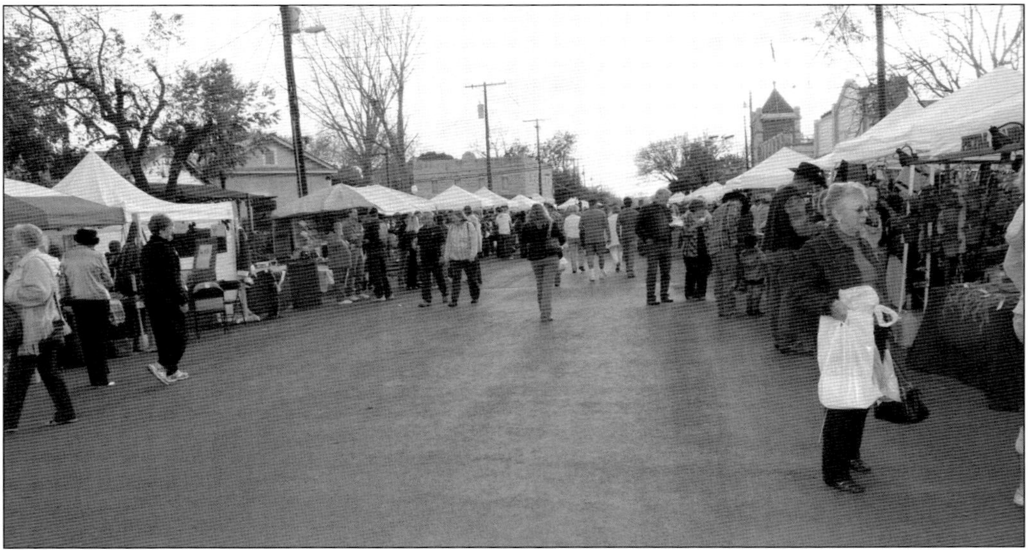

Six

Recreation

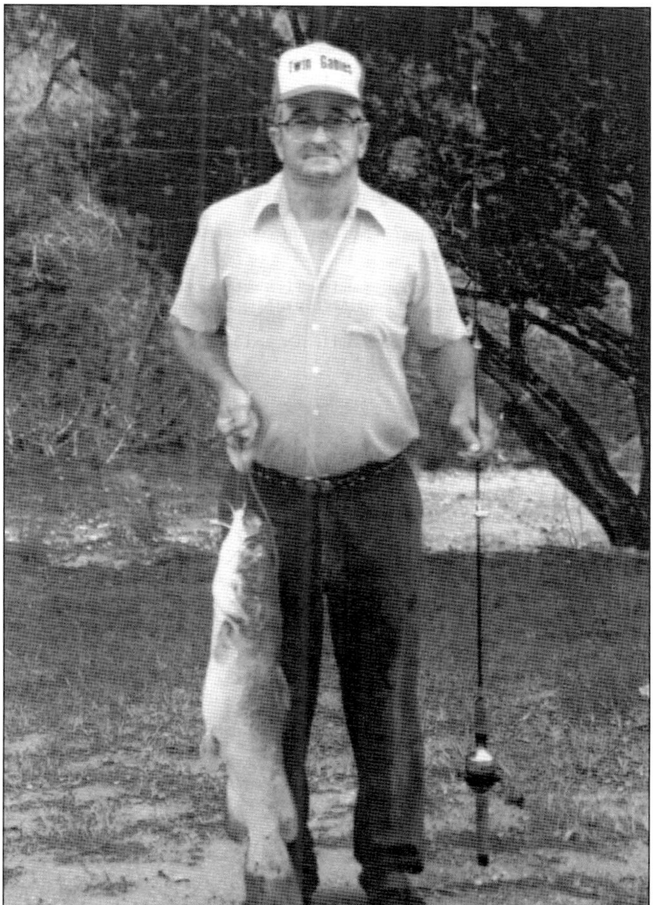

Fishing. The Guadalupe River and its tributaries provide opportunities for anglers seeking bass and catfish. The low-water crossings are favorite spots for healthy-sized catfish and occasionally large ones, such as this 22-pound specimen caught by Rudolph "Rudy" Kirchhoff near Ehlers Crossing of the Guadalupe River. (Myrtle Kirchhoff collection.)

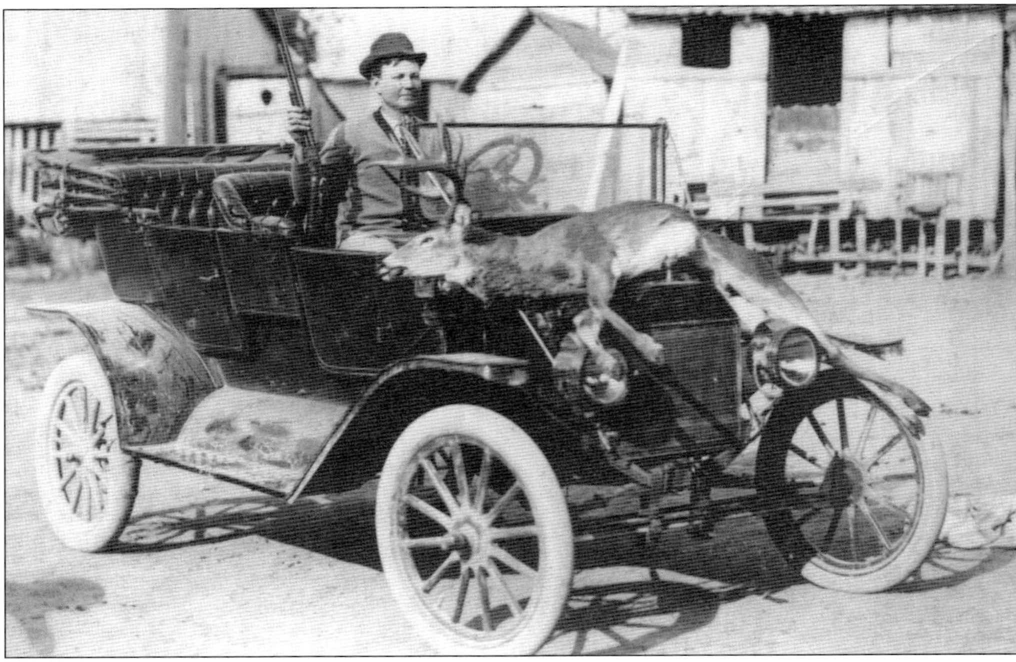

Hunting for Deer and Pigs. White tail deer and axis deer are abundant on the ranches in the area, and they often have 10 or more points on the antlers. Above, Edgar Holekamp has hoisted a 10-point buck on the hood of his touring car. Below, Oscar Lich and Hilmar Pfeiffer display their trophy deer. Though less in number, hunters also seek feral pigs and turkeys. (Both Comfort Heritage Foundation archives.)

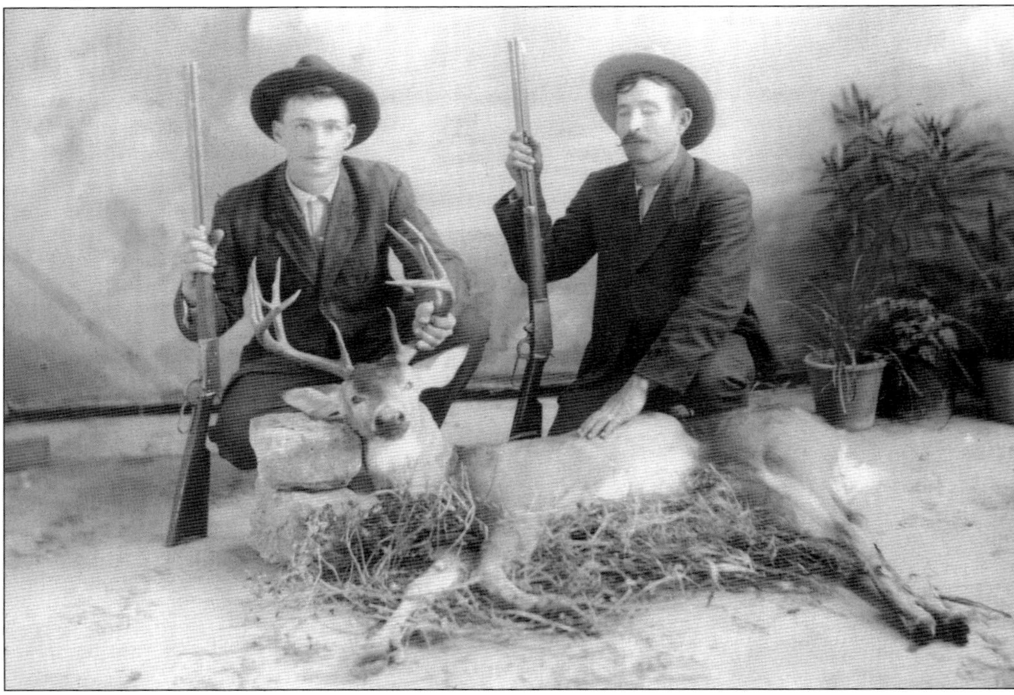

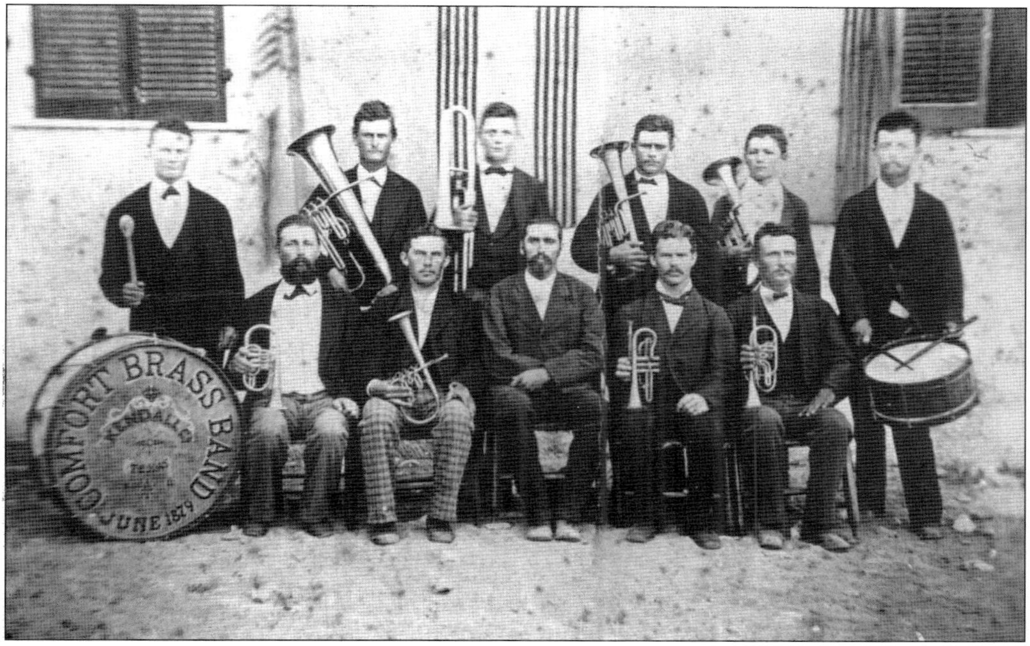

COMFORT BRASS BAND. The Comfort Brass Band of Kendall County, founded in 1879, consisted of eight horn players and two drummers. The band members are, from left to right, (first row) Julius Holekamp with flugelhorn, August Fisher with alto horn, bandleader Fr. Brunko, Albert Bodemann with cornet, and Julius Kott with cornet; (second row) Max Pankratz with bass drum, Frederick Boerner with tuba, Otto Boerner with trombone, Henry Spenrath with euphonium, Rudolph Flach with euphonium, and Ernst Flach with snare drum. In 1890, the band played at the annual school picnic in the Comfort Park. (Both Comfort Heritage Foundation archives.)

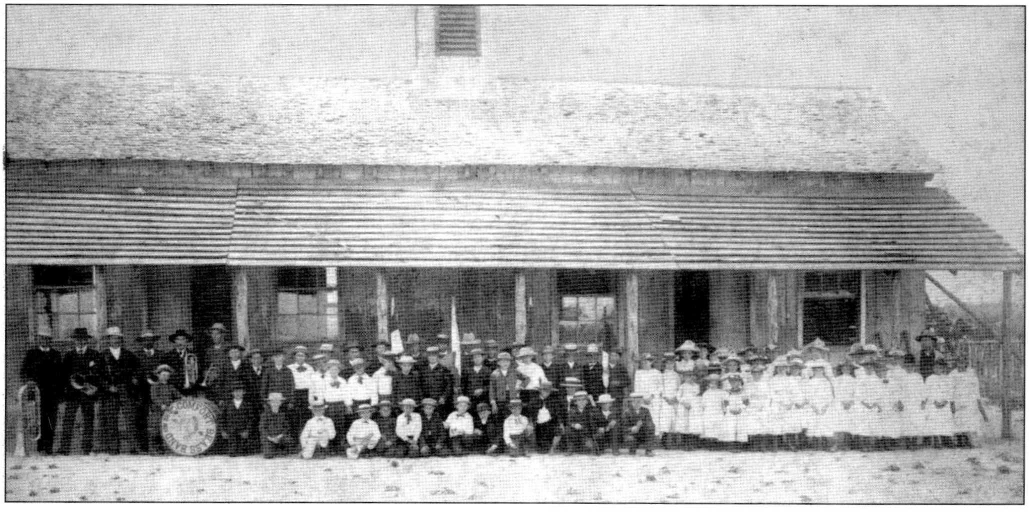

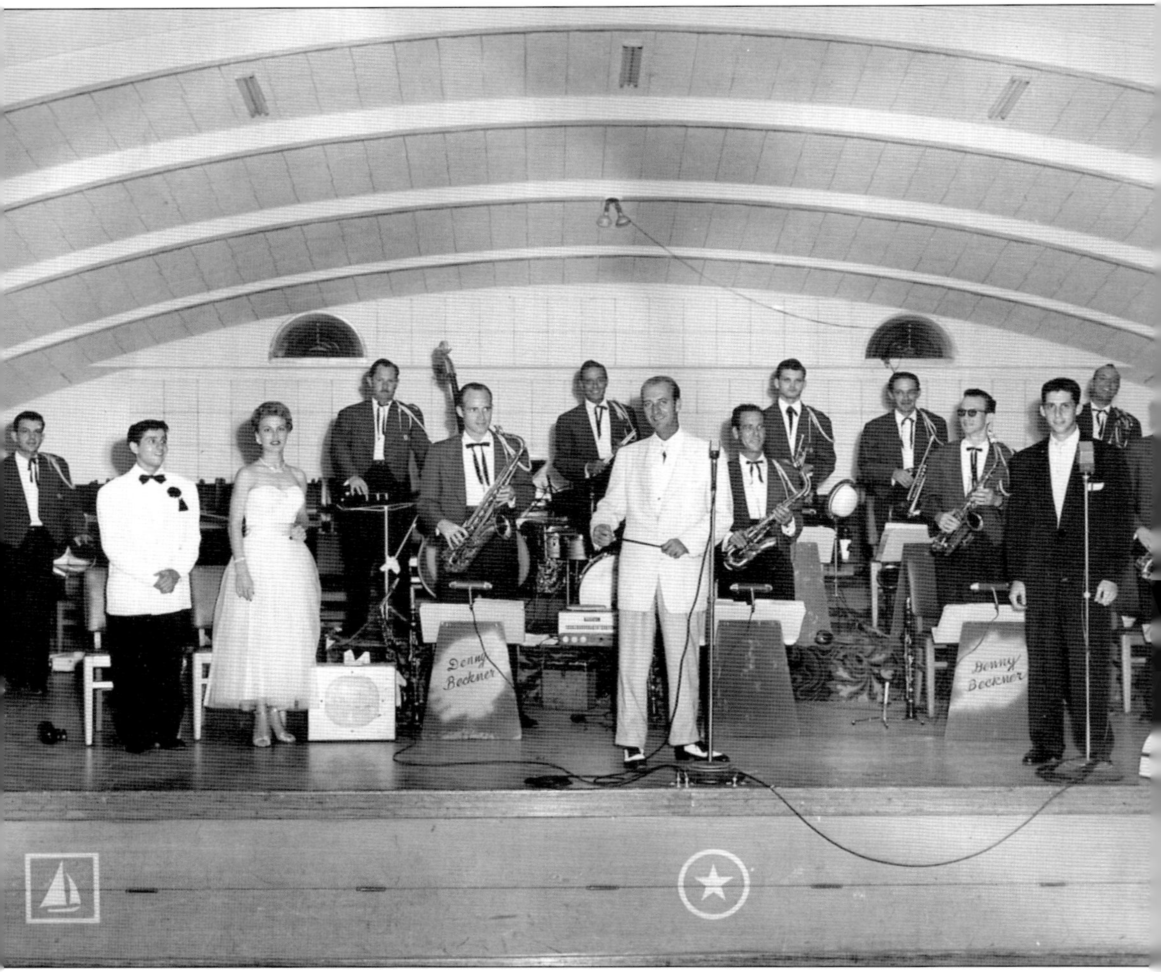

Denny Beckner Orchestra. A bandleader in the 1940s and 1950s, Denny Beckner lived in Comfort between tours. The band played at the Skyliner Ballroom at Fort Worth, the Pleasure Pier at Galveston, the Empire Room at the Rice Hotel in Houston, and also in New Orleans, Washington D.C., and New York City. He gave benefits for the Comfort Broncos baseball team in 1952 and 1953. (Al Olson collection.)

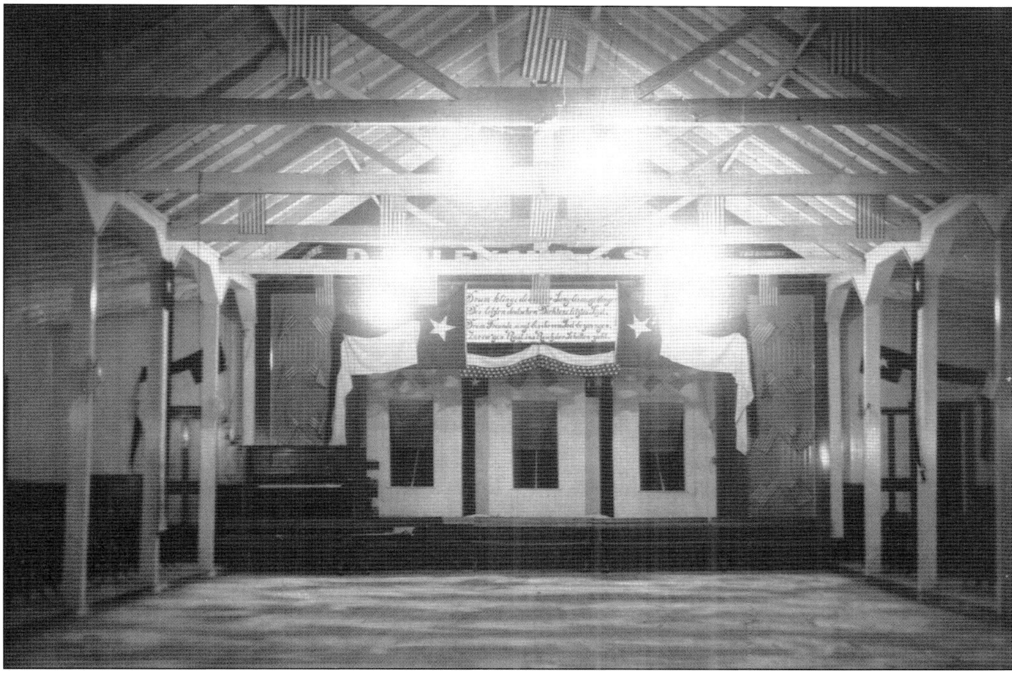

OPERA HOUSE. The stage setting has three panels with windows suggesting a house-like vaudeville skit. Above the stage is a German verse "*Drum klinge de [indecipherable] Lang bis ausgeklingen / Des letzen deutschen Dicter letztes Lied / Drum Fruende singts bis ihr rem Tod bezangen / Zur eur'gen Rast ins Reich der Schatten zieht.*" The German-speaking audience enjoyed performances in German. On the crossbeam is "Donely and Sons," who were probably the performers. A piano is at stage left. The U.S. flags have 48 stars dating the photograph to after 1912. Vaudeville had a wide range of acts—jugglers with Indian clubs, mimes who clownishly portrayed notable persons, and the popular mock wedding (at right) when a cross-dressed man (note the mustache, haircut, and big arms) would play the bride. (Both Comfort Heritage Foundation archives.)

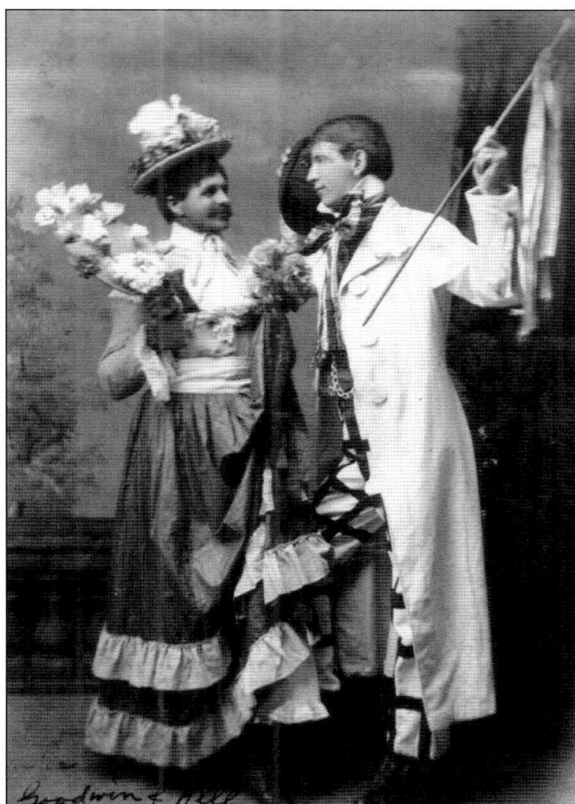

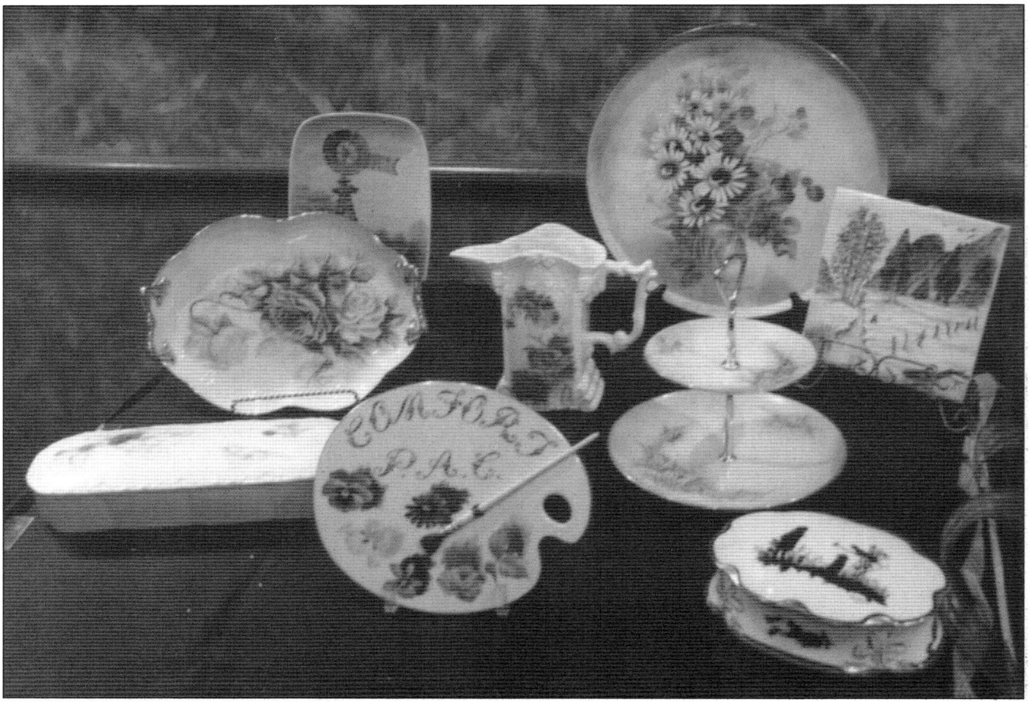

PORCELAIN CLUB. The Porcelain Art Club of Comfort began in 1971. With 18 members, they meet monthly with an instructor who is paid by proceeds from sales of their work. Hand-painted pieces are unique to the artist, using trays, vases, boxes, and serving dishes as the bases for country scenes, windmills, flowers, and vines. Each hand-painted piece is one of a kind. The dry paint is ground with a mixture of oils to become an open medium until fired. When painting china, members use several coats. Between each coat the piece is kiln-fired and checked for quality. The photograph below, taken at the Comfort table at the state convention in Bandera, shows treasurer Lillian Soell (left) and vice president Margaret Bendele (right) with president Ann Burnet. (Both Lillian Soell collection.)

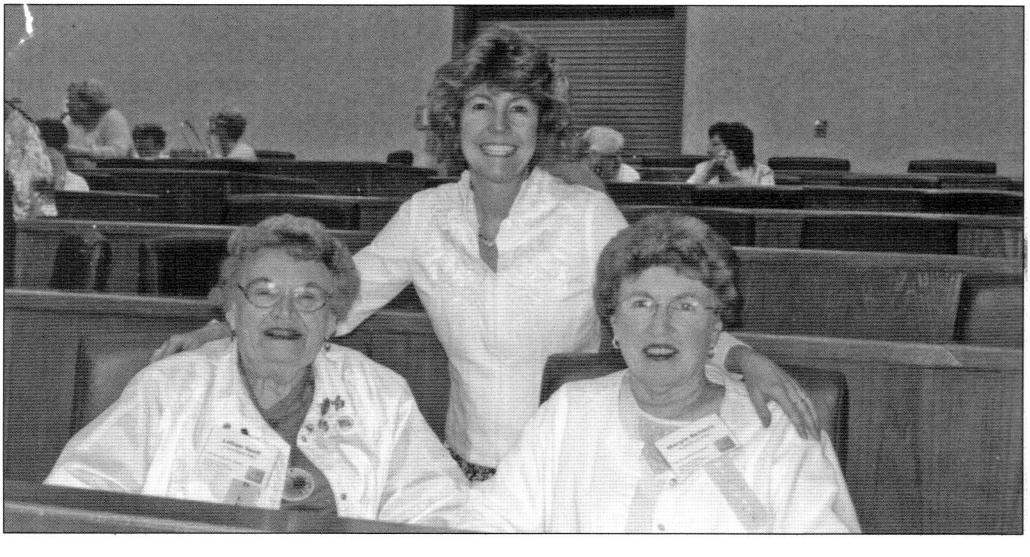

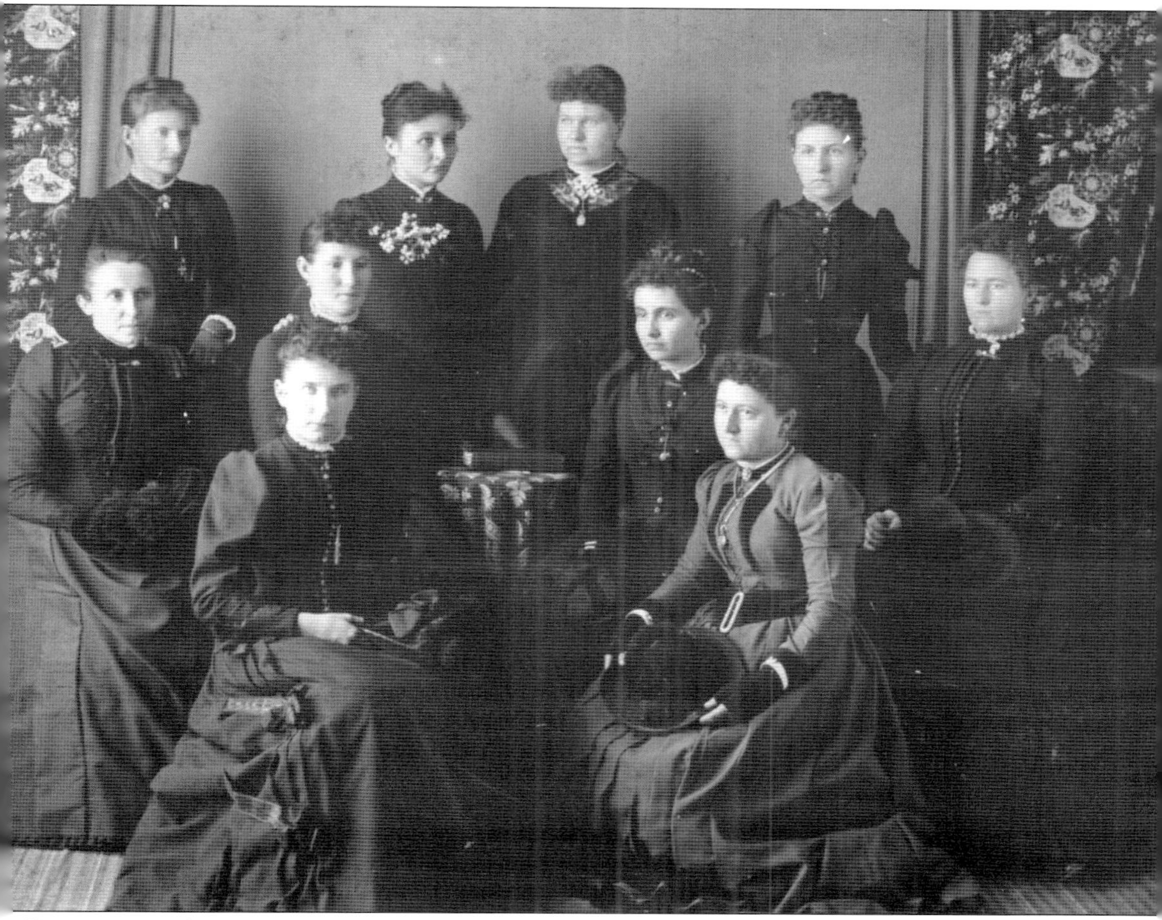

KAFFEE KREIS ("COFFEE CIRCLE"). This social group of the 1880s was made up of members from the early German family settlers in Comfort. Outsiders were never invited to join. Pictured here are, from left to right, (first row) unidentified and Emmie Kott Below; (second row) Agnes Wiedenfeld Doerffler, Anna Meyer Overmann, Ida Flach Ingenhuett, and unidentified; (third row) Leischen Serger, Toni Flach Brinkmann, Toni Maurhoffer Kott, and Toni Flach Ingenhuett. (Esther Wiedenfeld collection at the Comfort Heritage Foundation archives.)

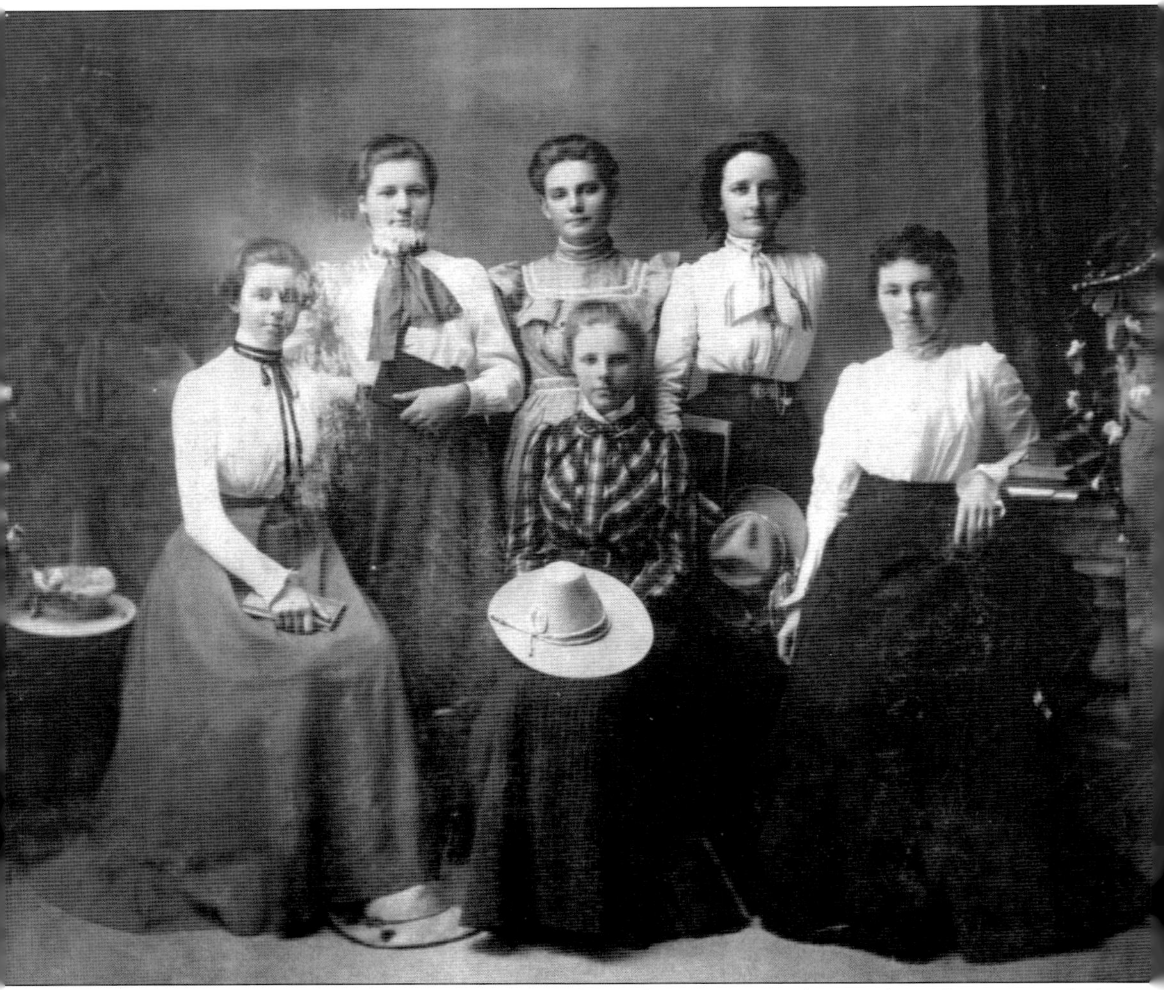

NIGHT SCHOOL, CLASS OF 1902. Many of the early German settlers, such as these young ladies, attended night school to learn English. The teacher for this group of girls was A. S. Wertheim Sr. Shown here are, from left to right, (first row) Helen Steves McFarland, Agnes Holekamp Codrington, and Julia Meyer Ellenberger; (second row) Betty Karger Flach, Igna Perner Seidensticker, and Martha Brinkmann Bierschwale. (Comfort Heritage Foundation archives.)

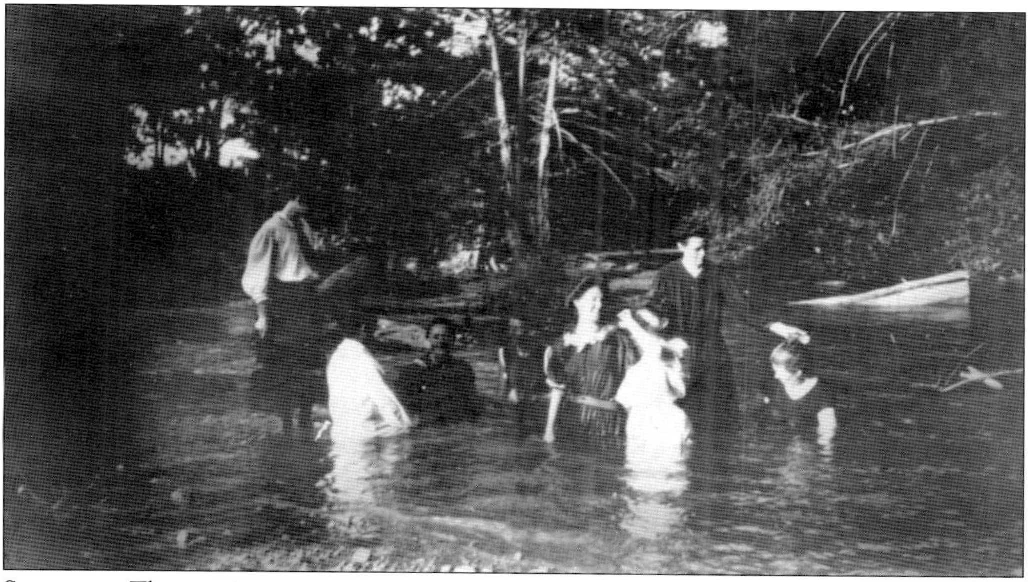

Swimming. The town's primary swimming site was the 40-foot-by-20-foot Gaddis Pool in Cypress Creek, which was 100 feet upstream from the low-water crossing. It had a rope swing on the bank and concrete steps along the edge with a picnic grove adjacent to the pool. According to Guido Ransleben, boys found oysters with pearls in both the Guadalupe River and Cypress Creek. No one was allowed in the water wearing a bathing suit. Local boys delighted in tying knots in the arms and legs of clothing of summer visitors, then dipping the clothes in the water to make it difficult to untie them. He recalled seeing some of them going up High Street to their hotels with one leg in the pants and their shirts over their shoulders. (Above, Tina Neumann collection; below, Comfort Heritage Foundation archives.)

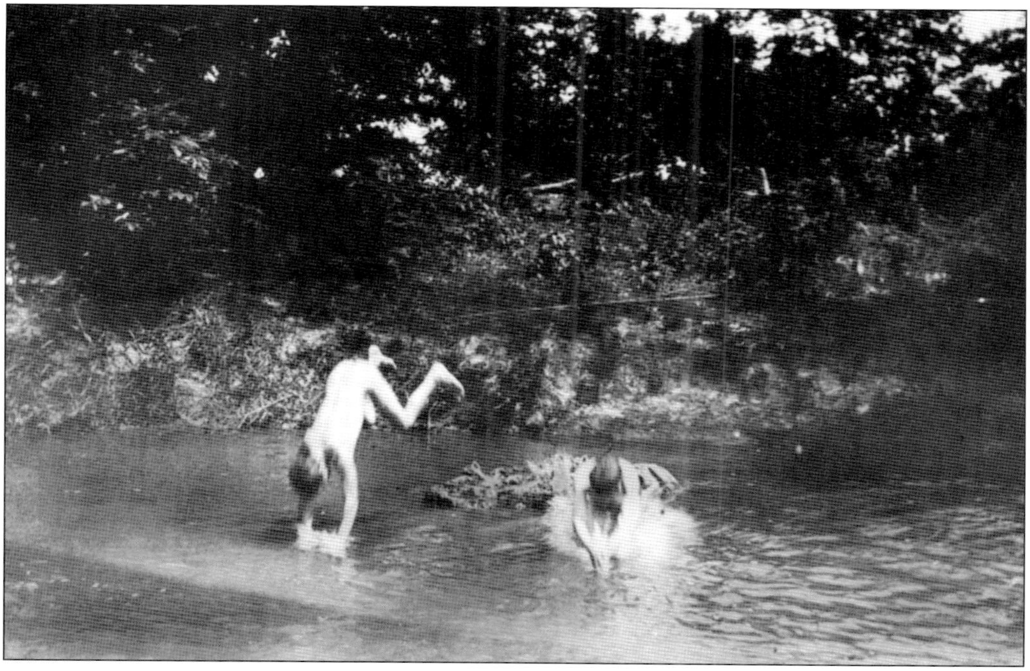

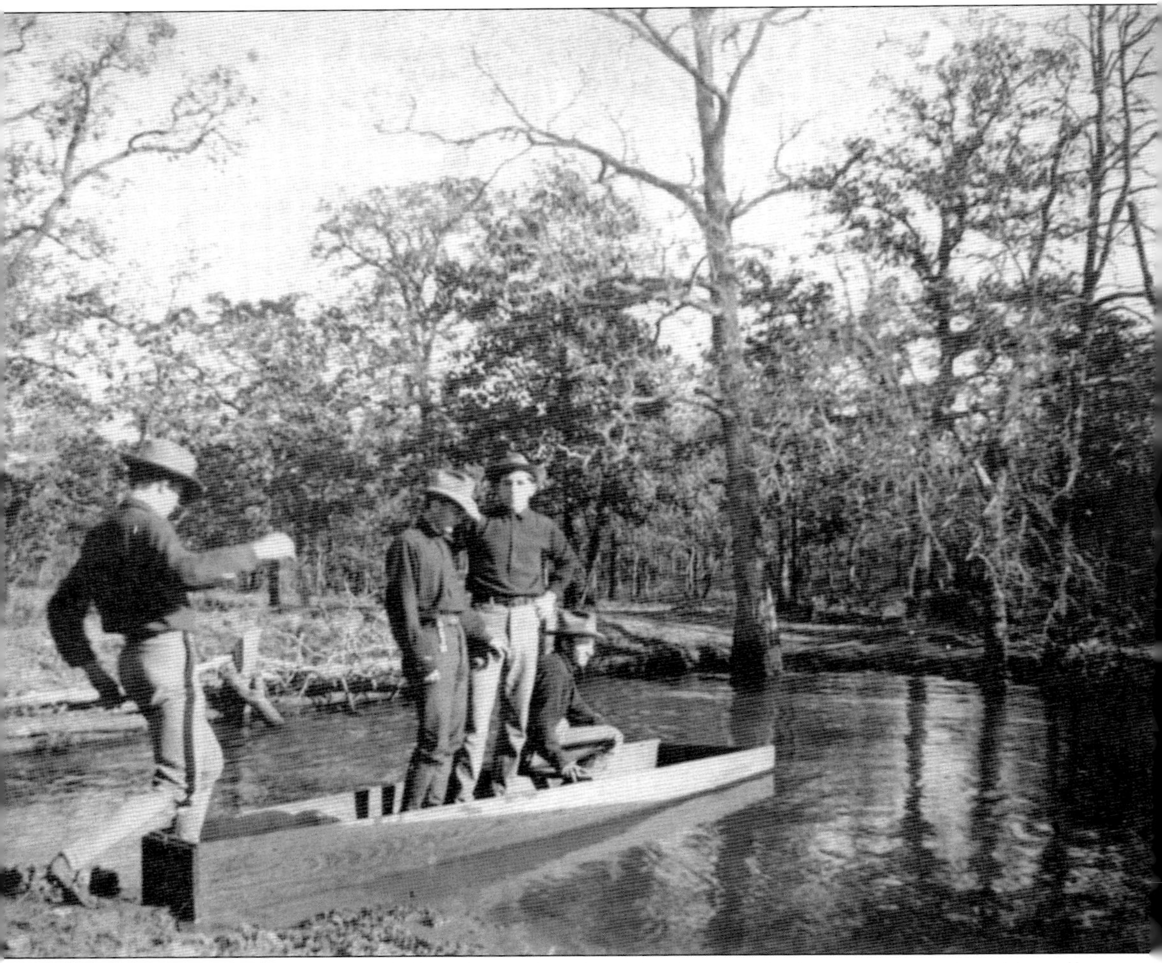

Boating. Four men in a skiff, including Michael Lindner, push off from a shore lined by tall trees on Thanksgiving Day 1904. Boating was a popular form of recreation on weekends, when families usually visited each other. (Ruth Lindner Zoeller collection.)

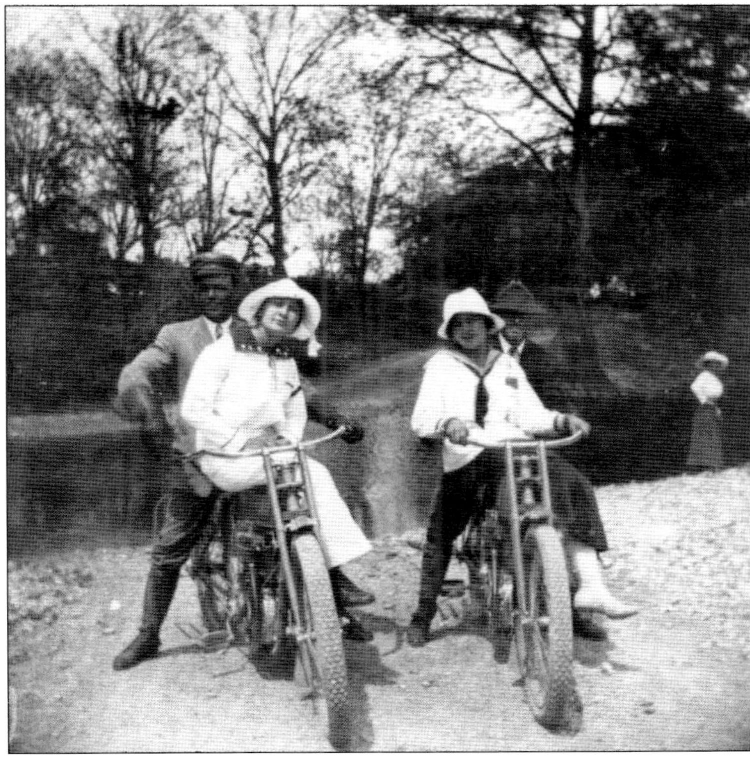

RIVER CROSSING. Sometimes the Guadalupe River was shallow enough to be forded by horse-drawn carriages and later by motorcycles. Heavy rains, however, could cause a sudden rise and flooding. These conditions continue, causing accidents and death when people are unaware of how high the water has risen in a short period of time. (Both Comfort Heritage Foundation archives.)

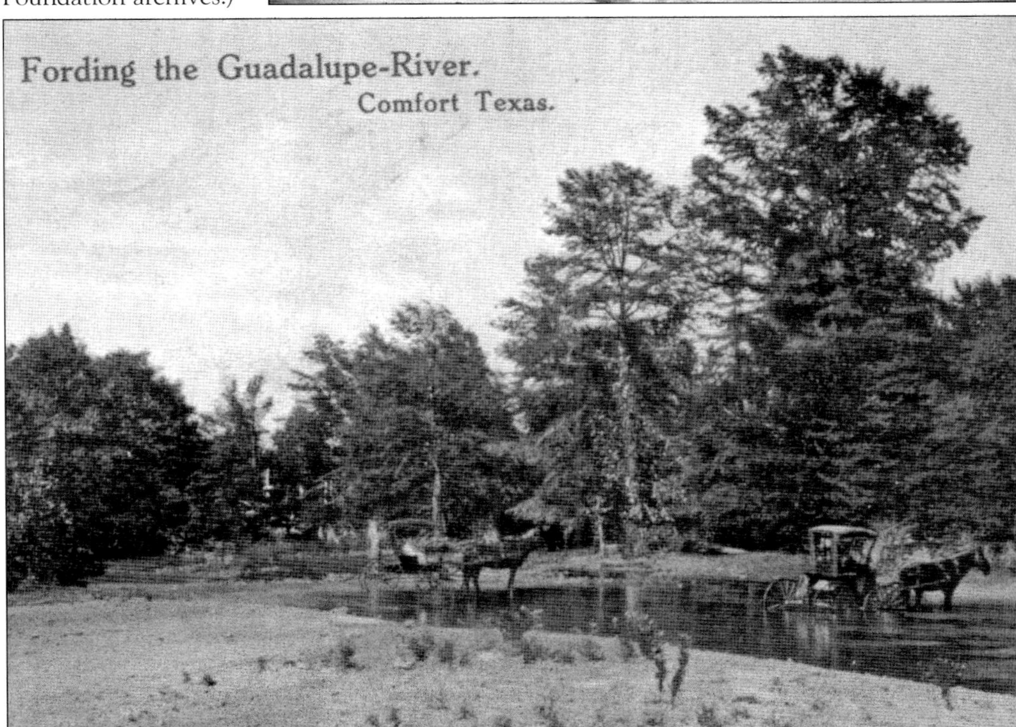

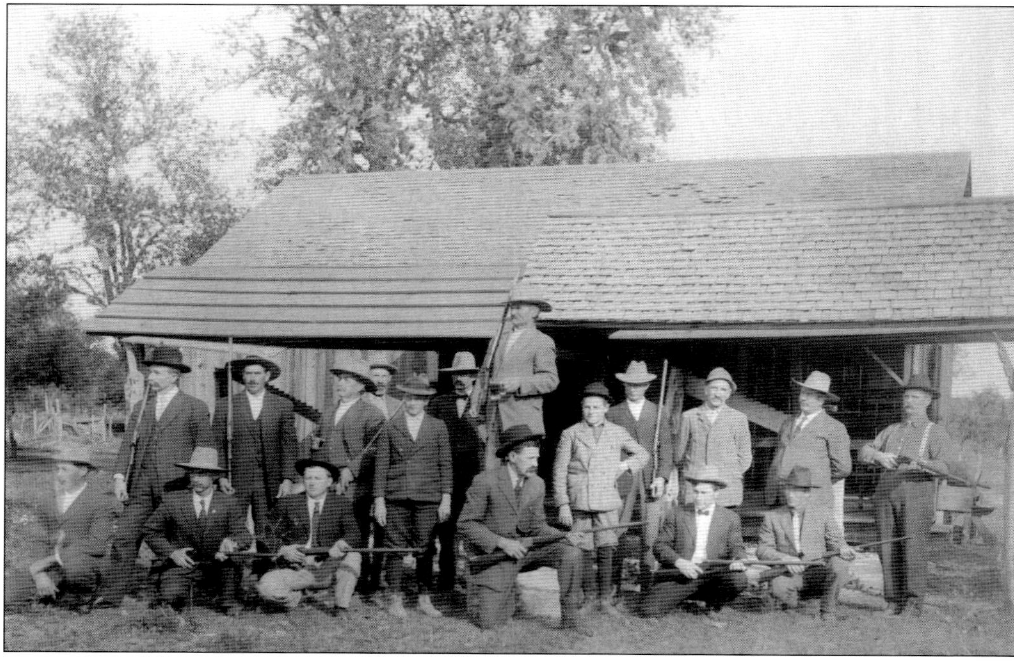

SCHÜTZENVEREIN. A schützenverein is a shooting club that continues a traditional activity from Germany. Members gathered on weekends to fire their long rifles from fixed gun rests at distant targets. These shooting clubs began in the late 1800s. The former North Creek (shown above) and Cypress Creek Clubs are defunct, but the Gillespie County Schützendbund is still active with Barons Creek, Bear Creek, Grapetown, Hubertus, Scharfschützen, and Tivy Clubs. Activities culminate in a joint club-firing contest, with crowning of the Schützenkönig. (Above, Roy Perkins collection; below, photograph by Ruth Kiel.)

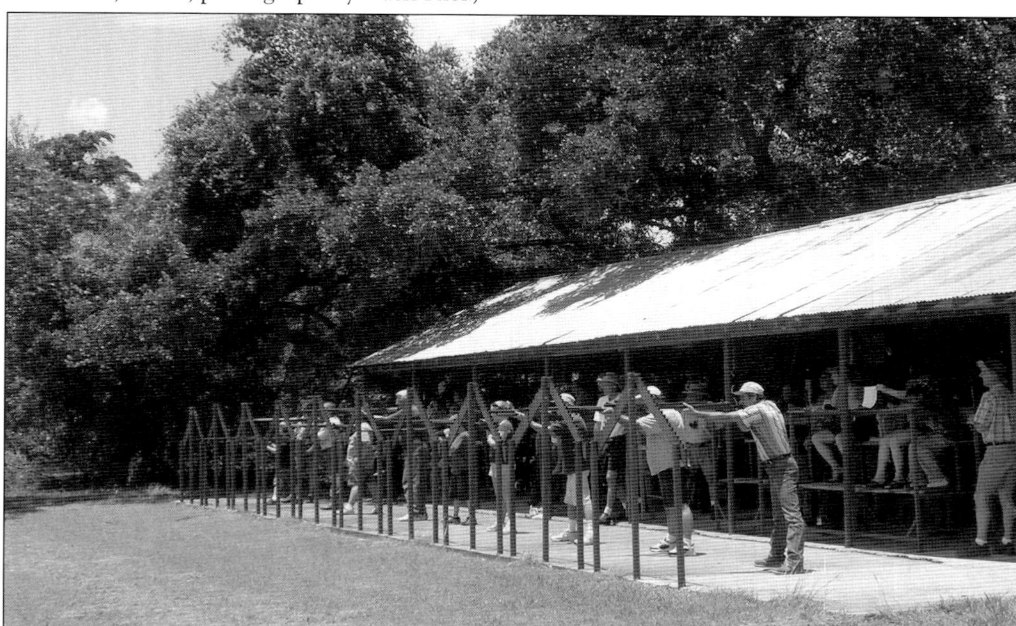

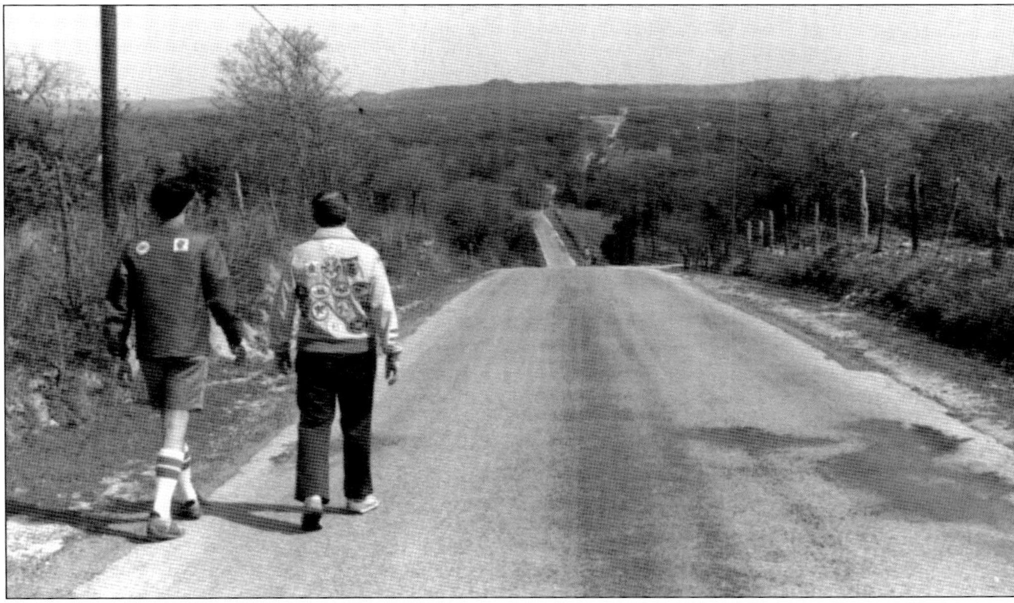

Volksmarch. The Comfort Guadalupe Gallivanters (also known as the Hill Country Volkssportverein) formed in 1979 to encourage walking. It sponsors an Easter weekend walk of 5 or 10 kilometers through scenic countryside around Comfort. Walkers look for the hidden colored eggs, for which prizes are given at the conclusion of the walk. A similar walk occurs at Halloween around Waring, often with costumed participants. Members of the club monitor the checkpoints. Shown below at the Brownsboro Cemetery checkpoint on a Halloween walk are, from left to right, club secretary Tina Bohnert with Frances "Fanny" Faltin Chamberlain and Frank Kiel. (Above, photograph by Gene Speirs; below, photograph by Ruth Kiel.)

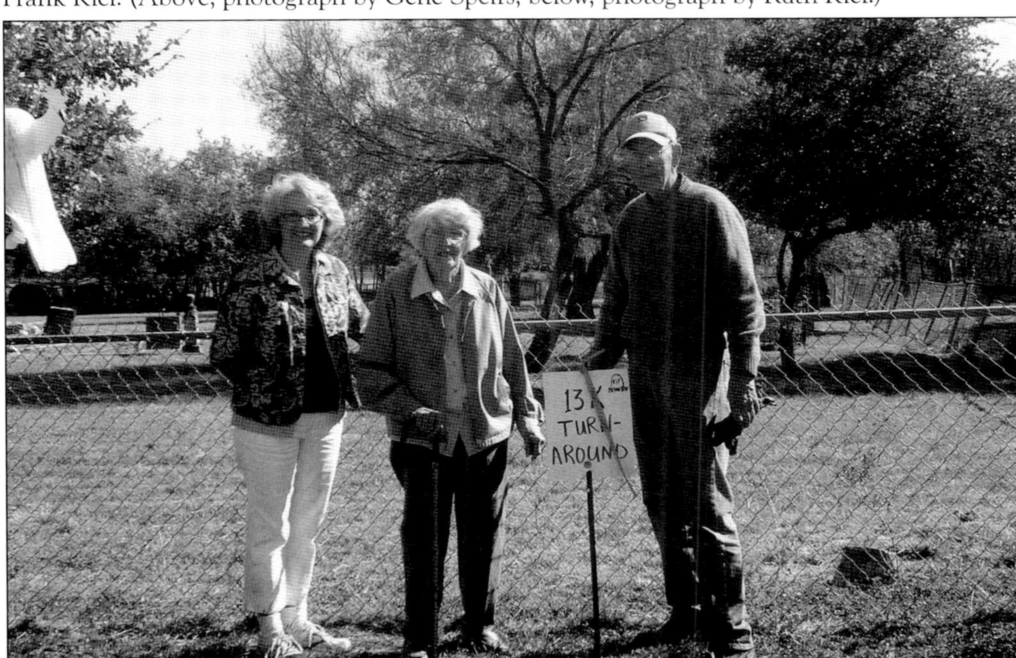

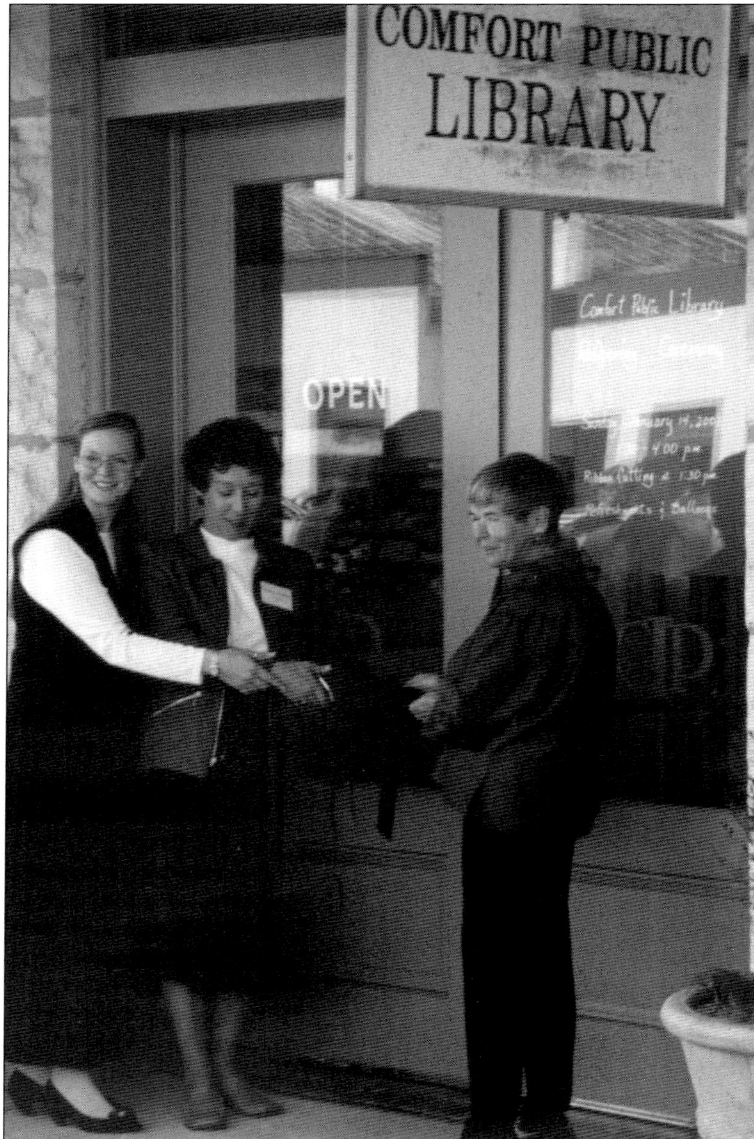

Comfort Public Library. Arno Schwethelm's mercantile store became the public library in 1985 when his descendants, Chester and A. C. Schwethelm, deeded the building to the library. A second renovation, including the addition of an elevator and enlargement of the mezzanine, occurred in 2000. The children's corner has low tables and chairs, puzzles, puppets, and a simple computer for young patrons. Children's Story Hour is a vital part of the program, encouraging children at an early age to use and enjoy the library. A couch and easy chairs provide a comfortable reading area near the newspapers, magazines, and new books. English as a Second Language (ESL) classes take place in a newly created meeting room on the mezzanine, which was designed as a quiet area for people doing research in the Texana and nonfiction sections. Seen cutting the ribbon here at the reopening are, from left to right, Marti Ashcroft, president of the Comfort Chamber of Commerce; Beth Borland, library director; and Ruth Kiel, library board president. (Photograph by Jeffrey Kiel.)

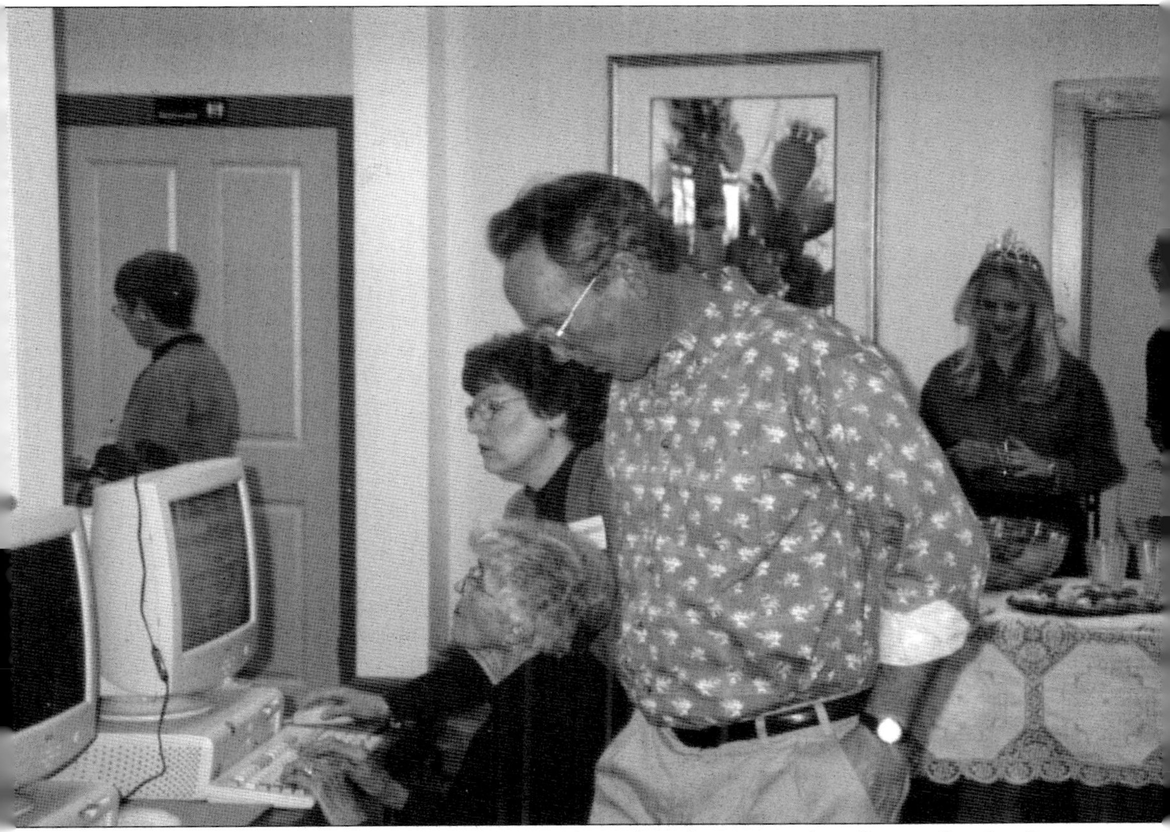

Reopening of the Comfort Public Library. Library board vice president Steven Borcherding is instructing Frances "Fanny" Chamberlain about usage of computers, while volunteer Bonnie Vernor looks on. With the reopening of the library, there were computers on the first floor where teenagers could get help with their homework or play games, where visitors to Comfort could check their e-mail, and where anyone could search the Internet. On the mezzanine, computer usage was designated for people doing research. Some patrons welcomed the addition of computers, but for others they were a mystery. The library offered classes for patrons with all levels of knowledge. Computer stations are usually full, especially after school. A large selection of videos and books-on-tape are available, in both English and Spanish. This historic building continues to be the literal and figurative heart of the community. (Photograph by Jeffrey Kiel.)

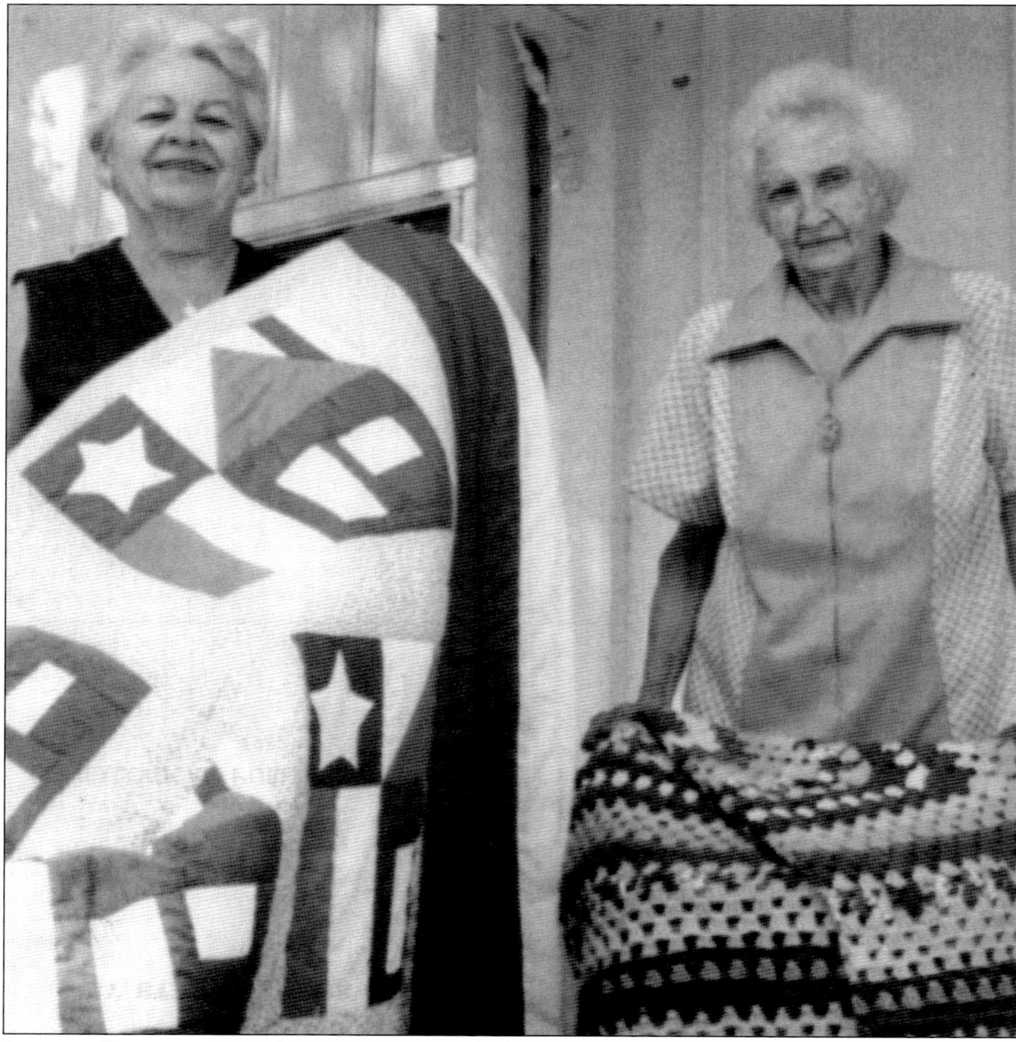

LIBRARY SUPPORTERS. Viola "Vy" Gass Frizzell (left) and Hedwig Doerffler display the handmade quilt and afghan to be raffled as fund-raisers for the Comfort Public Library. Frizzell was a board member and a longtime volunteer at the library. Doerffler was a seamstress whose bequest of her savings was the foundation of the Comfort Library Trust Fund. Interest from this fund helps to pay the operating expenses of the library. Only in an emergency can the principal be used. As part of the Kendall County library system, the Comfort Library receives some support from the county, but only with community support can it provide the services needed in this rural community. In keeping with Comfort's traditional respect for books and learning, donations and fund-raisers such as the used book sales, the raffle, and the annual Taste of Comfort dinner have provided money to supplement the Kendall County budget. (Comfort Heritage Foundation archives.)

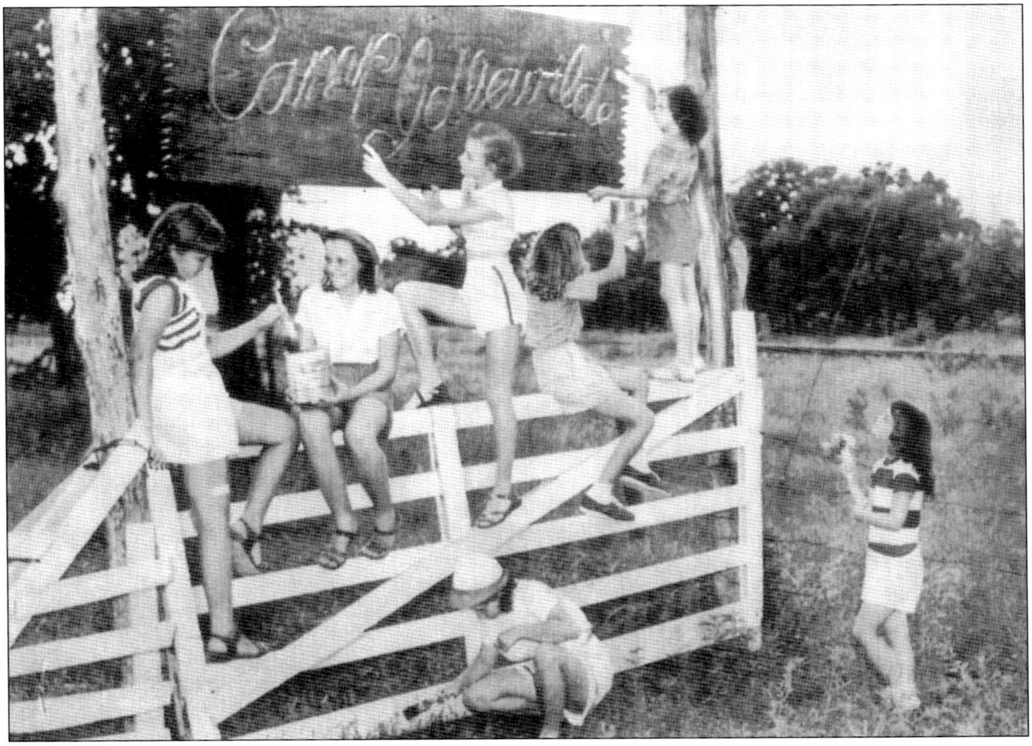

Summer Camps. Camp Idlewilde was first used as a spa in 1902. In 1906, the property became Camp Reliance, later Camp Good Times, and after 1918 the San Antonio YWCA Camp Idlewilde that received girls for 60 years. High school girls attended for swimming, tennis, and hiking. Working girls began their season in June. (Both Comfort Heritage Foundation archives.)

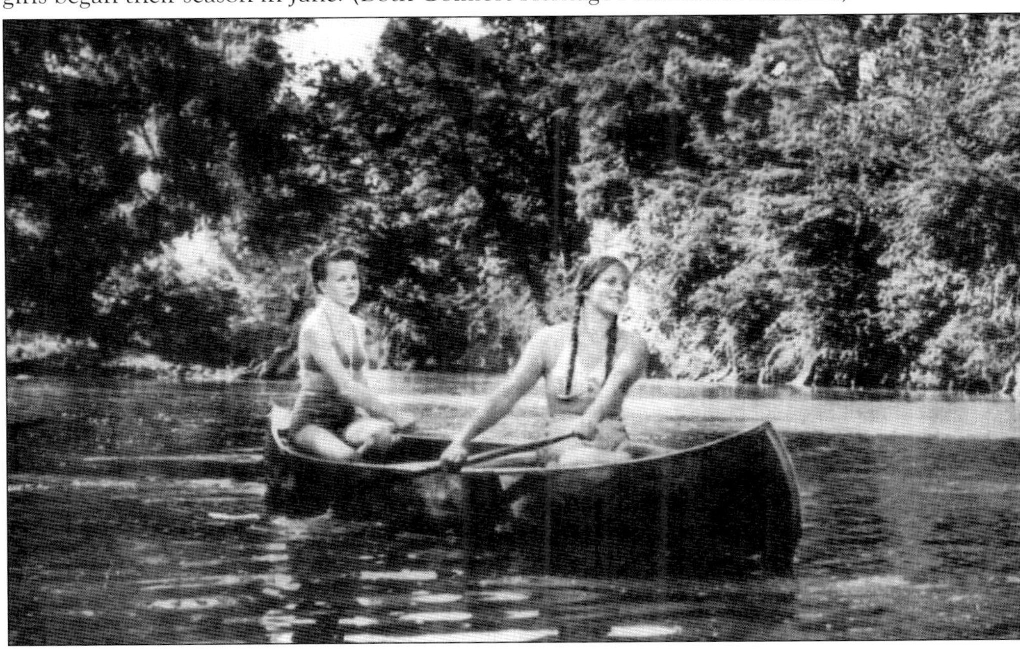

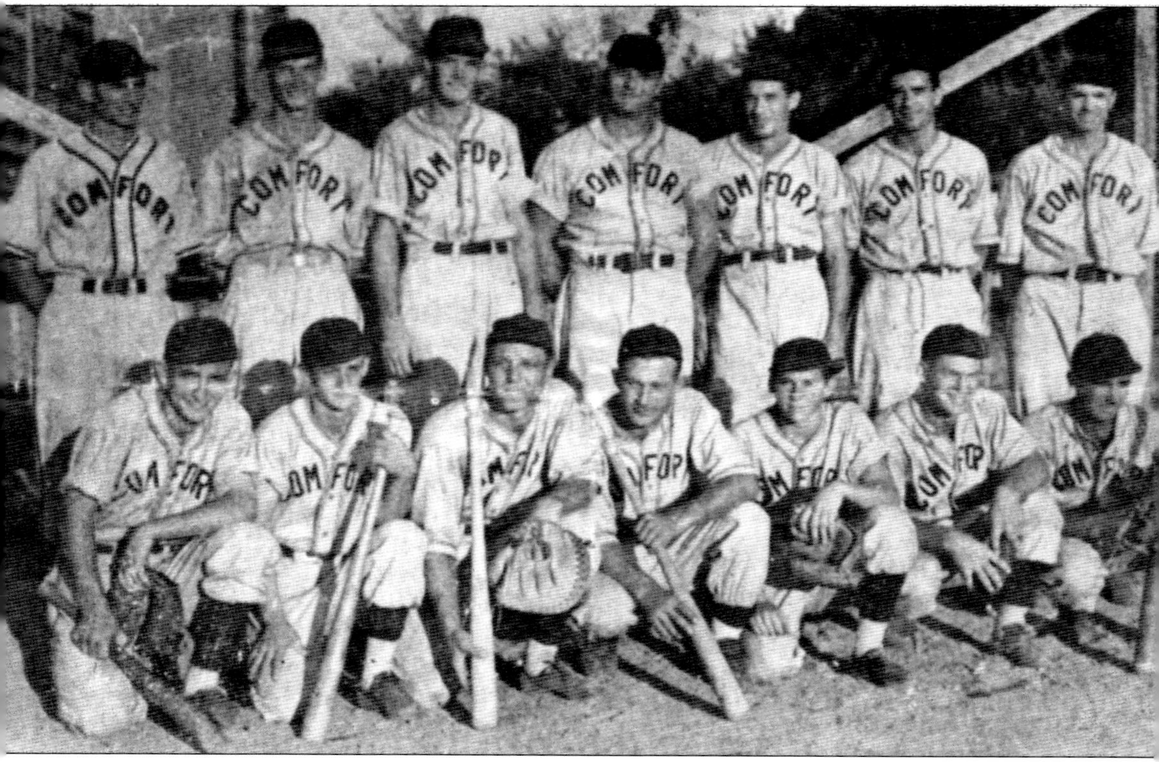

BASEBALL. The Comfort Broncos were founded in 1922 and played teams from Boerne, Kerrville, Fredericksburg, Camp Stanley, and Stonewall until 1958. Their records have a certificate from the National Semi-Pro Baseball League showing them to be part of the Hill Country Baseball League. The 1947 team included, from left to right, (first row) Rudy Kirchhoff, Raymond Kirchhoff, Clemens Heinen, Christie Lindemann, Howard Lewis, Dan Spenrath Jr., and Martin Spenrath; (second row) Joe Pankratz, Melvin Pankratz, Emil Habecker, Harry Merkel, Marvin Flach, August Pankratz, and Ernst Pankratz. (Marsha Habecker and Myrtle Kirchhoff collections.)

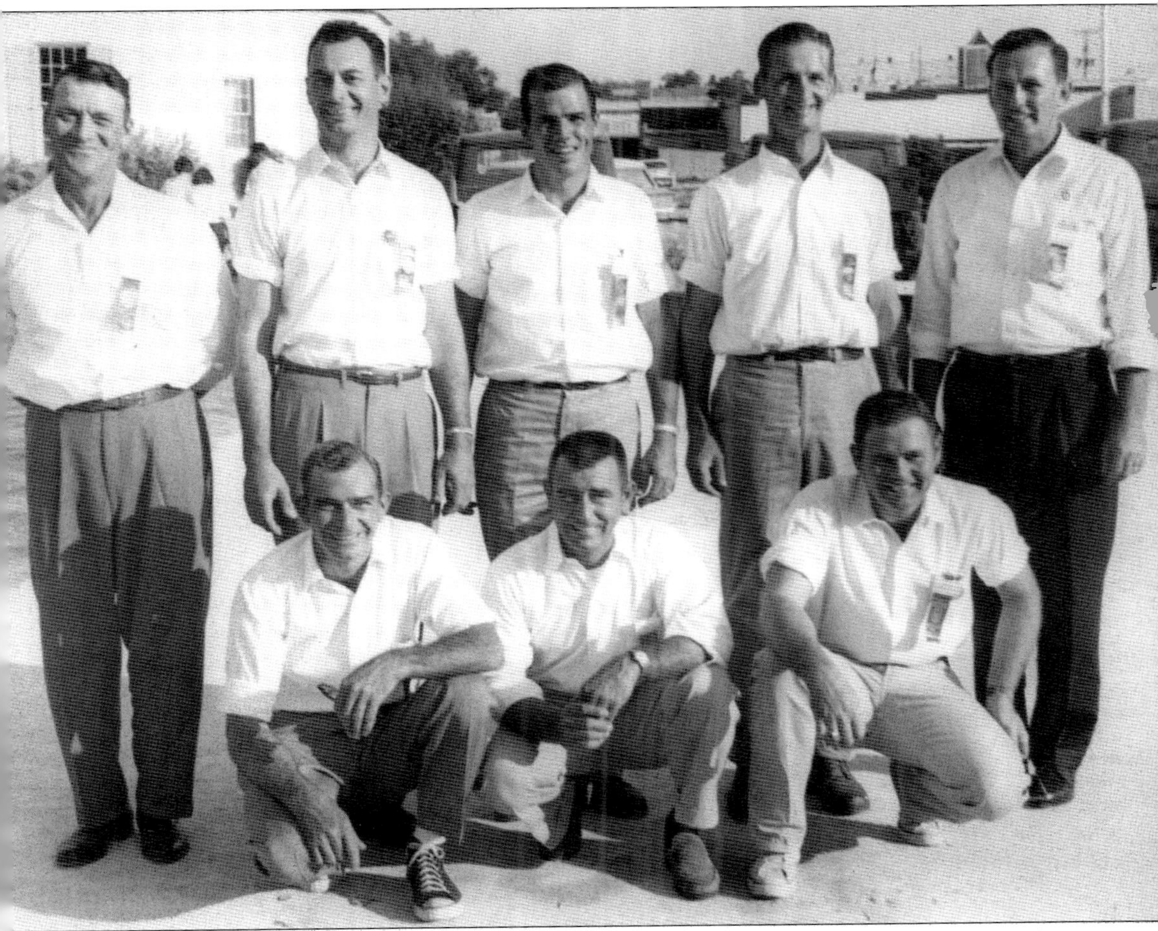

Pumper Races. Volunteer fire departments competed to determine who could fight a fire quickest with three-man and six-man teams. From the loaded hose box on the back of the fire truck, one man would pull the 2.5-inch hose to a 100-foot distant line, while others would uncouple the hose and attach it to the pumper truck outlet. When a continuous spray of water flowed out of the spout, the judge recorded the team's time. The Comfort team won first place at the Fredericksburg Pumper Race in 1963 with a winning time of 19.8 seconds. The team consisted of, from left to right, (first row) Manny Pankratz, Martin Spenrath Jr., and C. B. Chenault; (second row) Harry Meckel, Harold Spenrath, David Biermann, Melvin Pankratz, and Leroy Bohnert. (Comfort Volunteer Fire Department collection.)

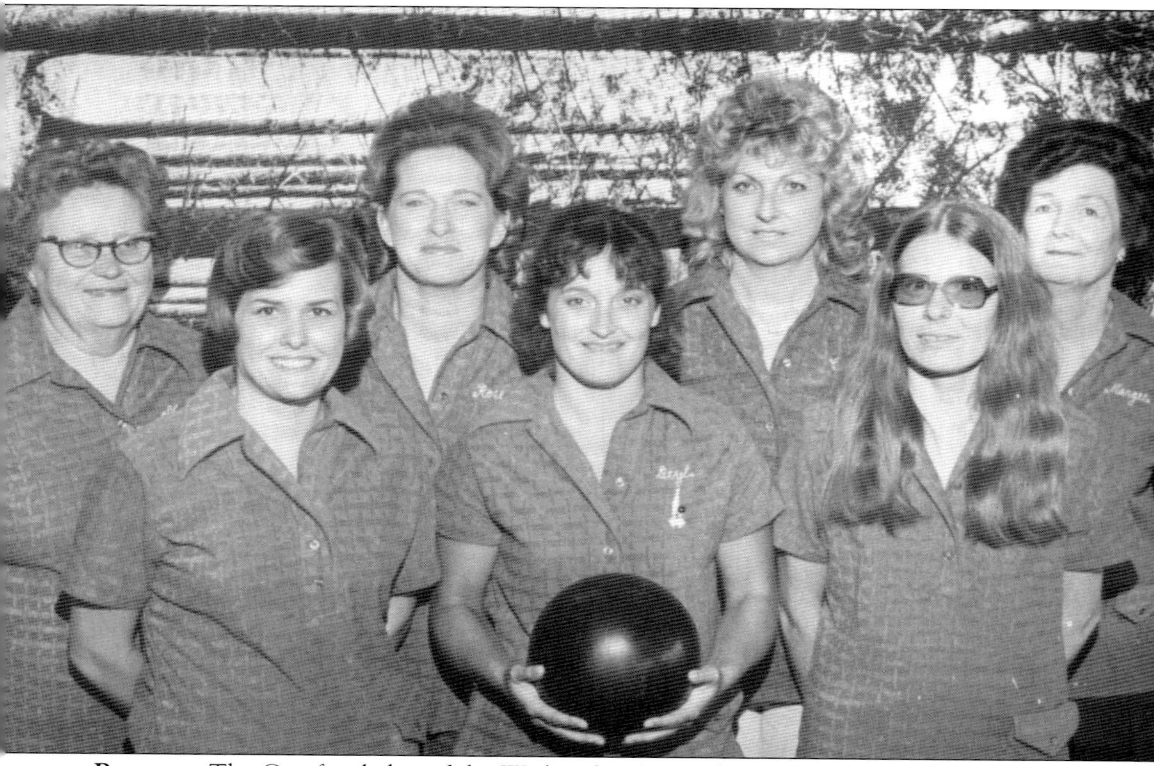

Bowling. The Comfort ladies of the Wednesday AM Ladies League won the competition at a tournament in Fredericksburg in May 1981. Team members pictured here are, from left to right, (first row) Cynthia Ingram, Deyl Reeh, and Kathy Waters; (second row) Norma Kirchhoff, Rose Mary Rausch, Cheryl Petty, and Margie Bartel. The *Comfort News* reported that in local competition at the Turnverein, the first-place men's team from the Comfort Hatchery dominated the action, being four games ahead of second-place Double D Restaurant, while Boerner's Team eased into third. (Comfort Heritage Foundation archives.)

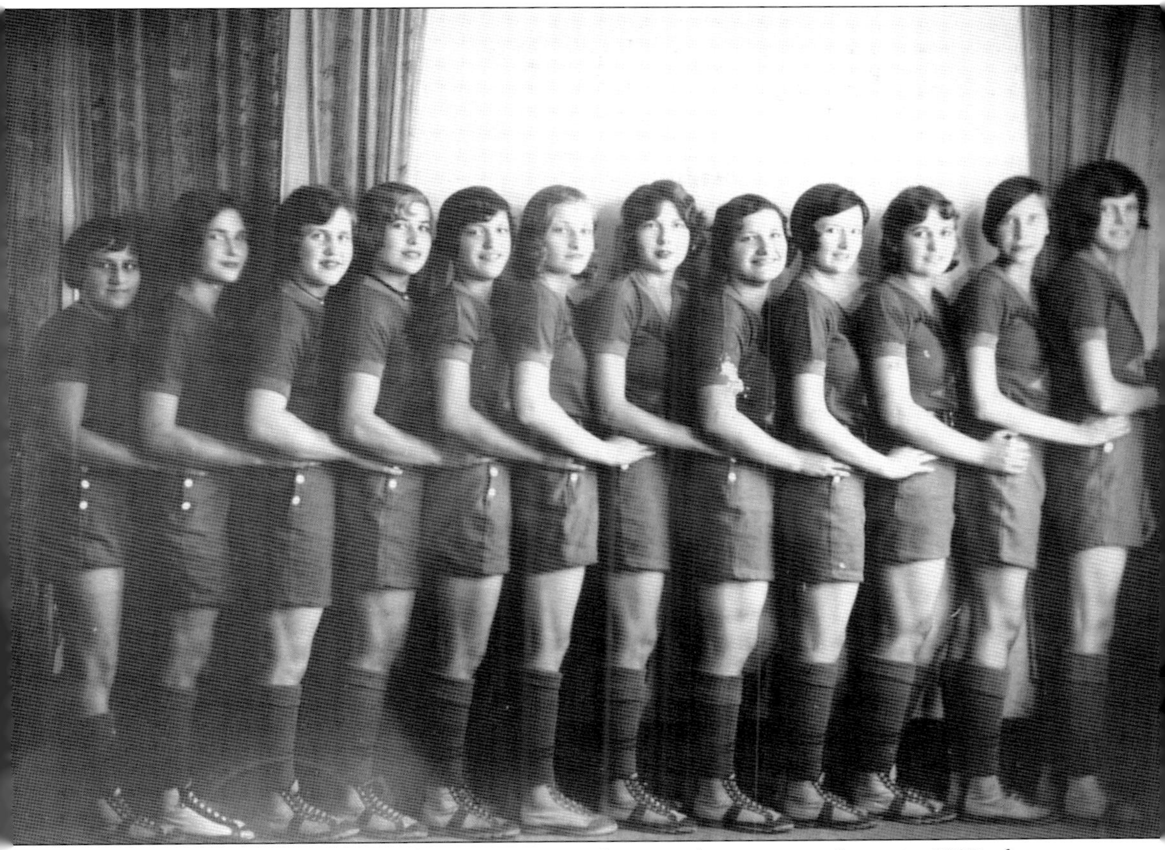

HIGH SCHOOL SPORTS. The Comfort Deer appears here in their new uniforms in 1930 after an undefeated season in 1928–1929, when they wore hand-sewn black bloomers and white blouses. They earned the money for the uniforms by selling "basket suppers." They also put on a play at the Rock Opera House. Their coach and English teacher, Marian Steves, directed it; boys refused to participate. The girls, wearing their new blue shorts and gold shirts, who can be identified include Leona Kott, Lydia Holekamp, Edna Stieler, Laura Gass, Mamie Flach, Gerda Rusch, Ellen Dietert, Ruby Flach, and Kathryn Schuetz. High school sports continue to be important events, especially on Friday evenings when Bobcat Stadium at Comfort High School is packed with loyal fans, families, and former players. (Comfort Heritage Foundation archives.)

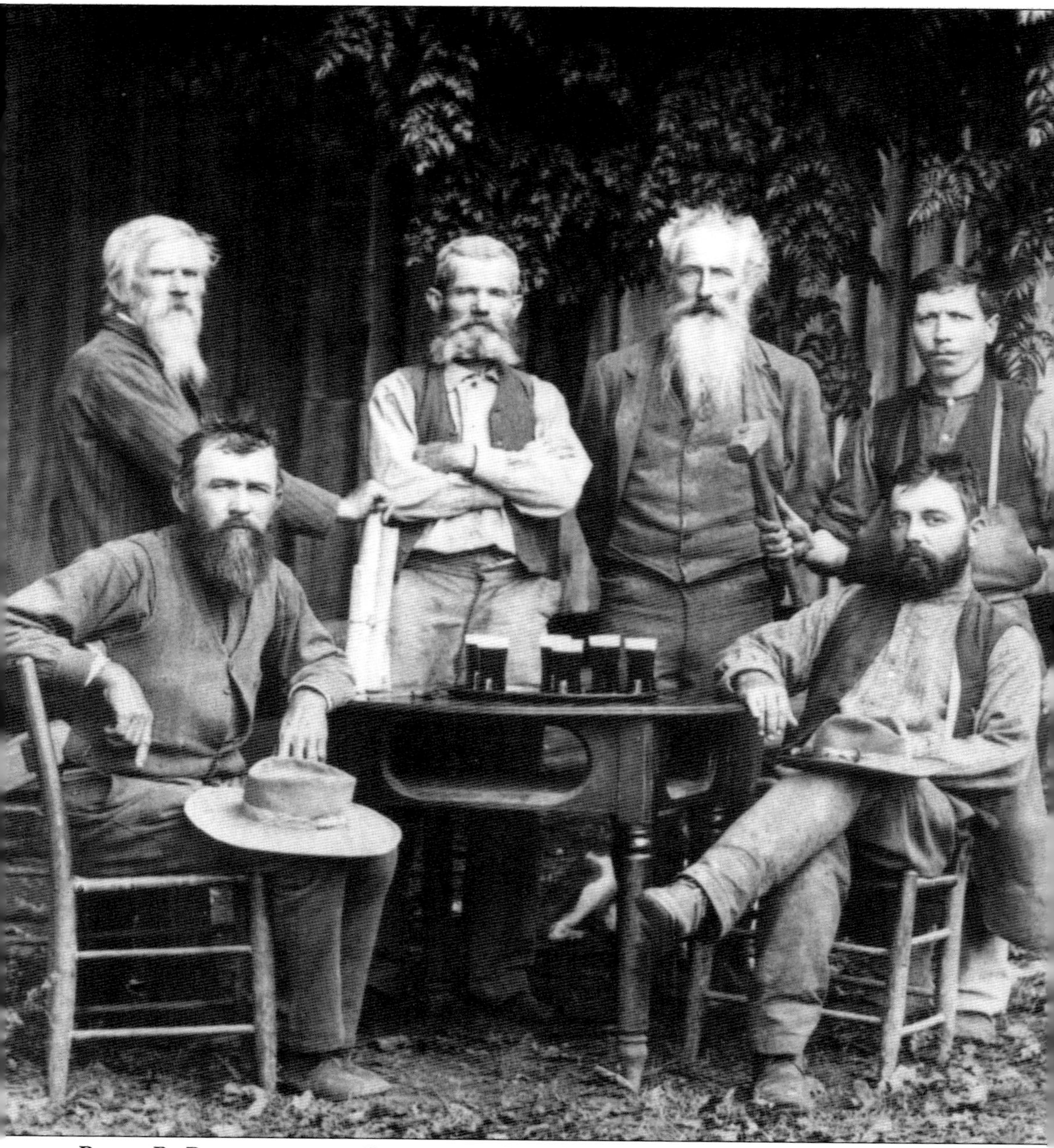

R AND R: RECREATION AND RELAXATION. In a photograph by Albert Glock taken about 1890 and now at the University of Texas Institute of Texan Cultures in San Antonio, men are pausing for *gemütlichkiet* (good-natured fellowship) in an unidentified beer garden. Seated are Charles Karger and Ernst Flach. Standing are Heinrich Boerner, Adolph Rosenthal, Otto Brinkmann, and Ludwig Hein. The probable location is the courtyard behind the Faust Hotel next to the Capitol Saloon, which at one time was managed by Karger. (University of Texas Institute of Texan Cultures at San Antonio collection.)

Seven

Outlying Communities

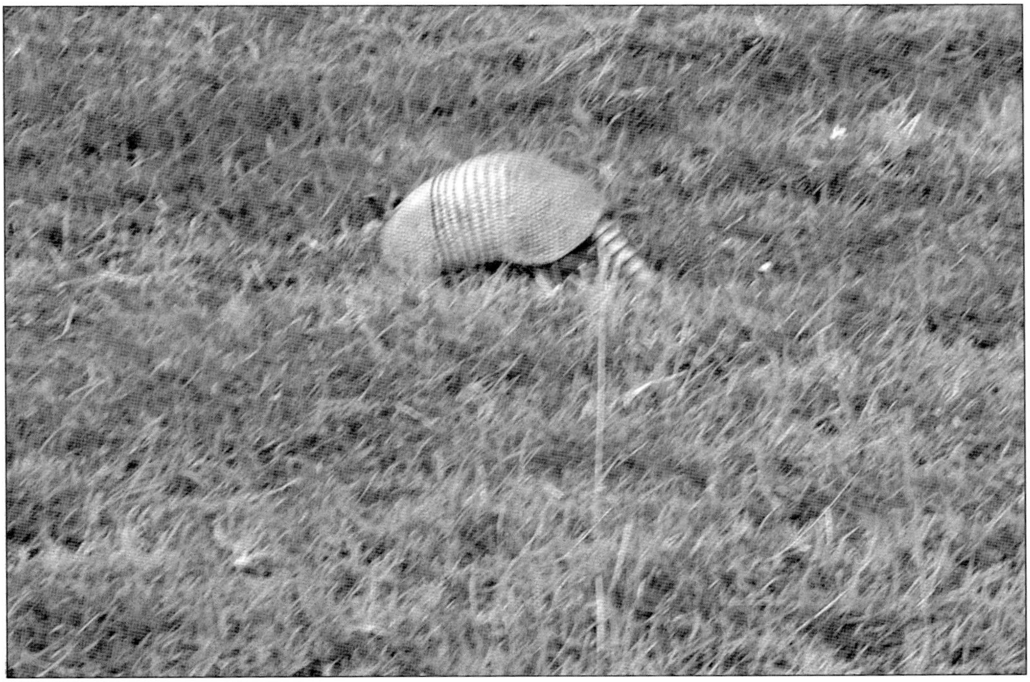

Armadillo Farm. The nine-banded armadillo (*Dasypus novemcinctus*) is a mail-clad mammal closely allied to sloths and anteaters. It was designated in 1981 the Texas state small mammal. The name derives from the Spanish *armado* (armored) and *dillo* (diminutive). Its armor consists of nine solid buckler-like plates linked by transverse bands. The three-banded armadillo and the six-banded armadillo are native to South America. (Photograph by Ruth Kiel.)

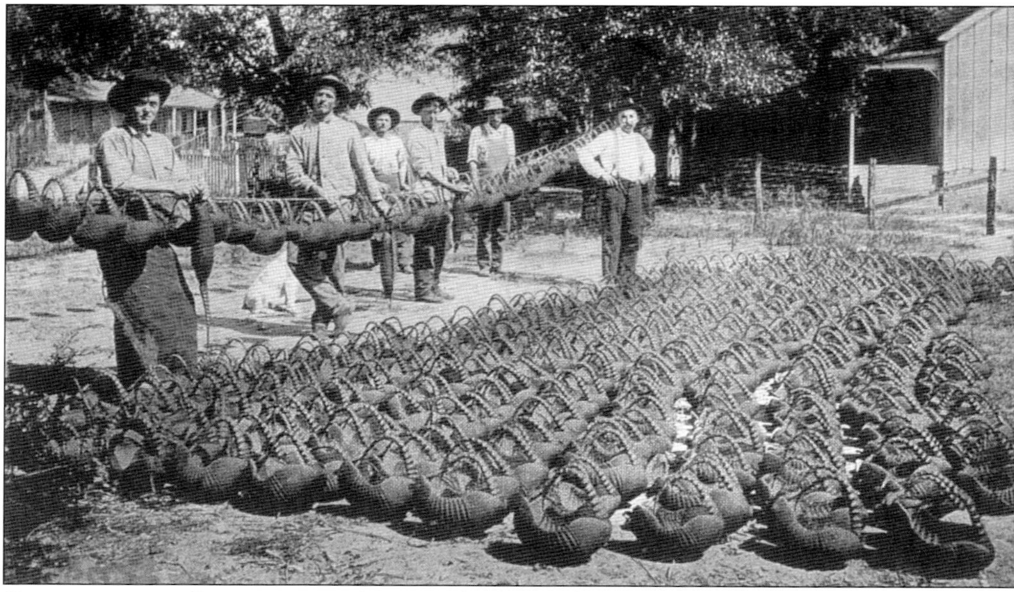

Collection and Processing of Shells. Charles Apelt (1862–1944) emigrated from Germany in 1887 and went to work on his uncle's farm near Comfort. He recognized the potential of a dried and curled armadillo shell as a basket and started a business to exploit the early-20th-century demand for curios. Rudolph "Rudy" Kirchhoff remembered that Apelt paid youngsters 50¢ for young armadillos and $1 for older and larger ones. Hunts for the animals were at night, often with a dog to help find them, but the dog was muzzled so as not to damage the shell. The hunters would pick them up by the tail and kill them by a blow to the head with a stick. (Comfort Heritage Foundation archives.)

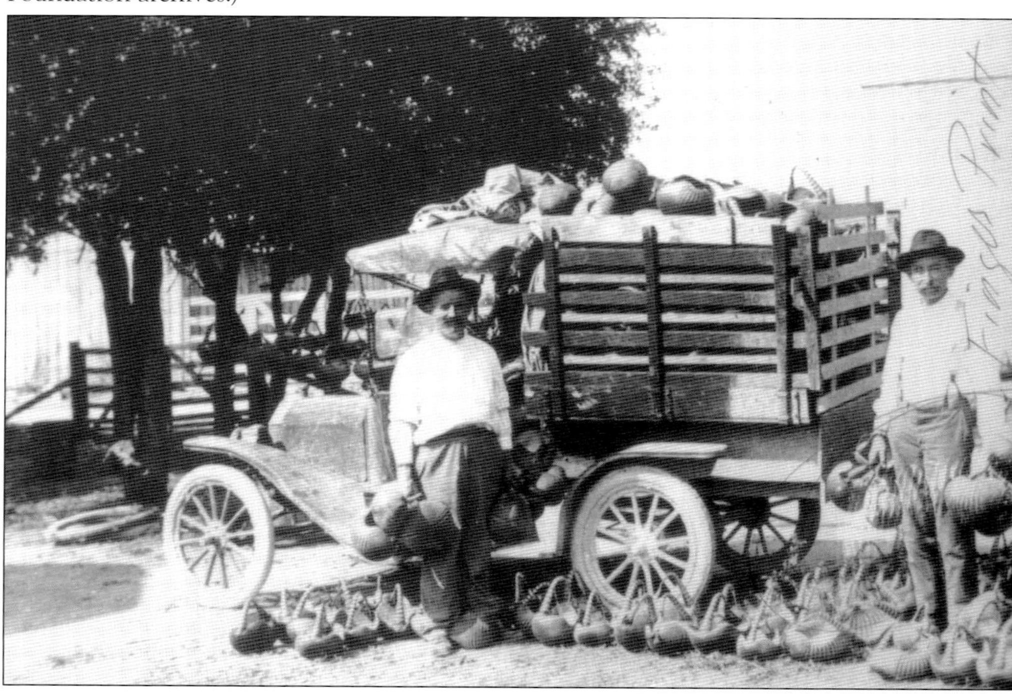

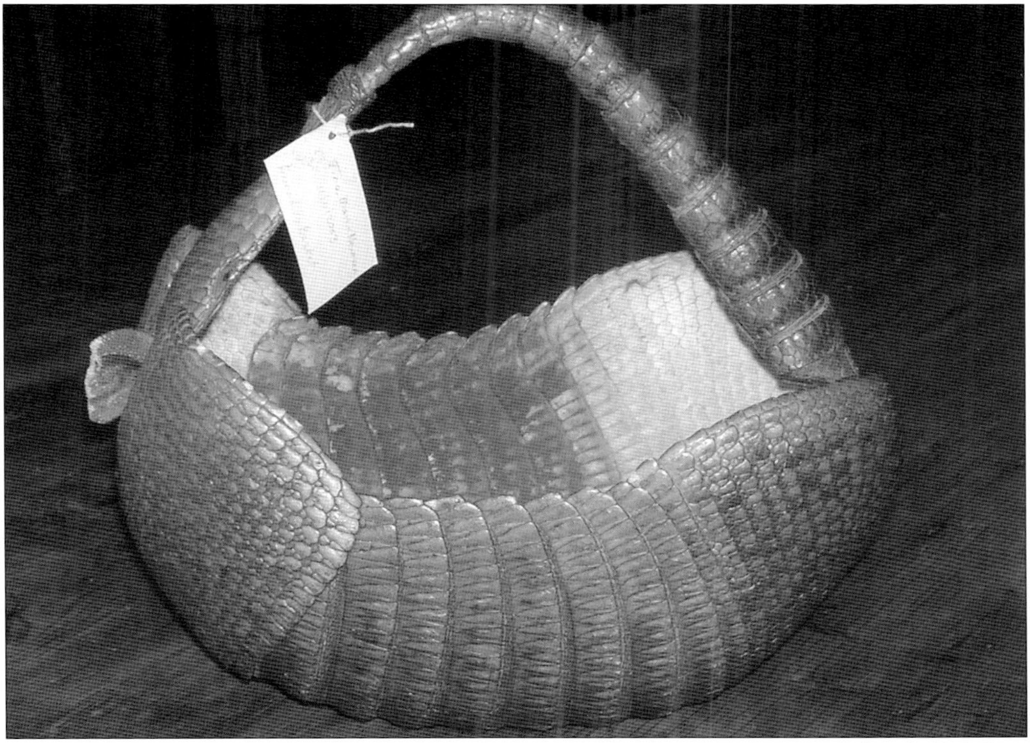

Armadillo Farm Products. The flesh of the armadillo was scraped out and the shells left to dry in the sun. The next step was immersion in water with minnows and fish that completed the cleaning of the shell. Subsequent treatment involved varnishing of the outer shell and lining the inner shell with silk or satin. The armadillo tail was looped to join the animal's head, forming a handle. They came in three sizes: an 11-inch-by-8-inch-by-10-inch large basket, 10-inch-by-8-inch-by-10-inch medium basket, and 9-inch-by-6-inch-by-9-inch small basket. In addition to the baskets that sold for \$3 and \$4, products included floor lamps with the armadillo shell as the lamp shade (\$20 with fringe, \$17 without fringe) and table lamps with wrought-iron stands using the armadillo tail as the upright stem (\$18 with fringe, \$16 without fringe). The Apelts also sold coconut lamps and starfish lamps, Indian blankets, and souvenir miniature cotton bales (10–20¢). (Above, photograph by Ruth Kiel; below, Comfort Heritage Foundation archives.)

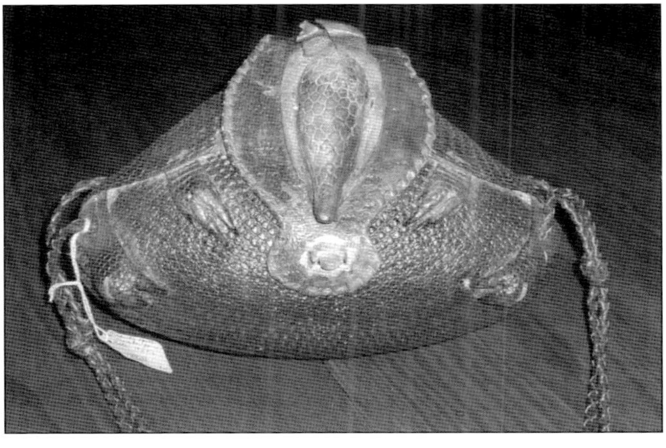

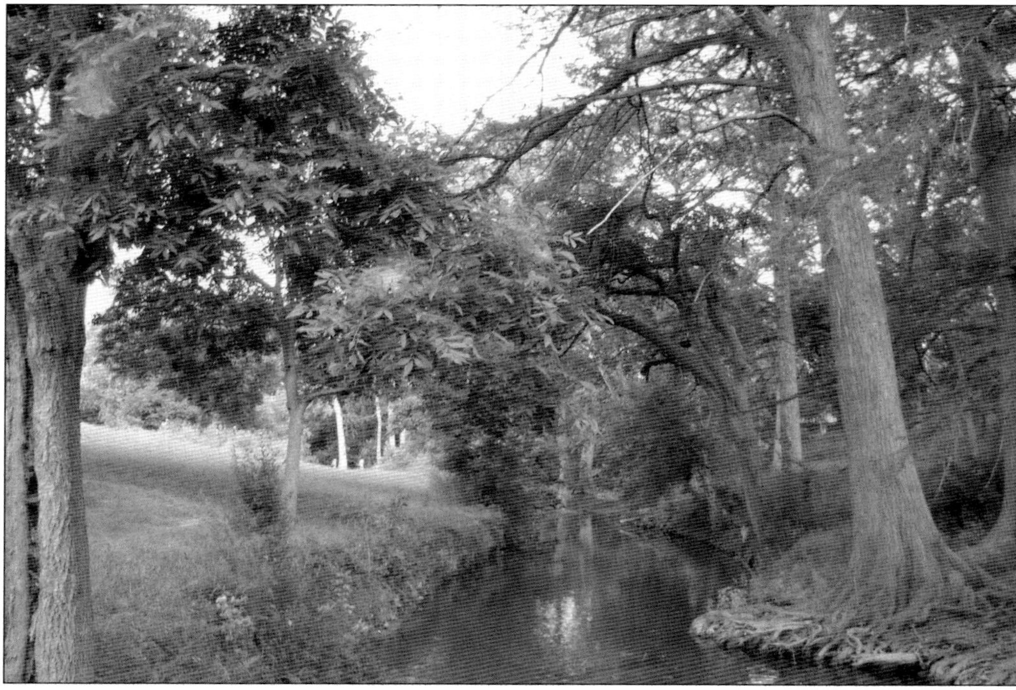

Cypress Creek Community. Cypress Creek flows east from the Third Creek-Cypress Creek Divide to join the Guadalupe River at Comfort. Pioneer German settlers of the Cypressville community, later known as the Cypress Creek community, formed a school district in 1879. The limestone structure seen below replaced the original frame schoolhouse in 1908. Built of limestone quarried on Otto Lich's nearby property, it was completed under the supervision of stonemasons Charles and Otto Bartel. Classes continued until 1942, when it consolidated with the Comfort School District. Today it is used as polling station for elections. Ranchers also meet there annually for a community picnic. They maintain a covered pavilion, the school, and the grounds. (Both photographs by Ruth Kiel.)

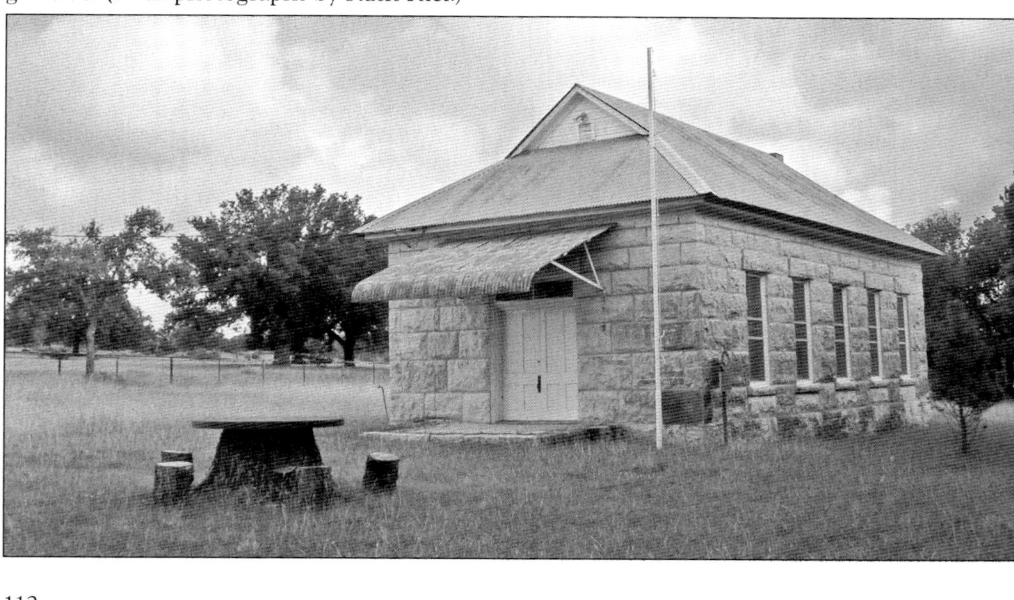

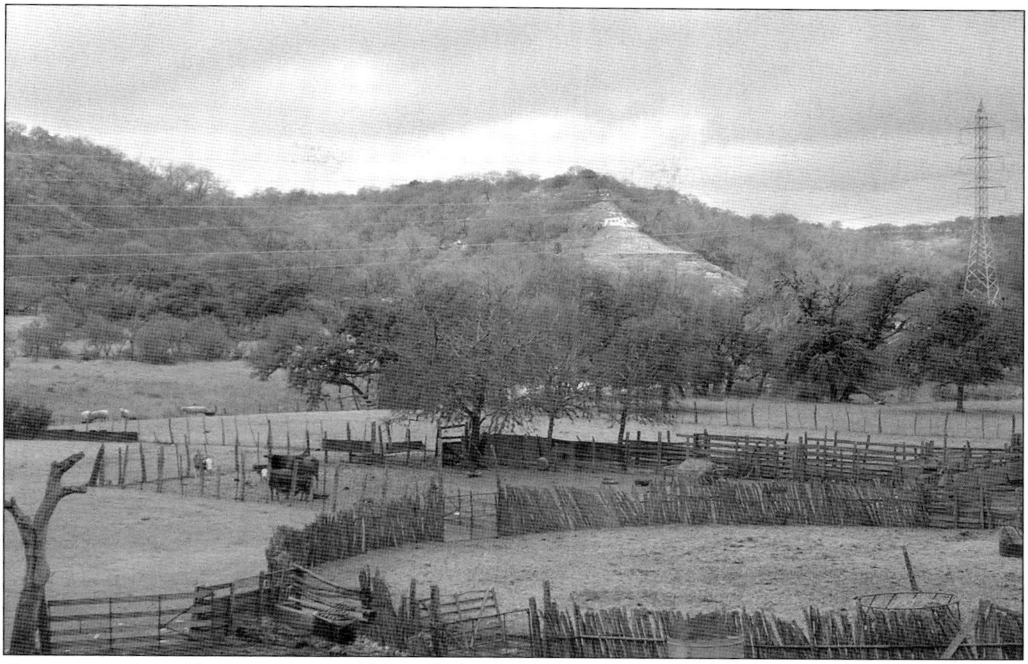

RANCHING AND CONSERVATION. Beyond Cypress Creek at the end of Lazy Valley Road is the Faltin Ranch, behind which is 1,900-foot Haddenbrock Hill, named after Franz Haddenbrock, who was the postmaster of Comfort 1865–1867. The gentle slope of the hill was similar to his long, thick beard. Children called him Weihnachtsmann (Santa Claus). The corral was originally on the Michael Lindner ranch. After Lindner's death in 1878, Faltin bought the corral and moved it to its present site. Windmill development in the late 1800s provided aquifer water to farmers, allowing them to move from streamside sites to higher land. (Both photographs by Ruth Kiel.)

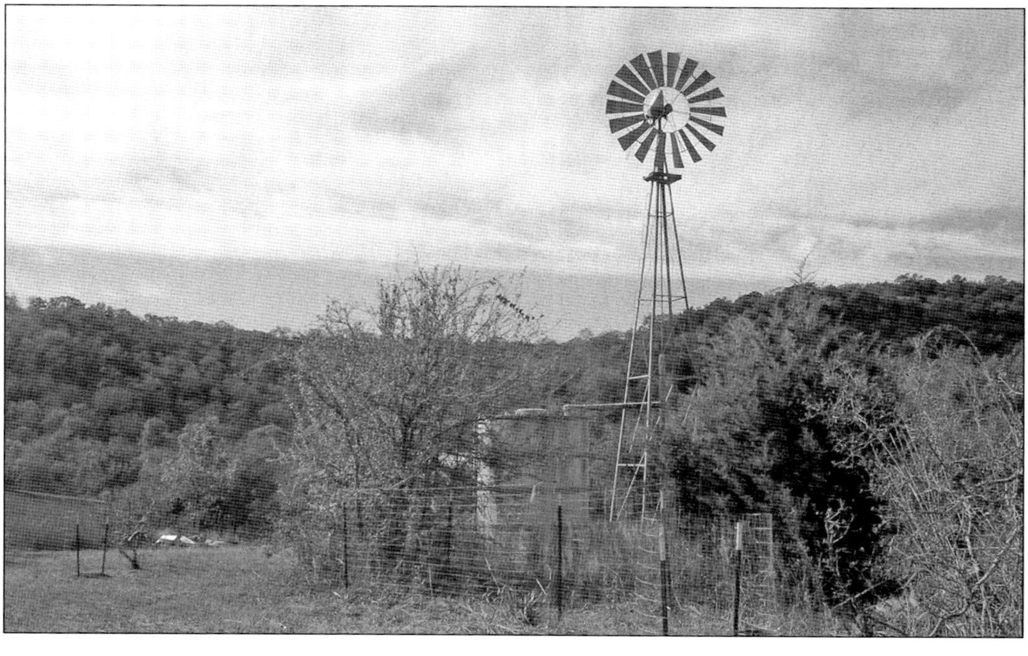

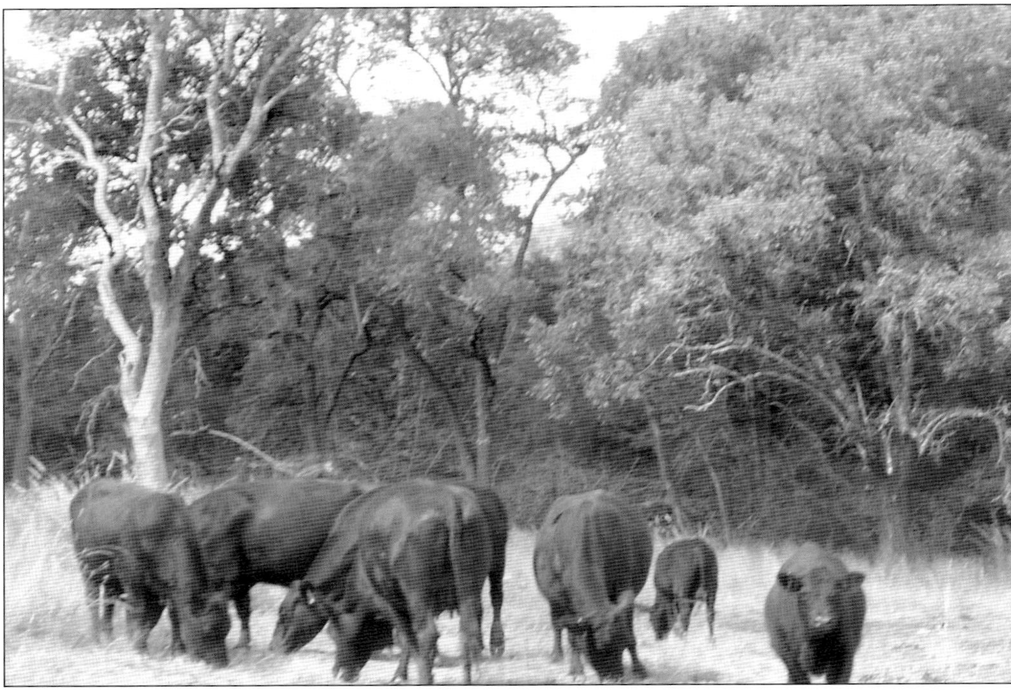

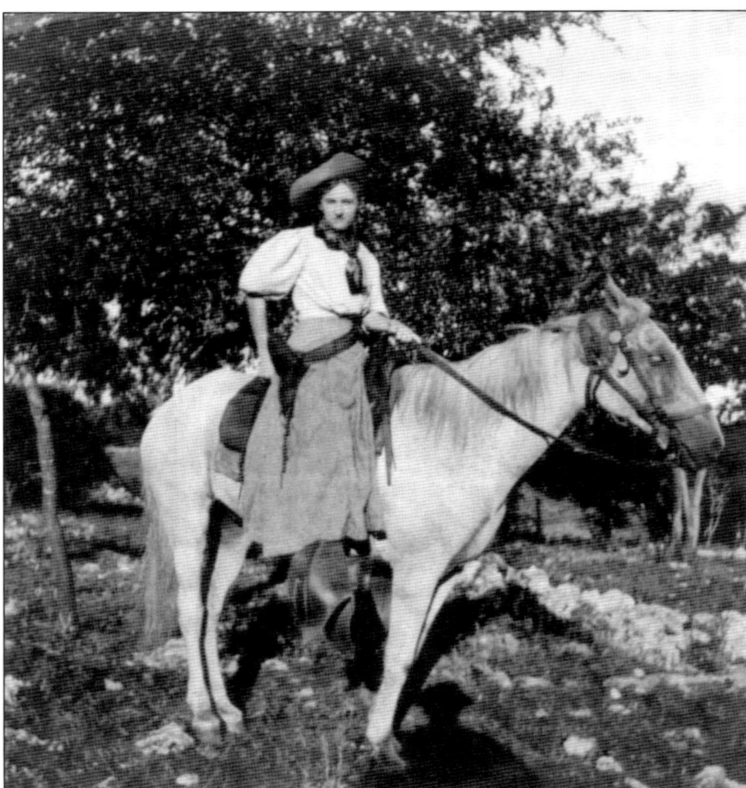

Cattle and Horses. Cattle, sheep, and goats are the common commercial animals; Black Angus cattle are popular, but also bred are Brangus, Charolais, Red Angus, and Santa Gertrudis of King Ranch. Texas long horns are not common. Horses are still used to manage cattle. Gretchen Faust Faltin (at left), with chaps and pistol, sits astride her horse. She was the wife of August Sedan Faltin and, according to Guido Ransleben, was known for her hospitality and friendliness. (Above, photograph by Ruth Kiel; at left, Tina Neumann collection.)

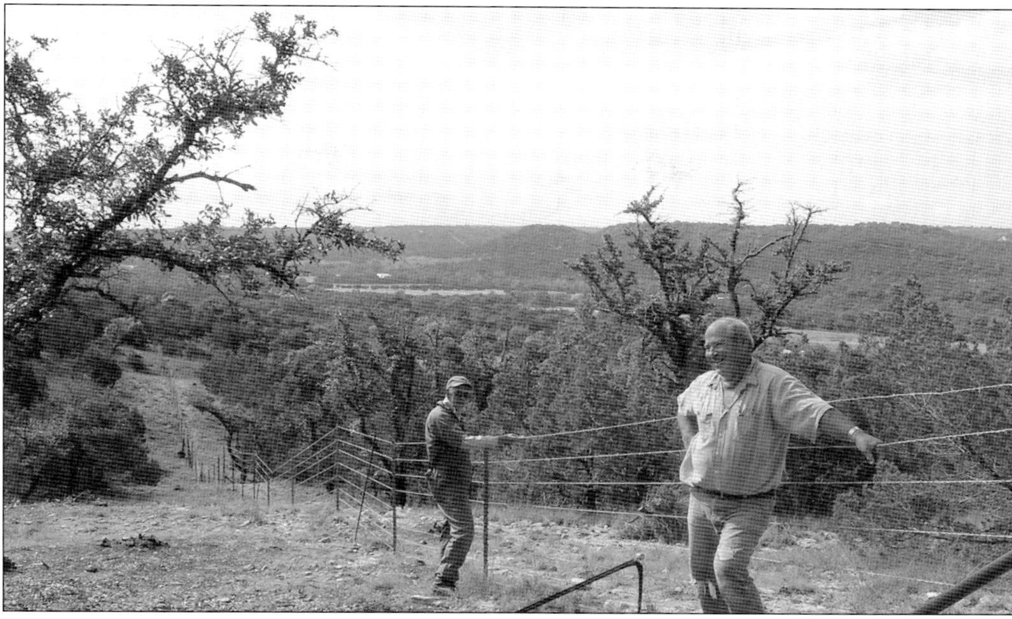

RURAL MAINTENANCE AND CLEARING. Recurrent tasks between seasonal haying and cattle handling include the need to build and repair fences, but only after clearing the fence line of encroaching ashe juniper trees, locally known as cedars, to provide a fire lane. Controlled burns are a common practice to kill weeds and cedar seedlings, but fire lanes are necessary to keep the burn from spreading. Seen above are Frank Kiel (left) and James "Butch" Lindner along a fence line. To meet the need of cedar cutters, the Charles Schreiner Company in Kerrville sold a light three-pound axe that evolved into the double-bladed Kerrville Cedar Axe. (Both photographs by Ruth Kiel.)

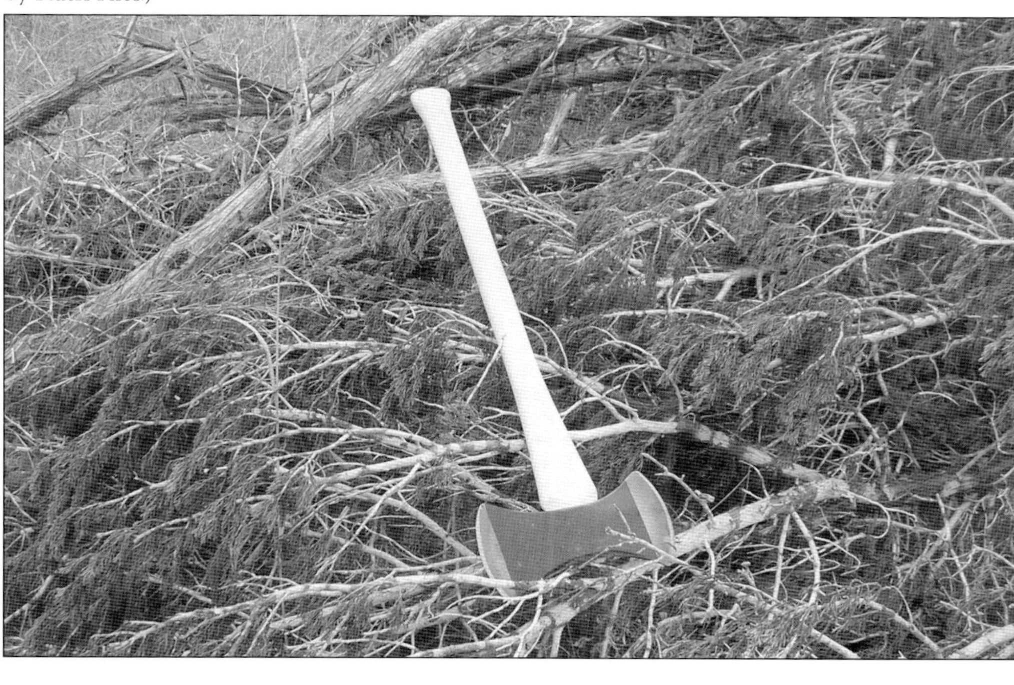

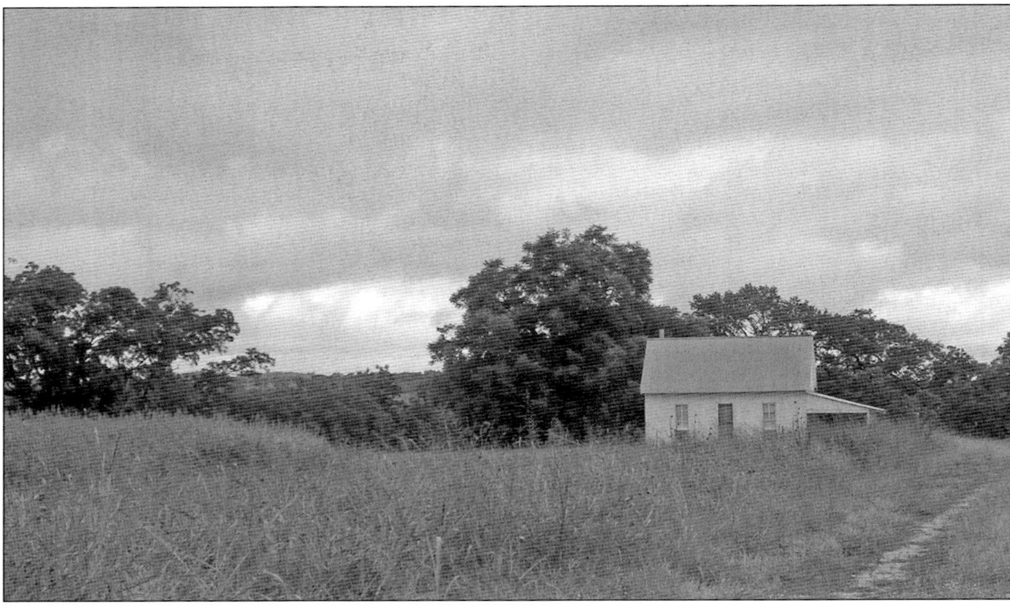

LANE VALLEY COMMUNITY. Part of the 1850s migrant group from Tennessee, Samuel Lane chose this valley for its rich soil and tall cypresses. Native Americans killed him while he was taking a turkey dinner to a friend in Comfort. The Lane Valley School adjacent to the Guadalupe River (above) taught in German until 1910. It closed in 1949, when students transferred to Comfort. It subsequently served as a polling station and community center. Emancipated slaves lived in the valley, and the small grave cluster is a reminder (below). One family, having no last name, became known as the Blank family. (Both photographs by Ruth Kiel.)

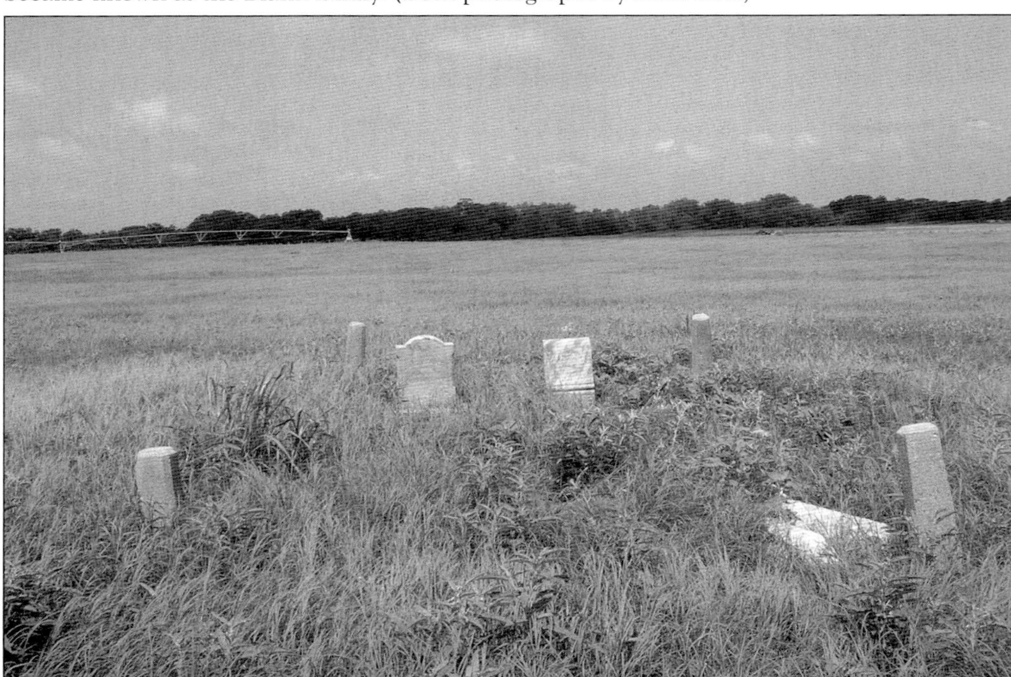

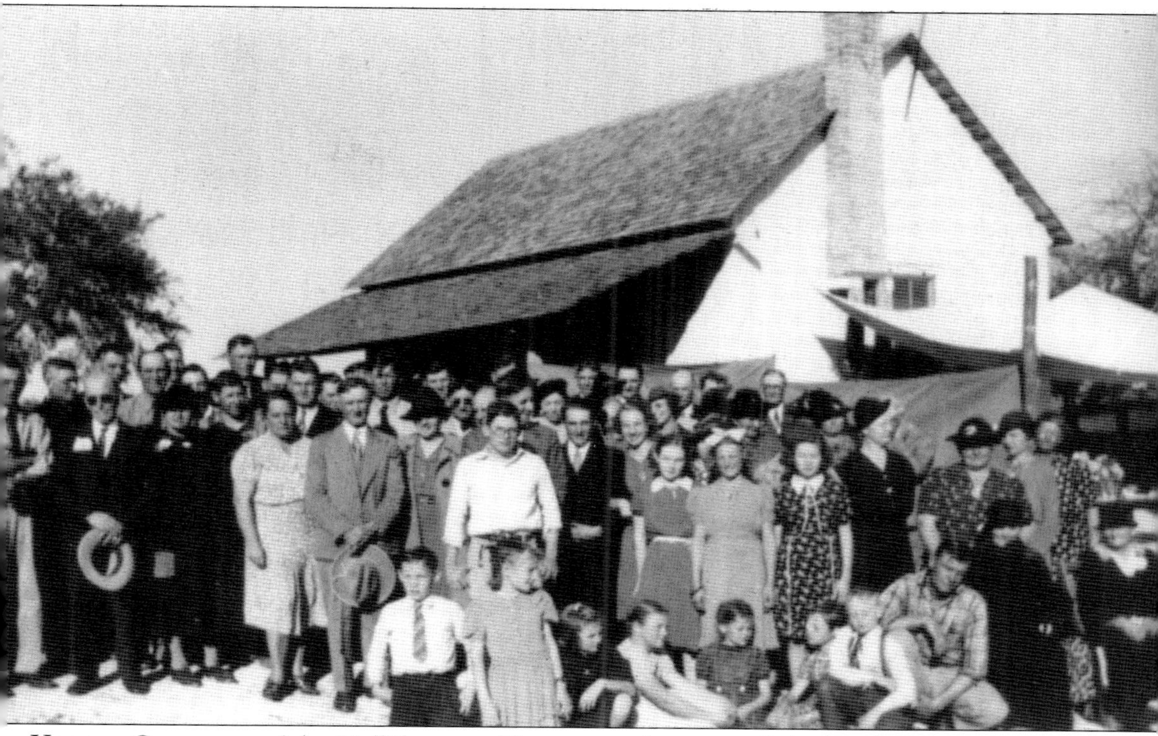

HOLIDAY COMMUNITY. John Holliday was a Tennessee volunteer at Goliad in the Texas War of Independence and also served in the Texas Revolutionary Army. He received a Texas veteran's 1,476-acre land grant in this area, extending from the Guadalupe River along this tributary now known as Holiday Creek (the variant spelling by the community). Early settlers built a school on the Lindner Ranch in 1889, which lasted until 1948. Hubert Heinen taught here in 1896 at a salary of $35 a month for an eight-month term. In 1939, graduates of the school held a 50-year celebration. The landowner moved the building and converted it into living quarters. (Photograph from the Joyce Behr collection.)

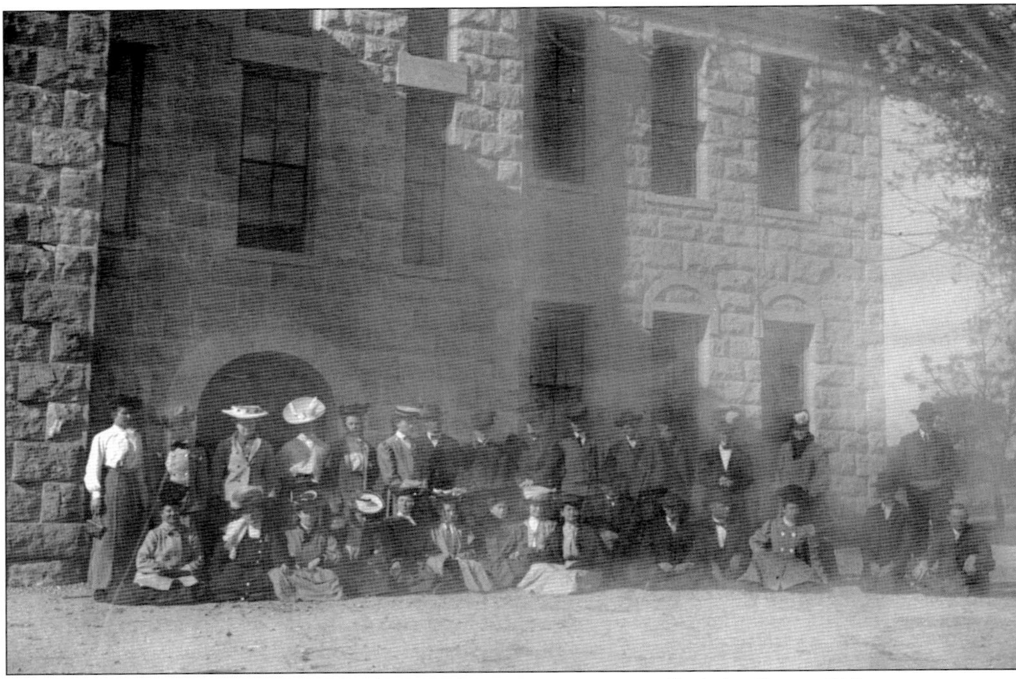

HERMANN SONS *ALTENHEIM*. The fraternal insurance group called the Sons of Hermann opened this building in 1915 as the Alten und Weisenheim for the aged and orphans. The title became Altenheim and is now Hermann Sons Retirement Home. Residents are from all over the state. The original German fraternal group, founded in New York in 1840, chose to honor the early German national hero Hermann (also known as Arminius) who in 9 AD formed an alliance of German tribes that defeated three Roman legions in the Battle of Teutoberger Wald (Teutoberg Forest). (Above, Comfort Heritage Foundation archives; below, Ruth Kiel.)

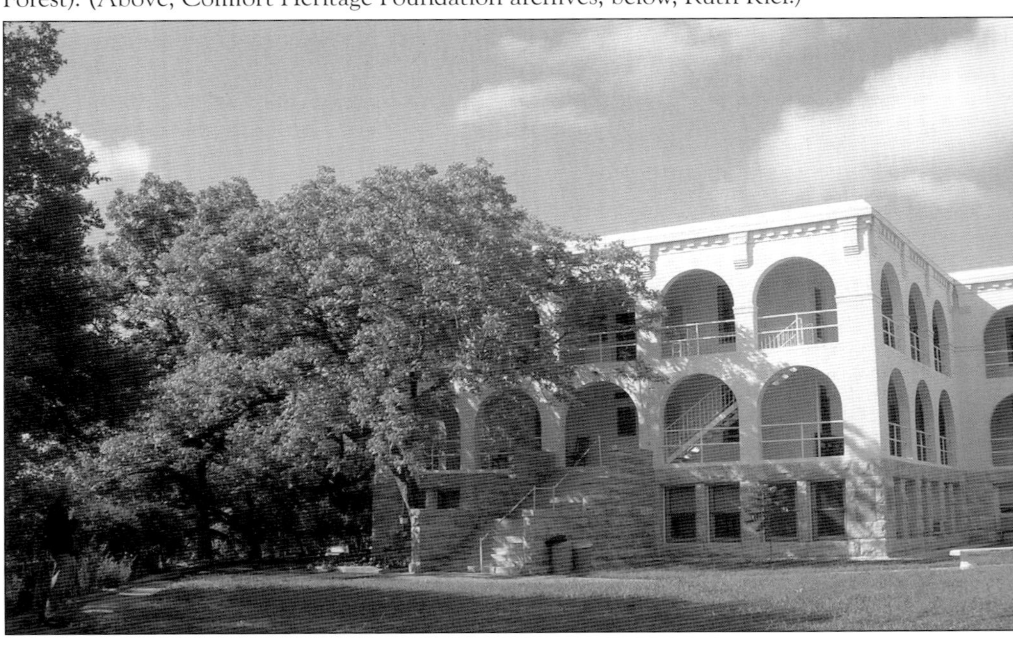

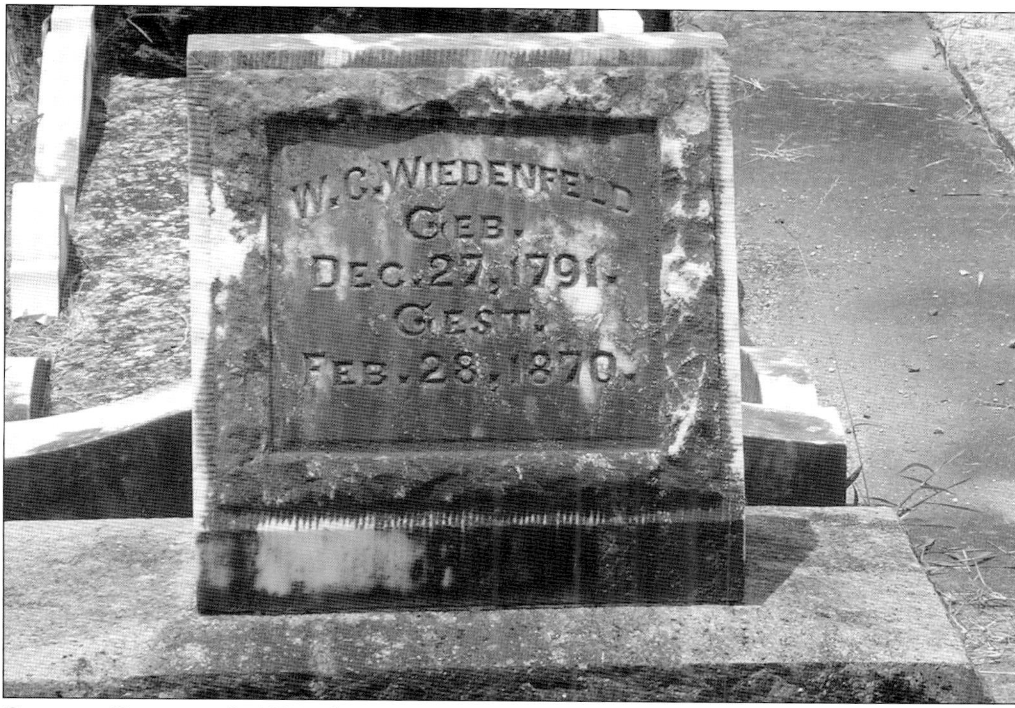

COMFORT CEMETERY. In 1854, when Ernst Altgelt laid out the town, he set aside 3 acres for a *friedhof* (cemetery) north of the main part of town. On the tombstones are many German names and German funerary phrases. The earliest tombstone-recorded death is John P. Heinen (1801–1860). W. C. Wiedenfeld (1791–1870) is the only individual buried here born in the 18th century. Seashell graves of Richard Doebbler (1847–1930) and Marie Doebbler (1867–1932) have concrete grave covers with embedded cockleshells from the Gulf of Mexico. (Both photographs by Ruth Kiel.)

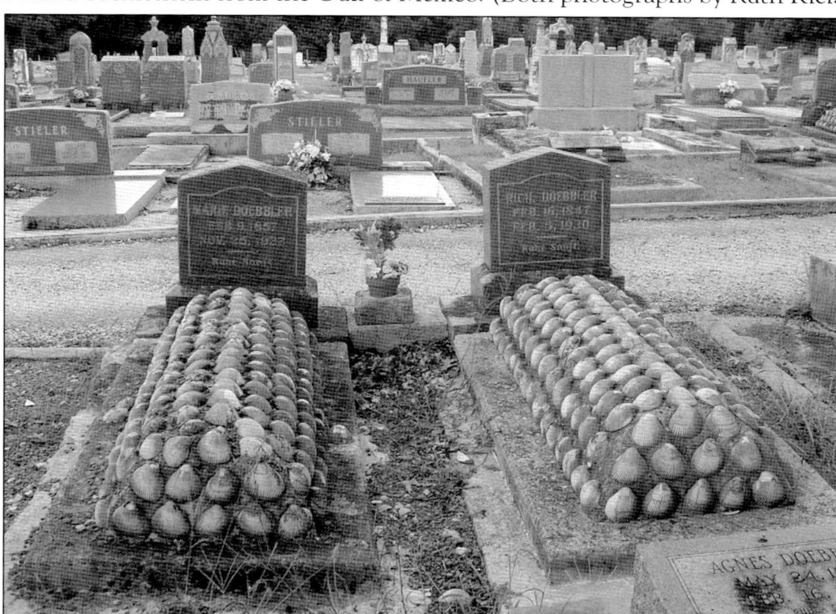

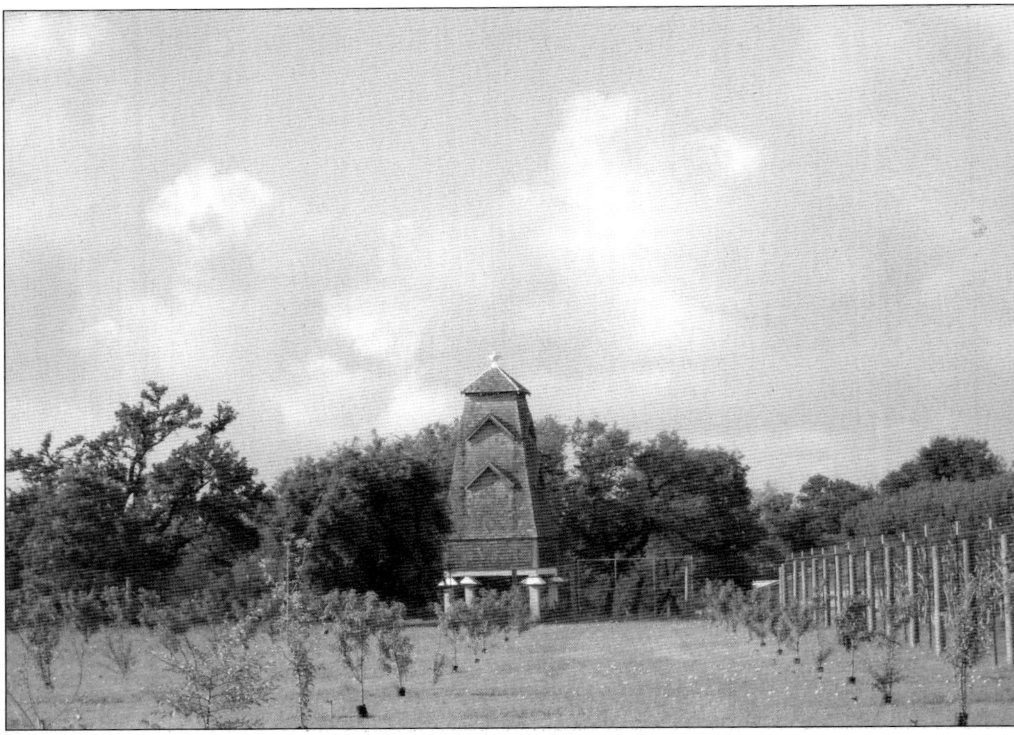

HYGIEOSTATIC BAT TOWER. Albert Steves had this shingle structure built in 1918 to attract bats that would consume mosquitoes, and thereby control the spread of malaria. Dr. Charles Campbell, a San Antonio physician, designed the tower. Sixteen of these towers were built between 1907 and 1929, including structures in Florida, Mississippi, and Italy. *Hygieiostatic* is an invented word, combining the Greek terms for *health* and *standing.* Although the bat tower is no longer active, the old 920-foot tunnel on Texas Route 9 that the Fredericksburg and Northern Railroad bored through the highest part of the Guadalupe-Pedernales Divide is now home to millions of Mexican free-tailed bats, which fly out at sunset looking for insects. (Both photographs by Ruth Kiel.)

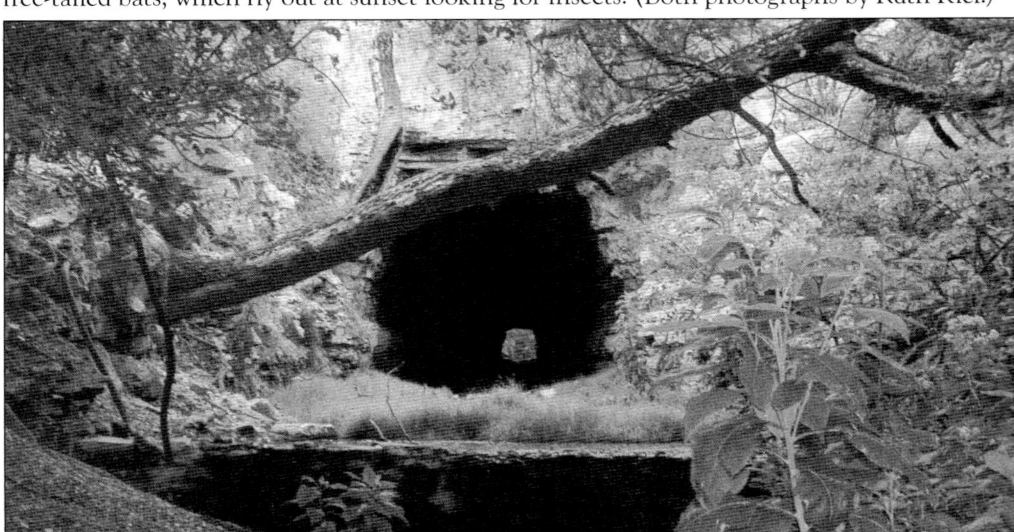

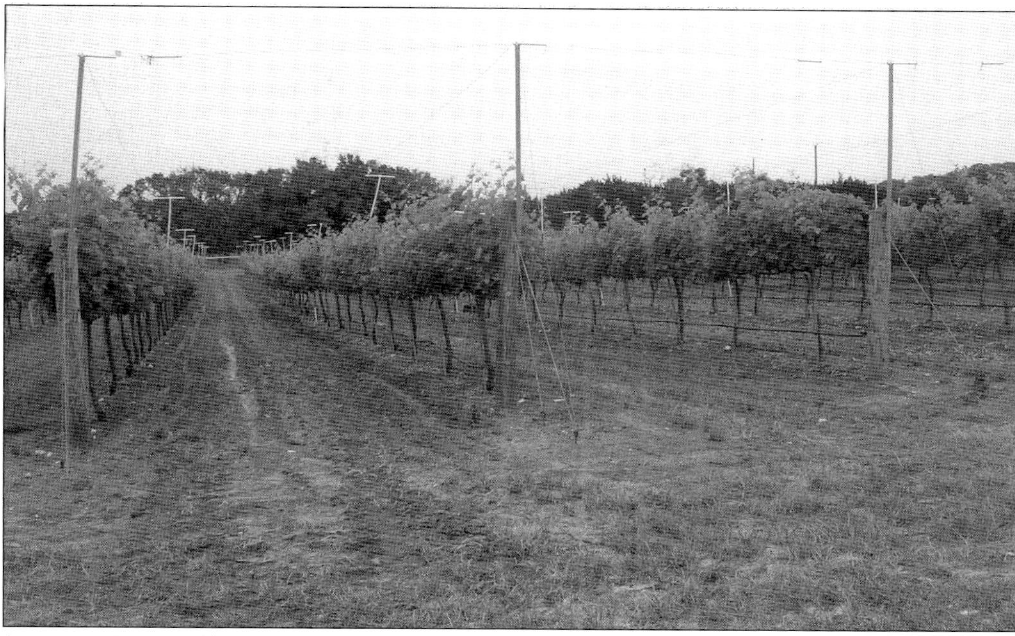

Singing Waters Vineyard. Richard and Julie Holmberg bought this land in 1993. They built their home and planted their first Merlot vineyard in 1998. Originally they made wine just for themselves and friends, but in 2004 they became a bonded winery, now producing Sauvignon Blanc, Merlot, a sweet dessert wine called "Sweet Lupe," and a prizewinning Merlot/Cabernet Sauvignon blend. They moved a historic Hill Country barn to the property for a tasting venue where they host musical events and art shows. Guests are welcome to bring picnic lunches to the banks of Bruin's Creek waterfall, the origin of the winery's name. (Both photographs by Ruth Kiel.)

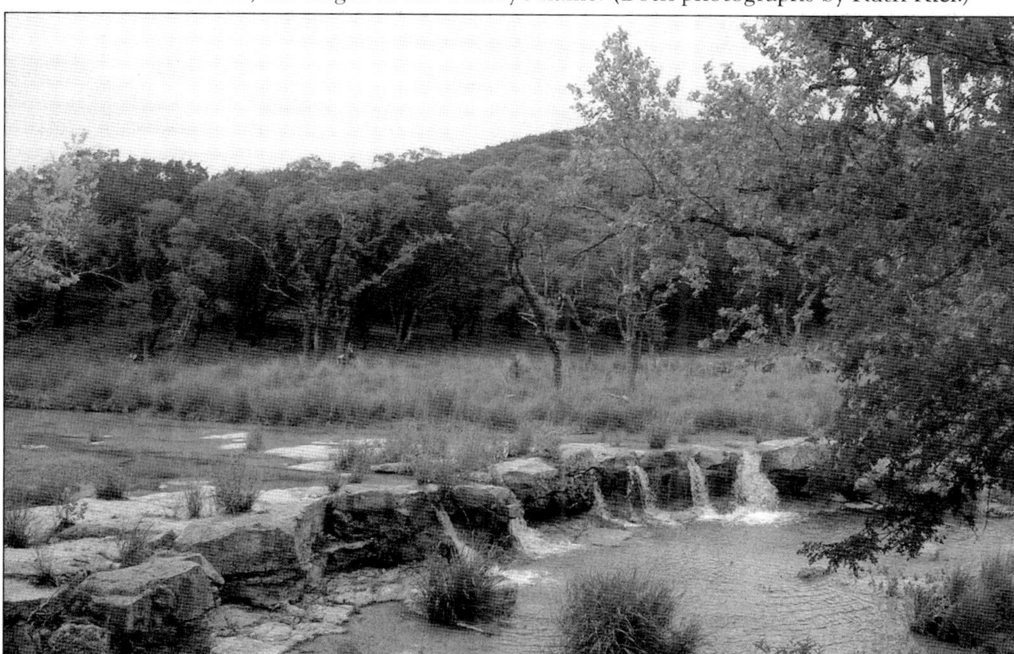

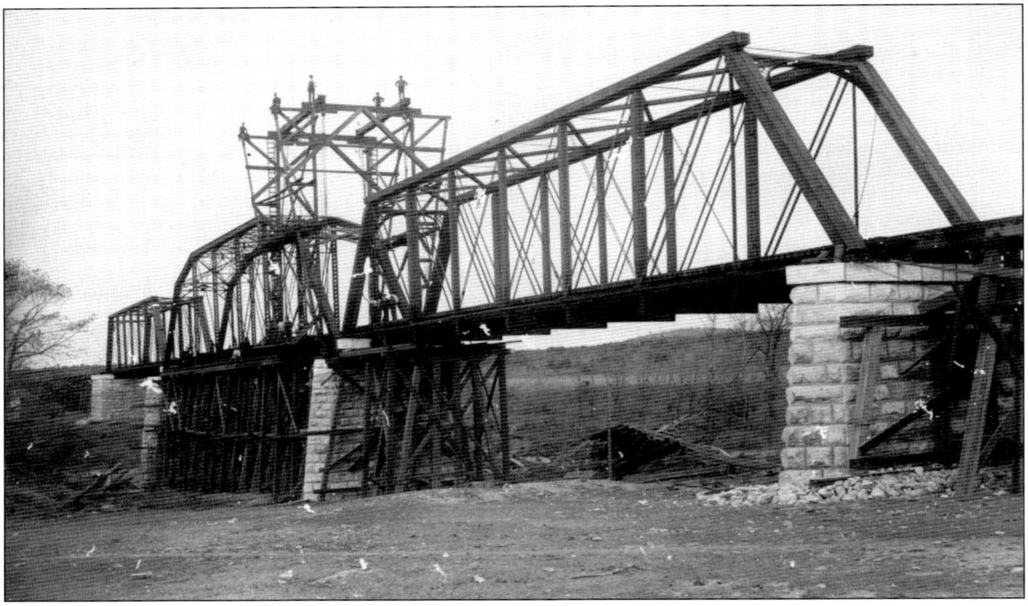

Old Railroad Bridge. The San Antonio and Aransas Pass Railroad served Comfort from 1887 to 1942. The Hill Country section went from San Antonio, through Leon Springs, Boerne, Welfare, Waring, Comfort, and Center Point, to Kerrville. Crossing the Guadalupe River was an obstacle, requiring big equipment and sure-footed men, such as those atop the temporary construction tower (above). Although the track was taken up for scrap metal in World War II, traces of the railroad embankments are visible, and the old bridge still stands. (Above, Comfort Heritage Foundation; below, photograph by Ruth Kiel.)

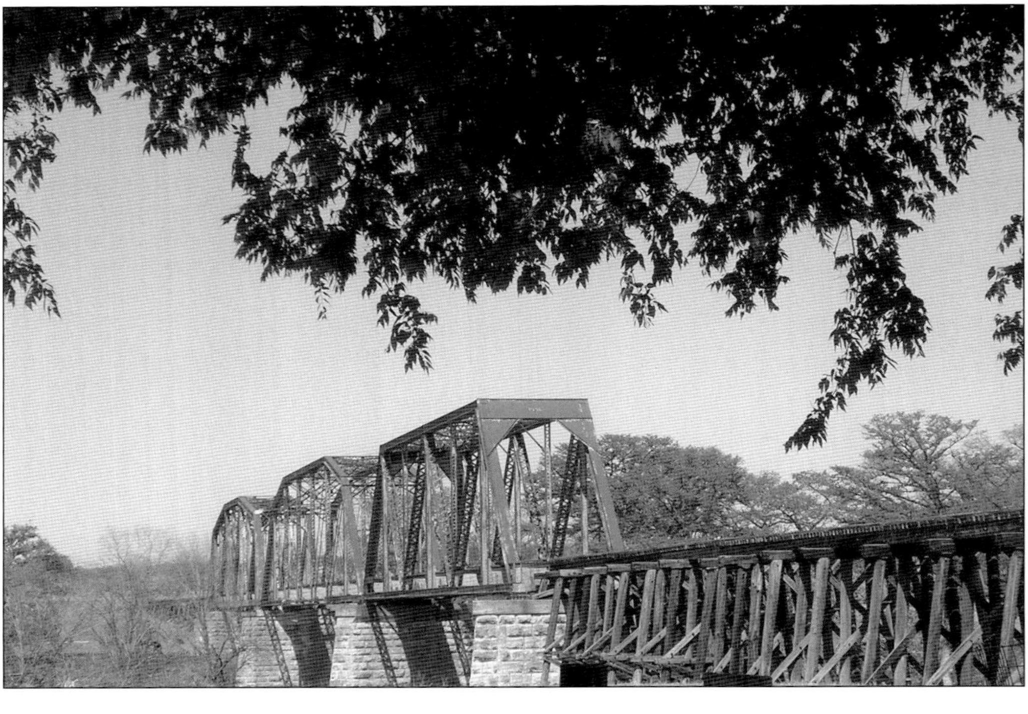

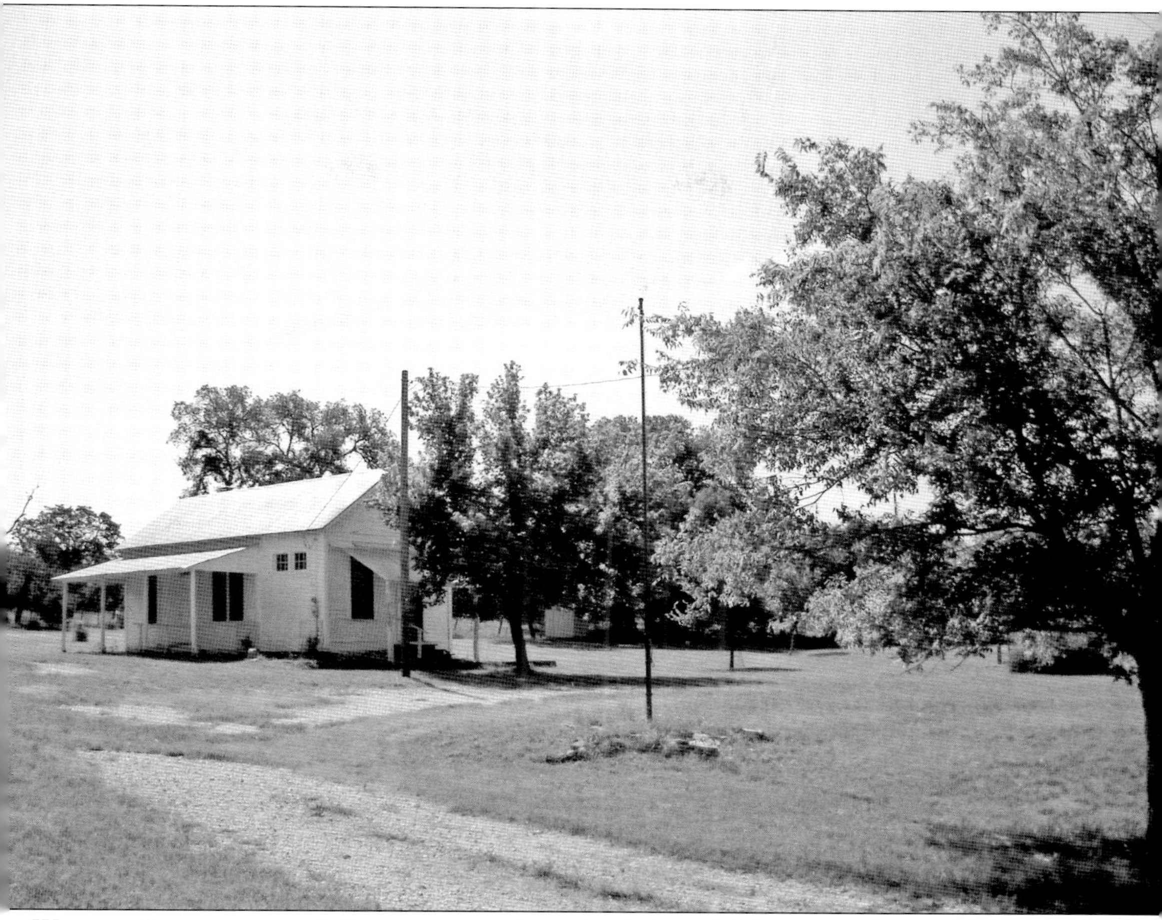

WELFARE SCHOOLHOUSE. Built as a one-teacher school about 1878 to serve the rural Welfare community, this building was originally on the west side of Joshua Creek. It was moved to this site in 1902. African American students had separate classes in this building. The structure served as a school until 1952, when students transferred to Comfort. The nearby general store, established by Ernst Beseler in the 1880s, became the community post office and tax center and is still in use now as a restaurant specializing in German food. (Photograph by Ruth Kiel.)

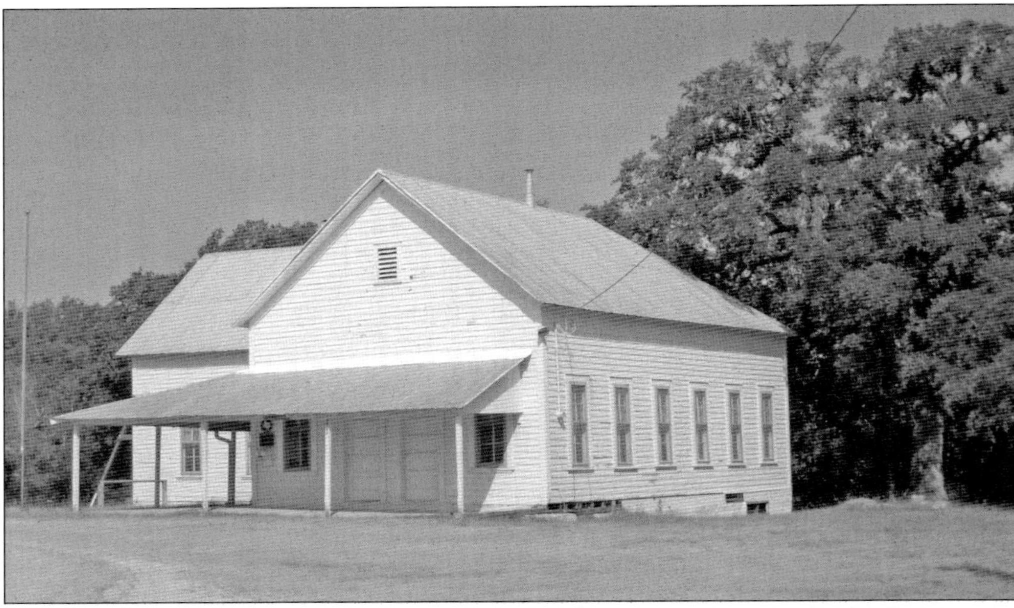

WARING SCHOOLHOUSE AND WARING HALL. Waring began as a train stop for the San Antonio and Aransas Pass Railroad and soon had a cotton gin, warehouses, two general stores, a saloon, a dance hall, and two boardinghouses. The 1892 schoolhouse closed in 1954, but it is still used as a community center. At the Waring Hall and Fire Station are two cast-iron eagles that Case Farm Machinery Company presented to honor outstanding performance by the local Rust Hardware Company. (Both photographs by Ruth Kiel.)

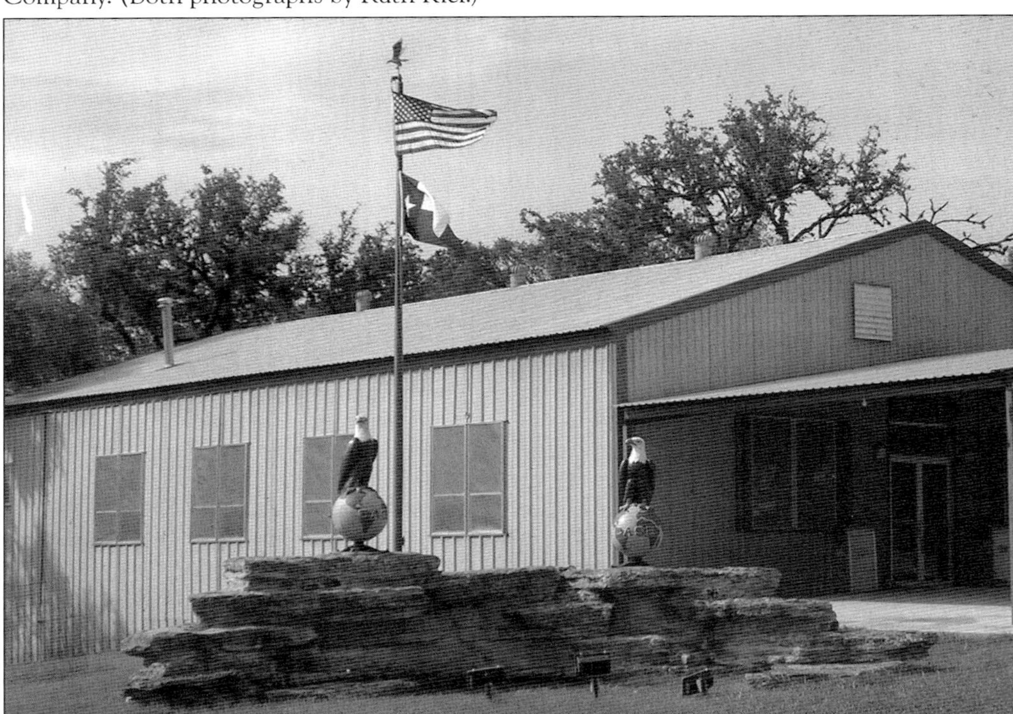

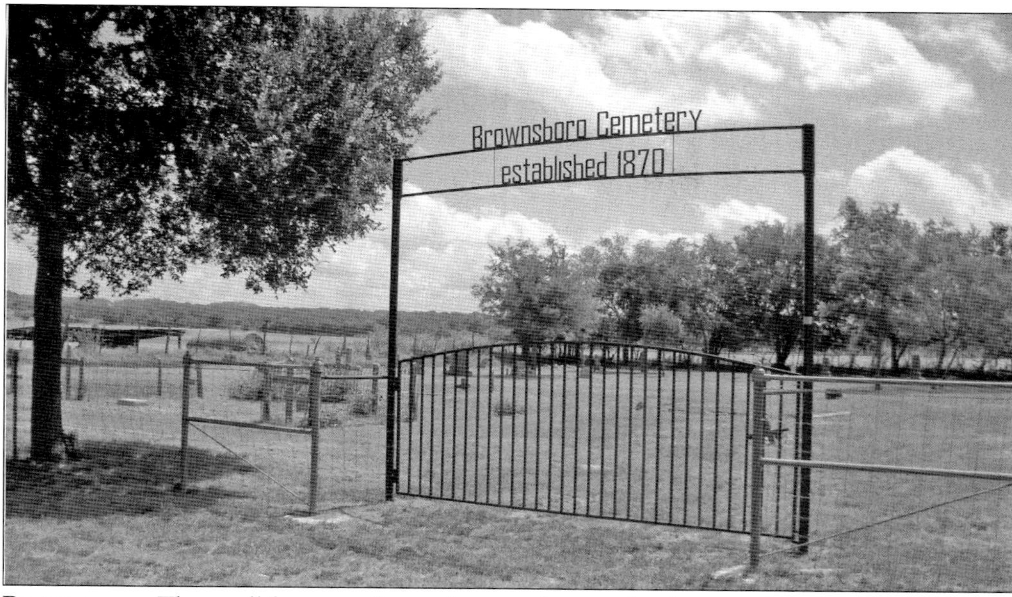

BROWNSBORO. The small forgotten Brownsboro settlement, 5 miles east of Comfort on River Bend Road with its church, graveyard, and school, was mainly a farming community. It was located on the San Antonio to Fredericksburg mail route and had a remount station where stagecoaches changed horses just north of the Guadalupe River ford. Only the cemetery remains; the school and church having been washed away in floods. Donated originally to the conference of the Methodist Church South, the cemetery is now the property of the Comfort Heritage Foundation. After restoration, the Texas Historic Commission designated it a Texas Historic Cemetery in 2008. The most recent survey recorded 79 burials, including 6 Confederate veterans. (Both photographs by Ruth Kiel.)

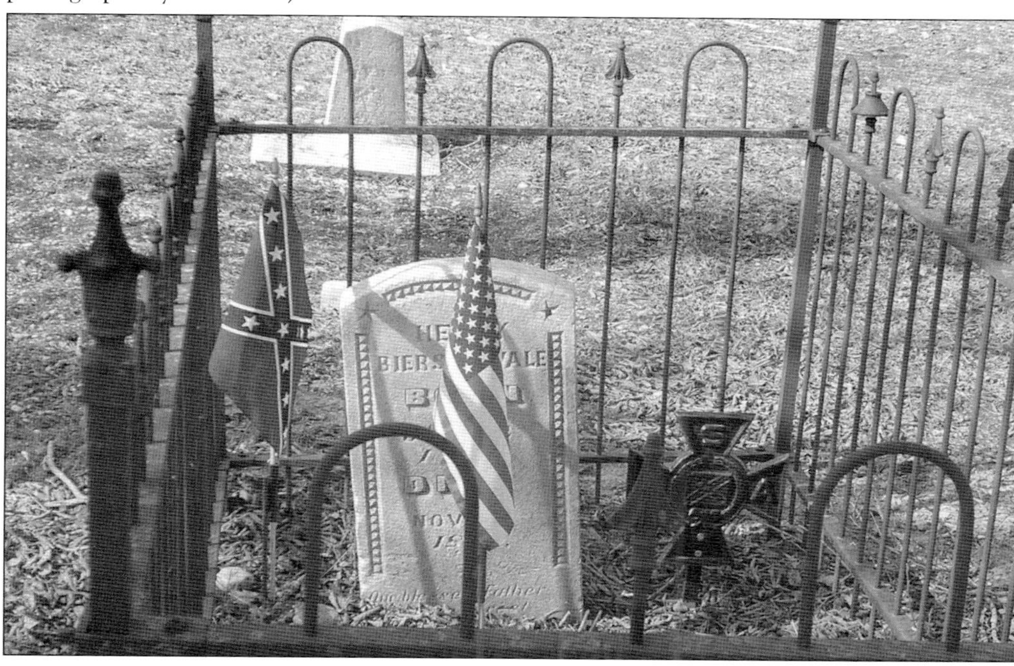

BIBLIOGRAPHY

Aldridge, Leon and staff of *The Boerne Star* comp. *Hill Country Views 1994: A Pictorial History of Kendall County, Texas*. Marceline, MO: D-Books Publishing, 1994.

Bennett, Bob, rev. ed. by Clara Watkins. *Kerr County 1856–1956*. San Antonio: Naylor Company, 1956, 1975.

Centennial School Building Book Committee. *Comfort Schools: A Proud Tradition*. Comfort, TX: Comfort Independent School District, 1993.

Jubilaeum Book Committee. *A History of Comfort's Business Buildings*. Fredericksburg, TX: Dietel and Son Printing, 1979.

Kendall County Historical Commission. *A History of Kendall County Texas—Rivers, Ranches, Railroads, Recreation*. Dallas: Taylor Publishing Company, 1984.

Kiel, Ruth and Frank Kiel. *Cypress Creek Travel Guide*. Comfort, Skyline Ranch Press, 2007.

———. *Guadalupe River Travel Guide*. Comfort, TX: Skyline Ranch Press, 2007.

———. *Hasenwinkel Road Travel Guide*. Comfort, TX: Skyline Ranch Press, 2007.

———. *Hermann Sons Road Travel Guide*. Comfort, TX: Skyline Ranch Press, 2007.

———. *Old No. 9 Travel Guide*. Comfort, TX: Skyline Ranch Press, 2007.

Lindner, Harvey E. *Memories, Opinions, and Other Things*. Austin, TX: Nortex Press, 2004.

Perry, Garland. *Historic Images of Boerne and Kendall County, Texas*. Boerne, TX: Perry Publishing, 1998.

Ransleben, Guido E. *A Hundred Years of Comfort in Texas: A Centennial History*. Rev. ed. San Antonio: Naylor Company, 1974.

INDEX